FAILING LAW SCHOOLS

THE CHICAGO SERIES IN LAW AND SOCIETY
Edited by John M. Conley and Lynn Mather

FAILING LAW SCHOOLS

Brian Z. Tamanaha

THE UNIVERSITY OF CHICAGO PRESS | *Chicago and London*

Brian Z. Tamanaha is William Gardiner Hammond Professor of Law at Washington University School of Law and the author of six books, including *A General Jurisprudence of Law and Society, Law as a Means to an End*, and *Beyond the Formalist-Realist Divide*.

The University of Chicago Press, Chicago 60637
The University of Chicago Press, Ltd., London
© 2012 by The University of Chicago
All rights reserved. Published 2012.
Printed in the United States of America
21 20 19 18 17 16 15 14 13 12   1 2 3 4 5

ISBN-13: 978–0-226–92361–1   (cloth)
ISBN-13: 978–0-226–92362–8   (e-book)
ISBN-10: 0–226–92361–4   (cloth)
ISBN-10: 0–226–92362–2   (e-book)

Library of Congress Cataloging-in-Publication Data

Tamanaha, Brian Z.
    Failing law schools / Brian Z. Tamanaha.
        pages cm. — (The Chicago series in law and society)
    ISBN 978-0-226-92361-1 (cloth : alk. paper) — ISBN 0-226-92361-4 (cloth : alk. paper) — ISBN 978-0-226-92362-8 (e-book) (print) — ISBN 0-226-92362-2 (e-book) (print)
    1. Law schools—United States—Finance. 2. Law—Study and teaching—United States.
3. American Bar Association.   I. Title. II. Series: Chicago series in law and society.
    KF272.T353 2012
    340.071'173—dc23

                                                                2012006829

♾ This paper meets the requirements of ANSI/NISO Z39.48–1992 (Permanence of Paper).

CONTENTS

Law schools today give the impression they are thriving. Many have magnificent facilities with state-of-the-art technology. Their resources are the envy of every department in the university. Law professors are among the best paid in the academy, with sparkling credentials, and are sought after not just as leading academic and legal figures but also as public intellectuals, as consultants, and for important state and federal government positions. The first decade of the twenty-first century has been a golden age of plenty for law schools.

Yet law schools are failing abjectly in multiple ways.

Annual tuition at over a half-dozen law schools topped $50,000 in 2011, with a dozen more poised to follow. After adding living expenses, the out-of-pocket cost of obtaining a law degree at these schools reaches $200,000. Nearly 90 percent of law students borrow to finance their legal education, with the average law school debt of graduates approaching $100,000. Many law graduates cannot find jobs as lawyers, enduring the worst market for legal employment in decades. Paying no heed to the adverse job market, law schools increased their enrollment in 2009 and 2010, which will send more graduates scrambling for scarce jobs three years hence.

A series of public revelations about widespread distortions and dubious activities damaged the credibility of law schools in 2011. Law schools across the country were advertising sky-high employment rates and triple-digit salaries for recent graduates when the reality was far different. They were criticized for offering scholarships to lure students who were unaware of the significant chance they would forfeit the scholarship after the first year. Two well-respected law schools admitted that they had falsely reported Law School Admission Test (LSAT) scores and grade-point averages (GPAs) to the American Bar Association.

Proud and dignified institutions that have long held themselves out as the conscience of the legal profession, law schools across the country have been engaging in disreputable practices. When called to account for these actions, law schools protest that they are just following the rules. They suggest that unhappy graduates should take responsibility for their poor decisions to incur such high debt. They universally place the blame for inflated employment numbers on the *US News* ranking, as if a magazine was responsible for their conduct. Elite law schools distance themselves from the worst offenders, conveniently ignoring that they too engage in questionable actions, merely to a lesser extent. Law schools at every level have been failing their ethical responsibilities, while pointing the finger at others.

In this book, I explore how law schools have arrived at this sorry state and the implications of this sad condition for the present and future. At the root of these problems is the way law schools today are chasing after prestige and revenue without attention to the consequences. The enviable resources law schools enjoy relative to their poor neighbors in economics and English departments are the riches obtained in the chase.

The economic model of law schools is broken. The cost of a legal education today is substantially out of proportion to the economic opportunities obtained by the majority of graduates. There are a few winners—graduates who secure well-paying jobs in corporate law firms—while a significant number end up with mountainous debt they will suffer under for decades with little to show for it. Law students in the anxiety-ridden job-hunting season speak enviously of classmates who won the "lottery." A lottery the job market has become.

Law school has always had winners and losers in job prospects among graduates. The difference today is that the enormous run up in tuition of the past three decades, and the student debt this produces, imposes a severe penalty on losers that did not exist in past generations. Formerly, a law graduate who entered the low-earning sector of the profession, or who did not land a job as a lawyer to begin with, or who never wanted to be a lawyer but planned to use the degree in other ways could still make a go of it financially. With the $100,000 debt common among law graduates today, that is much harder to do. The median starting salary of 2010 law graduates was $63,000—not enough to manage a debt that size.

The system of legal education is failing when a significant proportion of law graduates nationwide find themselves in financial hardship. Several dozen individual law schools, furthermore, are failing in the specific sense that a substantial bulk of their graduates suffer financial hardship. These law schools pile up casualties year after year among students who walk through their doors. If normal economic signals were operating, schools that fail to serve the interests of most of their students would not survive because people would stop enrolling. These law schools, however, are kept afloat by students making poor judgments to attend (encouraged by misleading job information from schools), while the federal government obligingly supplies the funds to support their folly.

Exposing the disconnect between the cost of a legal education and the economic return it brings and finding ways to fix it are the goals of this book. Various factors contribute to the problematic economic situation in complex, intersecting ways. The regulation of law schools, the work environment of law professors, the competitive pressures on law schools, the limited information available to prospective students, and the way law school is financed through federal loans are critical pieces.

The prologue begins with a brief account of the circumstances surrounding my interim deanship over a dozen years ago at St. John's University School of Law. It is difficult for outsiders to appreciate the unique workplace of professors. Telling this story allows me to convey vividly the dynamics at play. In part 1, I reveal how legal educators have utilized regulatory mechanisms time and again to further their own interests. I go on, in part 2, to describe what law professors do and how much we get paid and explain why the practicing bar and judges complain that law professors are out of touch and do a poor job of training lawyers. I explain why law schools are under the iron grip of *US News* ranking in part 3 and elaborate on the detrimental developments this has brought to legal academia. In part 4, I home in on tuition, debt, and the economic return on a legal education; I identify problematic features in our economic operation and offer proposals for improving the situation.

This is not a standard academic exegesis. I mix narrative with detailed facts and figures, description with occasional prescriptive commentary, hard information with grounded speculation about unknowns. Based on current trends, I make a number of projections about the short-term future for law schools and for the legal market.

What I write in these pages will affront many of my fellow legal educators. I reveal the ways in which we have repeatedly worked our self-interest into accreditation standards, from unnecessarily requiring three years of law school to writing special provisions to boost our compensation. We teach less and get paid more than other professors, and we earn more than most lawyers, yet we still complain about being underpaid relative to lawyers. I question the amount of money that goes into academic research. I challenge the efforts of clinicians to use accreditation standards to get job protection, and I question the economic efficiency of clinical programs. I identify schools that have dismal rates of success among graduates in landing jobs as lawyers, and I identify schools that publish highly unreliable salary numbers. I specify a set of characteristics of law schools that prospective students should be wary of attending. I argue that law schools extract as much money as they can by hiking tuition and enrollment, while leaving students to bear the risk, in the first instance, and taxpayers thereafter. And I propose changes to accreditation standards and the federal loan system that, if enacted, would drastically alter the situation of law schools.

This book challenges fundamental economic aspects of the operation of law schools, although I do not go deeply into pedagogical issues. What got us into this position is our hunger for revenue and chase for prestige. Some of what I write is intended to warn law schools about the coming financial crunch they will face from a continued fall in applicants and increasing attrition after the first year from students who drop out or transfer to other schools. Schools in a precarious position that do not alter their operation may literally fail, unable to bring in sufficient revenue to cover their expenses.

I do not believe law schools will reform themselves unless forced to. The situation is too comfortable and our interests too vested in the status quo. Thus one aim in writing this book is to reach beyond legal educators to prospective students and their parents, to external regulators, and to members of Congress to expose the depth of our problems and provide information that will facilitate better-informed decisions about how to respond. The federal loan program, though well intended, has devastating consequences for many students. Depending on a mix of considerations I will elaborate, for many thousands of prospective students it might be prudent to forgo law school at current prices.

Law schools, finally, are failing society. While raising tuition to astronomical heights, law schools have slashed need-based financial aid, thereby erecting a huge financial entry barrier to the legal profession. Increasing numbers of middle class and poor will be dissuaded from pursuing a legal career by the frighteningly large price tag. The future complexion and legitimacy of our legal system is at stake.

ACKNOWLEDGMENTS

In May 2006, I wrote my first blog post on the skewed economics of legal education, "A Peculiar Fairness Issue Brewing in Law Schools," on the group blog *Balkinization*. The post discussed spiraling law school tuition, the questionable economic return for many law graduates, and the dubious financial arrangement we create through merit scholarships "in which the students most likely to make the least money end up subsidizing the legal education of the students most likely to make the most money." I wrote more than two dozen *Balkinization* posts on various problems in legal academia in ensuing years, raising questions about the cost of interdisciplinary studies, expressing concerns about the increasing debt burden on law graduates, and exposing our industry-wide use of misleading employment statistics, among other topics. In a June 2010 post, "Wake Up, Fellow Law Professors, to the Casualties of our Enterprise," I spoke bluntly for the first time about the need for legal educators to take greater responsibility for the situation. I thank Fernando Rodriguez for jarring me out of my usual understated style of academic discourse to write more candidly and forcefully about these issues. This book elaborates on the same themes and is written in the spirit of that post.

Without the extraordinary assistance of Jeffrey Blackwood, this book could not have been completed in a timely fashion—thanks for always coming through, Jeff! I also thank John M. Conley, Bill Henderson, and Deborah Jones Merritt for their detailed critical feedback on the entire manuscript. Their comments improved the book in large and small ways. I thank my colleagues at Washington University School of Law for feedback at a faculty workshop on several chapters. I owe particular thanks to Peter Joy and Robert Kuehn. Long-time leaders in clinical legal education, Bob and Peter disagree with several of my positions, yet they have been unfailingly helpful. My law school dean, Kent Syverud, the incoming chair of the ABA Section on Legal Education and Admissions to the Bar, has steadfastly supported this project, notwithstanding my criticisms of the ABA and the potentially embarrassing things I say about law schools (including my own). Thank you, Kent, for encouraging me to remain true to the project. I also thank Paul Kirgis, David McGowen, and Jeff Sovern for their comments on early drafts. I thank Matt Leichter for his excellent work in pulling together essential statistics on legal business and legal academia. I thank Jolijt Tamanaha for preparing several possible designs for the book cover. I thank Kathie C. Molyneaux for helping me acquire background material from numerous sources. I thank Yvonne Zipter for her superb work editing the manuscript. I thank my editor, John Tryneski, for his enthusiastic support for this book and his helpful comments on the first draft.

To John Q. Barrett I owe special thanks. We started in legal academia as rookies together and forged a bond through our joint struggles. Years ago, at a critical time, John encouraged me to do what had to be done—he did the same again when I embarked on writing this book despite my reservations. Finally, I thank Honorata for everything. This book is dedicated to Brian M. Maeshiro. We met when we were eleven years old as opponents in a judo match (although our memories differ on who won that day). We became life-long Okinawan brothers, hanging out in high school, spending summers together, and traveling parts of the world. Thanks for the good times, Bo.

A Law School in Crisis (Circa 1997)

A raucous celebration outside faculty offices greeted me as I stepped off the elevator. It was early December 1997. Drawn by the commotion, I walked over. Two senior colleagues, a third joining them as I arrived, had plastic cups in hand, each with a shot of whiskey, raised in a toast, accompanied by laughter. The dean is done, I was told. His resignation was in our faculty boxes.

A tersely worded memo from the university president, Donald Harrington, announced that he had accepted Dean Rudy Hasl's resignation, effective at the end of the school year. President Harrington thanked Hasl for his contribution to the law school and announced that an immediate search would begin to find a new dean. Devoid of the obligatory flattery that adorns such announcements, the message of the memo was that Hasl had been fired, and good riddance.

Taking a seat at my desk, I immediately wrote to President Harrington:

Permit me to briefly introduce myself. I am an untenured member of the faculty, and have been at St. John's for two-and-a-half years. . . .

I do not question the appropriateness of the resignation of Dean Hasl. His position as leader of the faculty had become untenable. Nevertheless, the most serious problem we have at the law school is a grossly underperforming faculty. Several of the leaders of the drive to remove Dean Hasl are, in my opinion, among the worst offenders. My concern was—and remains—that the success of their initiative would be interpreted by them as confirmation that they could not be made to work harder for the school . . .

> It is crucial to our future that you send a strong signal to the faculty that the departure of Dean Hasl does not mean the end of efforts to improve the performance of the faculty. I urge you to make such a signal explicit, unequivocal, and soon. The final paragraph in your memo announcing Dean Hasl's resignation fell short of what is needed.

As I typed out these impetuous words, the faculty members I was referring to were carrying on in the hall. I showed a draft of the memo to a close colleague, encouraging him to talk me out of it, but he argued that it *had* to be sent.

The next day I was summoned to the president's office.

Father Harrington (a Vincentian priest) welcomed me into his office with a disarming smile and asked me to tell him what was going on at the law school. We were in a disastrous slide, I said. The law school had dropped a tier in the *US News* rankings the year before (as irate alumni donors regularly reminded him). In a belated attempt to improve our standing, Dean Hasl had begun prodding the faculty to do more. Many faculty members were hardly present in the building, coming in only to teach, leaving immediately thereafter. When they did stay on the premises, their office doors frequently were closed—an implicit "don't bother me" sign to students. Many faculty members were producing little if any scholarship; many hadn't written in years. A few had legal practices on the side—so busy that their "full-time" professor position had become their side job. A number were in semiretirement, though not officially. One appeared to have a drinking problem. Who knows what the others were doing. Out of a faculty of forty-five, perhaps a dozen were producing at a high quality as teachers and scholars. Student morale was low, sunk in a collective depression induced by the drop in rankings. Our fall from the third to the fourth tier in the rankings (out of five tiers at the time) led to an immediate drop in the quantity and quality of applications, which resulted, the following year, in a two-point reduction in median LSAT scores. A downward spiral of student qualifications loomed ahead. A proud institution with many accomplished graduates in New York, including two former governors and several sitting judges on the highest court, St. John's might take decades to recover.

It would be a mistake, I urged Father Harrington, to immediately hire a permanent dean to replace Hasl. Deans cannot continue in office against the wishes of the bulk of the faculty—that's what spelled his demise. What we needed was an interim dean who would clean house and raise the level of performance, giving the next dean a better chance to succeed.

Three months later I became the interim dean.

Drastic measures were called for because St. John's then was mired in a state of dysfunction. Although the situation was by no means representative of law schools generally, it merits retelling because what transpired there illustrates the lack of accountability law professors enjoy and the excesses that can result, and it reveals crucial dynamics that operate within law schools. The story can be told because St. John's today bears no resemblance to the place then: it is vastly transformed, with a dynamic dean and a critical mass of talented, hard-working faculty.

At a faculty meeting early that March, Dean Hasl announced that I had been appointed interim dean by the president (a closely held secret until that moment). The silence that greeted my name hung in the air as I walked to the podium. No one imagined that an untenured recent hire would be the one. I began: "Father Harrington asked me to be dean because he thought I was the person best able to bring us through this period of change. . . . What we are about to embark upon will be painful and difficult, and will require all of us to work harder—every one of us." My speech laid out three "nonnegotiable" points:

> First, we all have to work. This is a full-time job. We have an obligation to work at least forty hours a week on matters directly related to our responsibilities to the institution. . . .

> The second nonnegotiable point is that we are here to serve the students. They are the ones who pay our salaries. Our obligation is not just to teach them in the classroom, but also to answer their questions, to offer help when necessary, to serve as mentors, to write letters of recommendation, and more. To satisfy this obligation we must be here physically, in the building, and we must be welcoming to the students. Our doors must be open to them.

The final nonnegotiable point is that this is an academic institution, which by its nature requires that we are all teachers and scholars. We are in the business of conveying knowledge and teaching people to think. . . . That does not mean, however, that we cannot discuss different ways of living up to these requirements. We each have strengths in different areas.

It must seem ridiculous that a dean would lecture a faculty on the necessity to spend more time at the office, to work forty hours a week, to provide more services to the students, and to live up to our dual role as teachers and scholars. Things had gotten that bad.

The problems that St. John's confronted fifteen years ago are not unique. One can walk through the faculty corridors of many law schools and find lots of closed doors hiding unoccupied offices. Friday is an especially quiet day in faculty halls. The *only* thing we must do is show up to teach classes. On the list of great things about being a law professor, the freedom to decide whether or when to be at work (outside of scheduled classes) is at the top. We do what we want, when we want to, and no one—including the dean—tells us what to do. Some professors spend little time at school because they work more efficiently on scholarship at home. Some prefer to avoid the hassle of the daily commute. (Several law professors I know live in a different city, traveling to work by train or airplane.). A few go to an office where they carry on a legal practice in association with a firm. Whatever the individual reasons, getting the faculty to be present and available for colleagues and students can be trying. It's hard to create an intellectual community, or a community of any kind, when many people are not around much of the time.

These *are* full-time jobs, typically based on nine-month periods. The majority of law professors teach an average of six hours a week (per semester) for twenty-eight weeks a year; we also put in several hours of preparation per class (another eight to ten hours a week), perhaps two hours or so a week meeting with students and writing letters of recommendation, an unpleasant week or two each semester grading, and some committee service. A few professors give occasional talks at other schools, or at conferences, or serve on bar committees. When you add it all up and spread it out over nine months, that leaves a generous dollop of compensated time—say ten to fifteen hours a week—not taken up by teaching, committee service, and other work related activities. This ample time is for scholarship, yet virtually every faculty (except at brand-new law schools) has professors who don't write much.

Laments about this have been sounded for decades. Sixty years ago, the dean of the College of Law at the University of California, Berkeley, renowned scholar William Prosser, acknowledged,

> There is no law school, no matter how distinguished its reputation, that has not numbered on its faculty some such men as these. . . . The tragedy is that [owing to tenure] nothing much can ever be done about it. . . . All over the country there are many sad and wretched law schools in which the unhappy selections of some long-forgotten dean linger on year after year, too feeble, useless, and insignificant ever to receive an offer from another school, too satisfied ever to leave, and safe where they are until the age of seventy. Few die, and none resign.[1]

Harsh words, but true. In one respect, the problem has actually worsened since Prosser's woeful depiction: prohibitions against age discrimination give tenured professors license to keep their position indefinitely.

Deans have little leverage to get more out of malingering law professors—a group by no means limited to older faculty (and it must be emphasized that many older professors remain very productive). Abysmal performers can be fired regardless of tenure, at least in theory, but this is almost never done. Any attempt to revoke tenure would be controversial within a faculty; inevitably, the targeted professor would sue, claiming unjustified breach of tenure (correctly pointing out that other low producers have not been fired in the past). And the university would cut a check to settle. A range of slackers exists (as with any job), all of whom exact a cost in lost productivity, but not all of whom are bad enough to try to fix. As one might expect, a study found that a majority of law professors write less after obtaining tenure than before.[2] On most faculties, a minority of professors are disproportionally productive and the rest scatter across a spectrum from steady scholarly output to none at all.

A dean can withhold raises from poor performers as a sanction. Still, professors routinely get cost of living increases that keep them moving up the salary scale. The marginal difference between that and a merit raise provides negligible motivation to a professor on cruise control. (If you are wondering why a poor performer gets cost of living increases rather than nothing, remember that the dean's position becomes tenuous if too many faculty are unhappy. Nothing gets people more upset than pay issues.)

Deans wield small sticks for prodding—twigs, really—and consequently must resort to passing out goodies to get more out of people. They can try positive inducements, like offering paid research leaves or a summer research grant to encourage writing. This has the downside, however, of throwing more money at people who are already not doing what they should be. Morale issues develop within the faculty. Faculty members who have been working hard all along wonder why those putting in less effort obtain extra benefits. The dean, then, must hand out additional rewards to hard workers to maintain fairness and suppress grumbling.

Law schools, like universities generally, have resorted to offering generous buyouts to persuade ensconced retirement-age professors to leave. Tenure confers a property right—and professors can, and increasingly do, demand that they be paid to relinquish it.[3] It has become the professorial version of a golden parachute. Buyouts are costly and they are not as successful in inducing departures as one might think. Two years of full pay and six years of health benefits was the offer St. John's tendered in 1998, but initially not a single law professor took it. After all, the job is not taxing when done at a minimum level, the income is good, and professorial status is impressive. It makes sense that two years of free pay is not enough to give up a sinecure that only requires fifteen or twenty hours of work for half a year's time. And buyouts cannot solve the problem of underperforming professors who are not close to retirement age.

An effective way to wring more productivity out of professors who don't write is to ask them to teach an additional course. The standard load for most schools is four courses a year, which averages six hours a week of teaching a semester, or twelve classroom hours per year (more precisely, for twenty eight weeks). If a professor who is not writing is required to teach a fifth course, the school would gain another class at no extra cost. For every four professors who pick up an extra course, the school obtains the equivalent of another full-time classroom professor. At St. John's the faculty adopted this approach, enacting what we called the "alternative contribution system." Professors who were not inclined to engage in scholarship could choose instead to teach an extra course.

That is far easier to say than do. Law professors resent being asked to teach more than their customary, comfortable load. Adding a new course requires a lot of work the first time through. And worst of all, it is personally galling to teach more than one's colleagues, with a "nonscholar" stigma attached. Deans understandably would rather look the other way, absorbing the cost of underperformers rather than foist another course on them to their embitterment.[4]

After a year and a half as interim dean, I stepped down. Seven professors took the buyout, three more left on other terms, and five professors taught an extra course. The following spring the school jumped back up a tier per *US News*, remaining there ever since. Today, after subsequent waves of departures, the school is a changed place, with a highly productive faculty.

If this sounds like things worked out fine, that is only half the story. My term as dean was a miserable time for all. Among other measures, I froze faculty salaries (mine included), restricted travel, and eliminated summer research grants (except for new hires)—essentially taking money out of the pockets of professors—using the savings to boost scholarships for students and freeze tuition for a year. The faculty did not really have a choice when it "voluntarily" adopted the alternative contribution system. In an effort to increase accountability, everyone had to fill out a form specifying how many hours they spent on work-related activities (not surprisingly, nor credibly, every professor listed at least forty hours, and in most cases more). The palpable resentment these actions generated permanently altered my relationship with colleagues. Years later a colleague would occasionally remind me of the money I cost him over time owing to the one-year salary freeze. Another faculty colleague would not greet or speak to me, passing in silence in the halls or elevators for many years.

No dean who wants to remain the dean would have done these things. An official interpretation of the ABA standards accords the faculty significant power over the dean: "A dean should not be appointed or reappointed to a new term over the stated objection of a substantial majority of the faculty."[5] To understand the internal operation of law schools, one must keep this in mind.

I led off this book about law schools with a personal account of the circumstances surrounding my brief adventure as interim dean a dozen years ago because it is the best way to convey to readers the strange dynamics on law faculties. I must emphasize that many law professors at law schools across the country are conscientious and work hard. That said, the constellation of forces I describe in connection with the law faculty at St. John's operates everywhere. The crucial point I hope to get across through this story is that there is something unusual about a work environment that would allow a particular school to descend to such a condition. At almost any other type of job, people would have been fired long before, or the operation would have gone under. But in economic terms the professors and the law school were doing fine (notwithstanding the fall in rank). Many of the usual norms and incentives that govern workplaces do not hold for law faculties. At the heart of it lies this: law schools are run *for* law professors. This is not to say that the faculty runs the place. Individual professors have scant institutional power (though they can have personal sway with colleagues); the faculty collectively does not control the operation of the law school or its relationship with the university, although it has a strong say in certain institutional polices. The real power of law faculties lies in what can best be described as the all-pervading *faculty prerogative*—vague and unstated, yet unquestionably present.

No one tells law professors what to do. Law professors are superior to the students and served by the staff. They are the leading personages inside the law school and sometimes prominent outside as well. For a law school to function at a high level requires that individual professors be self-motivated, responsible, conscientious, and oriented to the common good even when that requires a sacrifice of their own self-interest. It requires, in other words, that law professors have better character than most human beings. Alas, we are fallible and self-oriented like everyone else.

PART I

Temptations of Self-Regulation

ONE

The Department of Justice Sues the ABA

In 1995, the Department of Justice (DOJ) filed a civil antitrust complaint against the American Bar Association (ABA), charging that "legal educators have captured the ABA's law school accreditation process."[1] This was an inglorious occasion for the ABA, a national organization of lawyers that claims to be the bastion of the rule of law. In the name of protecting the public, the ABA's Section on Legal Education and Admissions to the Bar, with the imprimatur of the US Department of Education, adopts and enforces accreditation standards for law schools to insure that they graduate knowledgeable, skilled, and ethical lawyers. Forty-five states, by order of their state supreme court, require graduation from an ABA-accredited law school as a prerequisite for admission to the bar.[2] Accreditation is therefore pivotal to law students and to law schools. A school seeking accreditation must meet a rigorous set of requirements; after accreditation is granted, schools undergo an extensive review by the Accreditation Committee every seven years, including an on-site visit by an inspection team.

The DOJ charged that the accreditation process had been subverted by legal educators to ratchet up their salaries and reduce their teaching loads. One accreditation standard established an eight-hour-per-semester limit on teaching loads.[3] Several provisions focused on securing adequate compensation for professors, and one standard required that faculty be given a "reasonable opportunity for leaves of absence and for scholarly research."[4] Although it says nothing about payment, "the Standard has been applied in practice to require paid sabbaticals, summer stipends, and other forms of research compensation."[5] Schools were at times "placed on report" when compensation levels were below that of peer schools.[6] Law professors thus enjoyed measures that inured to their financial benefit and insured they would not be subjected to onerous teaching loads.

A number of accreditation requirements imposed high costs on law schools. Law schools were required to have "adequate" facilities, substantial library collections, and low student-faculty ratios tallied on full-time professors in tenure-track positions (adjuncts or professors on short-term contracts did not count toward the ratio).[7] To maintain their standing as genuinely academic institutions, law schools were prohibited from offering bar preparation courses for credit (which helps prop up the lucrative bar review course industry). And several provisions jealously guarded accreditation itself by penalizing students at unaccredited schools. Accredited law schools were prohibited from accepting credits from students seeking to transfer from unaccredited schools. Graduates from unaccredited schools, furthermore, could not enroll in graduate law programs (LLM and SJD) offered by accredited schools. The standards barred them despite the fact that graduates from foreign law schools were freely permitted to enroll.

These various measures effectively kept out law schools built on a low-cost model, which emphasizes teaching rather than research, relies on a smaller core of full-time faculty without tenure at lower pay, uses a larger number of lawyers and judges to teach courses as adjuncts, possesses basic facilities and library collections, and focuses on teaching students practice skills and the core knowledge necessary to pass the bar exam. The DOJ antitrust investigation was prompted by a denial of accreditation to Massachusetts School of Law at Andover, a school that adopted the low-tuition model.

HOW THE INSPECTIONS WERE USED

The inspection arrangement invited abuse. A self-study would be prepared and provided to the inspection team by members of the faculty of the school undergoing review; faculty authors of the study would work faculty concerns into the study; the five- to seven-member ABA site-inspection team, typically composed entirely of law faculty, would interview various constituencies in the law school during their three-day visit; the report of the inspection team would reflect the agendas impressed on them during the process.

The findings of each accreditation review were sent to the dean of the law school and the university president. Legal educators who staffed inspection teams were naturally predisposed in two directions: favoring the law school in its relations with the university and the faculty in their dealings with law school deans. To the university president they would advocate the law school's interests—seeking to retain more funds and greater autonomy from the university.[8] To the law school dean they would press for compensation, research support, the extension of tenure, and other faculty-friendly conditions.

What accreditation amounted to was legal educators going around the country to school after school advancing the interests of fellow legal educators. As Ronald Cass, then dean of Boston University School of Law, observed in connection with the antitrust charges, "It always seemed that this was a process that was largely designed to help law schools extract funds from their host universities and to help certain groups within law schools extract funds from the dean."[9] (Dean Cass was doing fine himself, reportedly earning "$479,387 plus $23,173 in benefits in 1996–97.")[10]

While law school deans might have been pleased with the leverage this arrangement lent them against the university, they became fed up with accreditation demands. The American Law Deans Association was formed in 1994 to advocate changes in the accreditation process. Deans objected that "the process of accrediting law schools—ABA approval and AALS membership—had become unduly intrusive, burdensome, and unrelated to the actual quality of legal education. . . . Accreditation had become mainly focused on the inputs of legal education—such as space in the library or the level of pay for faculty—and . . . accreditation seemed increasingly to apply the same input formula regardless of the nature and mission of the particular school."[11] Reflecting its overreach, in 1994 "about 50 law schools, including many of recognized high quality, were on report [by the Accreditation Committee] for allocating inadequate resources to their law program."[12]

The ABA entered into a consent decree on the antitrust charges, agreeing to halt its offending practices. The ABA would no longer collect and share salary information and would no longer refer to compensation in connection with accreditation. The ABA would no longer exclude for-profit law schools or prohibit transfer students or graduates from unaccredited schools from moving to ABA-accredited schools. The Accreditation Committee and the Standards Review Committee could not have more than 50 percent of their membership made up of legal educators; site-inspection teams would henceforth include a university administrator from outside the law school and a lawyer or judge or lay member. The ABA would be subject to regular reviews from an antitrust compliance review officer. For ten years the consent decree would remain in effect, during which period the ABA would comply with all DOJ requests for interviews and information.

A humiliating capitulation by the ABA this was. But ABA President George E. Bushnell declared unrepentantly, "We absolutely, categorically deny [the antitrust allegations] and believe we're right."[13] To explain its agreement, the ABA mimicked the complaint uttered by every defendant who pleads nolo contendere to a charge: it did not contest the charges because the legal expense of proving its innocence would be too exorbitant. (A delicious irony: the preeminent professional organization of lawyers complaining that it must endure an injustice because legal costs are too high!) When insisting on the ABA's innocence, Bushnell did not deny the underlying factual allegations; rather, he contended that these actions did not violate antitrust law.[14]

THE FOCUS ON PROFESSOR COMPENSATION

University of Texas law professor Millard Ruud—the former consultant on legal education to the ABA and, later, the executive director of the Association of American Law Schools (AALS)—incensed by the unjust charges, defended the focus on faculty salaries. "It is beyond dispute that a law school's compensation structure directly affects the quality of those whom it can recruit and retain. Is it mere coincidence that the law schools that compensate its faculty best are also those that have the most highly regarded programs of legal education?"[15]

This defense betrays the flawed mindset of the people involved. Ruud is correct that professors at elite programs have higher pay, but that is irrelevant to the purpose of accreditation. Accreditation is justified as a means to insure a sound program of legal education that produces competent lawyers. This requires that salary be set at a level sufficient to attract capable law teachers. Insisting that faculties should be compensated at levels comparable to their peers, however, is about matching pay among professors. To determine whether faculty pay levels are adequate one must look at the supply of candidates seeking jobs as law professors—which was highly competitive in the 1980s and early 1990s when these accreditation actions were in full bloom.

The official interpretation of the accreditation standard relating to faculty compensation failed to heed this obvious point, stating: "A law school's faculty salaries, especially of full and associate professors, which remain unfavorable in comparison with the national median and with faculty salaries at approved law schools in the same geographical area may not be sufficient to attract and maintain a competent faculty."[16] This language suggests that anyone below the comparable median—half of the law faculties at any given time—might be inadequately compensated. Another official interpretation asserted, "A faculty salary structure which ranks at the very bottom of salaries at ABA approved schools is non-competitive and presumptively in non-compliance with the Standards."[17] This assertion is absurd on its face because there must always be schools at the bottom. An upward spiral follows from the combined operation of these interpretations: faculties below the median, especially those at the bottom, get moved up with every inspection, thereby raising the median and bottom for the next round. It was a fantastic arrangement for law professors.

Two years before the DOJ complaint, the *National Law Journal* ran an article on a recent run-up of law professor salaries. "During the past five years, faculty pay scales at most American law schools have gone up, and in some cases they have gone up by more than 50 percent, to the point that it's not uncommon for full professors to make, with perks, upward of $200,000."[18] "For example, in 1988–89, Seton Hall paid its full professors an average $71,900. In 1992–93, the average was $107,283. . . . At the Fordham University School of Law, full professors averaged $89,700 in 1988–89; by 1992–93 the figure had jumped to $125,250." These salaries, the article added, were supplemented by summer research grants of up to

$20,000 and fringe benefits that ranged from 20 to 38 percent of base pay. Funding these salary hikes, average tuition at private law schools rose by an average of 10 percent each year between 1988 and 1992 and, at public schools, by a yearly average of 11.7 percent.[19]

The article identified several factors that contributed to the rapid increase in faculty salaries, including making up for lagging law professor pay in the 1970s, setting attractive compensation levels to recruit talented professors, and rewarding productive professors with raises. "Another reason for the increase," the article explained, "is that the ABA, through its accreditation process, put pressure on schools to raise faculty salaries, according to several deans."[20] This article, remember, was written two years before the DOJ suit. The practice was an open secret.

CLINICAL TEACHERS REVOLT

A revealing twist to the DOJ suit exposes a deep rift within law schools that will come up again in this book. As required by antitrust procedures, the DOJ solicited comments on the consent decree. Several of the harshest condemnations of the accreditation process came from a subgroup of legal educators, clinical law professors. Clinical law professors objected to the consent decree for not going far enough, thereby allowing law professors to continue to control the process for their own benefit.

The Clinical Legal Education Association (CLEA), an organization of clinical teachers (with four hundred members at the time), asserted, "because . . . the accreditation process has been dominated by academics and deans, it has not been able to serve the function of insuring that students are adequately prepared to practice law."[21] CLEA worried that university administrators on site-inspection teams "are apt to pursue the goal of improving scholarly output as their highest priority," failing to appreciate the importance of skills-training programs. More important, according to CLEA, the consent decree failed to

> change or challenge existing standards and practices which enhance the power of academics at the expense of the needs of students and their future clients. For example, the existing standards mandate that legal academics be granted tenure, but do not provide this protection

to many clinical teachers who are involved in preparing students to practice law. The standards also require law schools to permit legal academics to participate in the governance of the law school, but have not been interpreted to mandate that clinical teachers be allowed to partake in governance. This differential treatment serves to preserve the status quo in which the research and other needs of academics are given priority over the needs of students and their future clients.

These views were repeated by other clinicians who submitted objections to the consent decree, prominently including John Elson of the Northwestern University School of Law, a leading voice among clinicians and a veteran participant in accreditation proceedings. Professor Elson confirmed, in bitter language, that legal academics have captured the process and "naturally seek to maintain a system of accreditation that reinforces their notions of 'quality' legal education. Those are notions that have elevated the production of scholarship as the highest law school priority and relegated students' professional preparation as an obligatory burden that should not interfere with academics' higher intellectual calling."[22]

Two aspects of these assertions stand out. CLEA suggests that law schools, dominated as they are by neglectful "academic" professors pursuing their scholarly indulgences, are not training competent lawyers. The DOJ never contended that law schools were failing this badly. The second striking aspect is the transparent attempt on the part of CLEA to use accreditation for the benefit of *its own* interest group—to enhance the status and employment conditions of clinicians. Clinicians must be given tenure and an equal say in governance, CLEA argued, if law schools hope to train competent lawyers.

The airing by clinicians of their grievances exposes a schism that lies below the surface of many law faculties, one that goes to a fundamental divide over whether law schools are academic institutions or exist to train lawyers. As we shall see, this divide has had enduring significance for law schools.

The entreaties of clinicians were rejected by DOJ as raising law school policy issues irrelevant to accreditation. Academic law professors were enviably successful at using the accreditation process to enhance their conditions of employment, and clinical professors were attempting to use the antitrust suit to accomplish the same—in both instances law professors presented their arguments in the name of the public interest.

THE HIGH PRICE OF ACCREDITATION

For an ignominious postscript, at the close of the ten-year period covered by the consent decree, the ABA was brought back to court by the DOJ for six violations of the court's order. Among these violations, the ABA had failed to insure that no more than half of the members of the Standards Review Committee were law school deans or faculty, and in multiple years the site-inspection teams did not include university administrators from outside the law school. These breached requirements were reforms designed to prevent legal educators from capturing the accreditation process. Judge Royce Lamberth found that "on multiple occasions the ABA has violated clear and unambiguous provisions of the Final Judgment," and he ordered the ABA to pay $185,000 in attorney's fees and costs to cover the expenses incurred by the antitrust division in uncovering the violations.[23]

While the blatant use of accreditation to benefit faculty is in the past, the enduring legacy of these actions was to entrench a culture within legal academia that presumes that a legitimate law school *must* be academically oriented.[24] Former Cornell Law School dean Roger Cramton objected (in 1986) to ABA accreditation decisions that "delayed the continued approval of sound law schools devoted to training practitioners for local practice"; "inspection reports criticized the nature and quality of scholarship as insufficiently theoretical or challenging and the failure of the schools to provide summer stipends or other measures supportive of research."[25] These attitudes continue to dominate legal education. Law schools at every level (except for unaccredited schools) allocate significant resources to faculty scholarship today because that is the prevailing norm of what it means to be a legitimate law school.

This has costly consequences. Take the example of Atlanta's John Marshall Law School, which had operated since 1933 as an unaccredited law school serving working-class students. Starting in 1987, the Georgia Supreme Court required graduation from an ABA-accredited school for bar membership, a shift in policy that forced John Marshall to seek accreditation. An inspection report in 1998 recommended against ABA accreditation, in part because it "deemed the school's teaching load, at eight hours a week, too high."[26] After being taken over by a for-profit company and implementing a host of changes to meet the standards, the school finally obtained full ABA accreditation in 2009. Tuition was $32,250 in 2010. John Marshall students graduated with an average law school debt of $123,025, among the highest in the country. Many graduates did not get jobs as lawyers. Whether accredited or unaccredited, the school remains at the bottom of the Atlanta-area law school hierarchy and its students have limited opportunities for employment. Now, however, students must pay a premium that attaches to accreditation, not just because it costs more to run an accredited law school but also because the market-based tuition price of an accredited law school is at least $10,000 higher than an unaccredited school.[27]

Why Is Law School Three Years?

"In the first year they scare you to death; in the second year they work you to death; in the third year they bore you to death." The truth in this old saw about law school is evidenced by perennial calls to abolish the third year. Larry Kramer, dean of Stanford Law School, remarked in a 2010 speech, "One of the well-known facts about law school is it never took three years to do what we are doing; it took maybe two years at most, maybe a year and a half."[1] Three law schools—Northwestern University School of Law, Southwestern Law School, and University of Dayton School of Law—have recently begun to offer two-year JD programs. These are not genuine two-year programs but three years of courses (and tuition money) crammed into two. Washington and Lee University School of Law transformed the entire third year into a practice setting, while still collecting full tuition.

A 1971 study by prominent legal educators, the Carrington Report, faced the issue head on: "Law faculty who have long wondered what to do with the third year must require of themselves an answer to the more basic question, why must there be a third year for all?"[2] The third year is unnecessary and should be abolished, the report concluded. Students learn enough in two years to prepare them for most legal practices. The report proposed a JD course of study that takes two years, available to students who have completed three years of undergraduate study. A law degree could then be completed in five years of education (three undergraduate plus two law school) rather than the current seven years (four undergraduate plus three law school), eliminating two years of tuition and living expenses and reducing opportunity cost. Students or returning lawyers who wish to specialize could add a year of concentrated study in their desired subject. This alternative is preferable to the current system, the report argued, because the expense of seven years of education inhibits people from poor families from becoming lawyers, resulting in reduced availability of lawyers with an understanding of the problems of the poor.[3]

If many legal educators think two years is sufficient, why is law school three?

The third year exists for reasons almost wholly detached from substance: at the turn of the twentieth century a determined effort by elite law schools used the ABA and the Association of American Law Schools (AALS) to entrench the three-year standard.

ELITE LAW SCHOOLS WRITE THE STANDARDS

The closing decades of the nineteenth century were a troubled time for the bar and legal academia. The legal profession was held in low esteem by the public, with lawyers being perceived as shysters engaged in unethical practices. Law schools were proliferating. "From 28 schools with 1600 students in 1870, the number jumped to 54 schools with 6000 students by 1890, and to 100 schools with 13,000 students by the turn of the century."[4] Night law schools taught entirely by legal practitioners and cheap to attend sprouted in major urban centers, producing a flood of graduates from recent immigrant families (Eastern Europeans, Italians, and Jews). Elite legal professionals who controlled the ABA worried that these new lawyers would further tarnish the already sullied reputation of the bar.

University-affiliated law schools, for their part, had trouble attracting students because a law degree wasn't required by any state for admission to the bar. (The traditional path to the bar was serving an apprenticeship in a law office.) The bar and elite legal academia thus shared a confluence of economic and professional interests in setting higher standards for legal education. Solidifying this alliance was an undercurrent of racist and nativist attitudes. The dean of University of Wisconsin Law School, voicing an often-repeated concern of the legal establishment, charged that night law schools enrolled "a very large proportion of foreign names. Emigrants and sons of emigrants . . . covet the title [of attorney] as a badge of distinction. The result is a host of shrewd young men, imperfectly educated, crammed so they can pass the bar examinations, all deeply impressed with the philosophy of getting on, but viewing the Code of Ethics with uncomprehending eyes."[5]

Legal education had not yet become standardized. A variety of programs and degrees were awarded in law—LLB, LLM, ML, DCL—ranging in duration from one to three years. Most programs did not require any college training for entry and many did not require a high school diploma. Before the turn of the century, the overwhelming majority of schools had two-year programs.[6] Harvard established a three-year program in 1878 (although mandating only eighteen months in residence), followed in the subsequent decade by Columbia Law School, University of Pennsylvania Law School, and a handful of others. The success of these schools encouraged more institutions to add a third year—with the obvious attraction of another year of tuition revenue—but two-year programs continued to thrive.

The ABA Section on Legal Education was created in 1893 at the urging of legal educators in the ABA who wanted a committee devoted to law schools. The schoolmen who dominated the section, dissatisfied that they remained at the margins of ABA concerns, invited representatives from laws schools to attend the 1900 annual meeting to create a second organization, the Association of American Law Schools. The two organizations were closely intertwined at the beginning, holding joint meetings for thirteen years (until the ABA inconveniently moved its annual meeting to October, in the middle of the academic calendar), with prominent legal academics circulating through AALS leadership positions and the ABA Section on Legal Education.[7]

The inaugural 1900 Articles of Association dictated that all AALS member schools require matriculating students to have a high school degree or its equivalent. The articles also imposed the three-year standard: "The course of study leading to its degree shall cover at least two years of ten weeks per year, with an average of at least ten hours required class-room work each week for each student; provided, that after the year 1905 members of this Association shall require a three years course."

Schools with two-year programs, then still the majority, were allowed to join the association immediately, with a five-year allowance to add the third year.

A delegate objected on the floor to the standard on grounds that still resonate today:

> I do not care at this time to go into the question as to whether a three-year or a two-year course is the more desirable. I do want to say that there is a very great difference of opinion among educators on that question; that in the opinion of many educators of wide experience two years spent at a law school and one year in an office is the best education a student can have. . . . I am not arguing against the existence of those great schools which with their endowments and able faculties, large attendance of students with ample means, may think it is desirable to have three-year courses. But it is an entirely different question whether you shall say that every law school ought to have a three-year course and that the student cannot have the benefit of the two-year course if he desires.[8]

Echoed by other lawyers at the meeting, this objection proved unavailing.

The schools that aggressively promoted the three-year model, with Harvard taking the lead, self-consciously styled themselves as *academic* institutions that provided their students a broad education in legal principles (or legal science, as it was called), which is inculcated through lengthy instruction from scholarly professors. The dean of Harvard asserted that "if law be not a science, a university will best consult its dignity in declining to teach it;"[9] Columbia's dean said the same: "It is only by regarding law as a science that one can justify its being taught in a university."[10] University-affiliated law schools were sensitive about this issue because law had widely been considered a trade best learned by working alongside a lawyer in an office—the Abraham Lincoln way.

Many law schools at the time, in contrast, saw their role as training students for the practice of law. Proponents of this view asserted that legal training was less about theory than about the fundamentals necessary for practice, which could be ably conveyed to students by experienced practitioners and judges in a two-year course of study, supplemented by work in a law office. Cheaper, shorter, and more narrowly focused, this delivered students what they needed and no more. The dividing line was not just economic but also geographical: all of the Southern law schools, including elite institutions, had two-year programs at the time. In 1905, when the grace period for current members expired, the AALS took a hard-line position, expelling schools that did not complete the transition to three years (University of Tennessee College of Law got the boot despite a plea for more time).

It was not necessary to force a choice between these two alternatives. Both could coexist. A 1921 study commissioned by the Carnegie Foundation, written by Alfred Reed, argued that law was a differentiated profession, which should be matched by a differentiated system of legal education. Local law schools have a practical curriculum that trains students in what the law is.[11] National law schools were training not just lawyers but people who would become the leaders of society. "Its primary interest is not with the law as it is, but with the law as it may become. . . . It sends into practice, into the legislature, on to the bench, men who, understanding the ideal as distinguished from the actual law, recognize their responsibility as parts of a general law-making machine and are animated with the ambition not merely to utilize the law as it is, but also to convert it into a more efficient instrument of justice."[12] It is a mistake to insist on a unitary set of standards, Reed argued, because the "two types of law schools serve distinct social purposes."[13] To modern ears these words perhaps sound elitist, but his argument was a defense of keeping access to the legal profession open to the poor and recent immigrants by allowing a cheaper model of legal education to exist (assuming basic standards are met) alongside academically oriented law schools.

The leaders of the bar and legal academia rejected Reed's proposal out of hand.[14] Law is a unified profession that requires uniformly high standards, they insisted. Shortly after the release of the Reed Report, the ABA promulgated its first ever accreditation standards for law schools, including these provisions:

(a) It shall require as a condition of admission at least two years of study in a college.

(b) It shall require its students to pursue a course of three years duration if they devote substantially all of their working time to their studies, and a longer course, equivalent in the number of working hours, if they devote only part of their working time to their studies.

(c) It shall provide an adequate library available for the use of the students.

(d) It shall have among its teachers a sufficient number giving their entire time to the school to ensure actual personal acquaintance and influence with the whole student body.[15]

The combined efforts of the AALS and the ABA Section on Legal Education, with some of the same people serving on both, produced these standards—which embraced and enforced the academic model of law school.[16]

This was a resounding victory for university-affiliated law schools. By this time most of the academic law schools—spurred by the 1900 AALS standards and the success of the three-year programs—had already made the transition to three years, but they did not yet hold a monopoly. Although it would take a couple of decades before the majority of states adopted graduation from an ABA-accredited school as a prerequisite for sitting for the bar, with the enactment of these standards the cast that would mold contemporary legal academia was set.

At the 1921 meeting on the standards, a Chicago lawyer, Edward Lee, summed it up: "That the contest brought to a culmination here today is the result of a deliberate purpose on the part of the great law schools of the country, comprising the Association of American Law Schools, to thrust out from the teaching of law all other schools not in that Association, and to put an anathema on them."[17] Urban part-time schools that served working people were the obvious target. The new standards, he objected, would "deprive masses of people in our large cities, many of them of foreign extraction, from access to our courts and legal aid for want of lawyers familiar with their language and distinctive customs."[18] Another critic at the meeting labeled it a "reactionary" proposal that would make it harder for less privileged people to follow what had been a traditional path of upward mobility in America.[19]

A UNIFORM ACADEMIC MODEL FOR A DIFFERENTIATED PROFESSION

Law school thus became what it is now: a three-year course of study taught by full-time academics. Justifications offered at the time in support of the third year are surprisingly thin for so momentous a decision. The only explanation provided in the ABA Report proposing the standards is that legal education must produce knowledge of legal principles and develop in students a mind attuned to the common law. "The process of assimilation and of mental growth must be orderly and comparatively slow."[20] It also invoked professional pride, noting that the American Medical Association had proposed a four-year standard for physicians; since it is self-evident that law is more complex than medicine, legal studies should be no less than three years. These were the total of the arguments for the third year.

When legal academics today debate whether the third year should be abolished, the old arguments are rehashed with little awareness of these historical circumstances. Professor Dan Solove of George Washington University Law School, for example, defended the third year in familiar terms:

> Some assume that the goal of a legal education should be to teach people practical skills so that when they leave law school, they can start practicing law like a pro. I don't agree. . . .
>
> We are training people who will be in profound positions of power—future lawyers, judges, politicians, policymakers, and so on. It is important for all of society that these individuals be given a legal education that consists of more than just taking a few key classes and rushing off into the practice of law. Law school is, for many, one of the few times that they reflect more broadly on the law, on justice, on how the law ought to be, on what works and doesn't work well in the legal system. It is a chance to learn about the history of law, the philosophy of law, law and literature, law and sociology, law and economics, and more. I believe that these things make students be better lawyers—wiser, more creative, more well-rounded. When we train lawyers, we're training people who will be shaping our society, and I

think it is imperative that their legal education be a robust extension of a liberal arts education, not simply a trade school education.[21]

As Reed pointed out nine decades ago, however, not all lawyers are leaders shaping society. Most lawyers engage in routine tasks that require diligence, care, and a strong sense of responsibility. Why, then, force all students to undergo a third year for intellectual "enrichment" at the cost of their financial impoverishment? Graduates of two-year programs, once given the opportunity to begin a career as a lawyer, may still go on to play important leadership roles in society. A number of twentieth-century legal luminaries, including Dean Roscoe Pound of Harvard Law School, Justice Benjamin Cardozo, and Justice Robert Jackson, did not attend three years of law school.

Those who wish to preserve the third year as a standard for all law schools must defend not the third year itself, which can be useful to many, but the model of the *unitary profession*, which requires the third year of everyone. Elite law schools can be free to offer a three-year program to students without every law school being compelled to do so. The legal profession has never been unitary in the nature of the work done by lawyers or in their compensation.

Liberal egalitarians will likely protest that the no frills law school argued for in the previous chapter and the two-year law school advocated here would be dumping grounds for the middle class and the poor. This is true. Few children of the rich will end up in these law schools, if they are allowed to exist. But a more apt description than "dumping ground" would be "affordable access to becoming an attorney." As things now stand, the "dirty, not so hidden secret in all this is that 'the heaviest debt burdens the lawyers least able to pay.' "[22] The real enemy of the middle class and poor is the expensive academic model that discourages many from going to law school at all and imposes a crushing debt on those who do attend.

THREE

Faculty Fight against Changes in ABA Standards

Law faculties across the United States erupted in protest in spring 2011 against a set of proposed changes to the ABA accreditation standards. Seventy law faculties ("and counting") passed resolutions "vigorously opposing the proposed changes to ABA Standards 206, 405, and 603 that would end the legal academy's commitment to the system of tenure and security of position for law school deans, traditional faculty, clinical faculty, legal writing faculty, and librarians."[1] The Association of American Law Schools (AALS) sent a ten-page letter on behalf of the organization detailing objections to the changes. The Society of American Law Teachers (SALT) sent a five-page opposition letter. The association of clinical professors), CLEA, sent an eleven-page opposition letter. Dozens of letters and resolutions have been submitted in opposition from individual law professors and other law faculty–related organizations.[2] Much of legal academia was up in arms against the proposed reforms, painting frightful visions of the deterioration of legal education that would follow if the reforms were enacted.

What got law professors so riled is that the proposed changes dared to address the sacred pillar of academia: tenure. Tenure is terrific. The holder has a job for life with absolutely no worries (except for the rare occasion that a school fails). Few American workers enjoy such luxury. Tenure is justified as essential to academic freedom—the lifeblood of the academy—necessary to promote the open expression of controversial ideas. (Another argument sometimes offered in support of tenure is that it enables universities to pay faculty lower compensation in exchange for ironclad job security and a longer work horizon.)

The proposed changes to the ABA standards do not abolish tenure. Rather, they suggest that a law school is free to hire full-time faculty in non-tenure-track positions. Previously the standards had been understood to require that the main law faculty must consist of tenured positions. The interpretation of the newly proposed standard loosened this: "A system of tenure earning rights, *while not required*, can be an effective method of attracting and retaining a competent fulltime faculty."[3] The mere suggestion that law faculties need not be predominantly tenure-based is abhorrent to academics—hence the firestorm.

This language was less a radical proposal than a concession to reality. At universities generally, although tenure is still the official norm, the trend for decades has gone the other way. About 65 percent of teaching positions at colleges today are nontenured, with many classes taught by graduate students, adjuncts, and instructors on contract.[4] Law schools have also drifted in this direction, though not as far, held back by the ABA standards. A significant proportion of courses in law schools are taught by adjuncts, visiting professors, legal writing professors and clinical professors on contract, faculty fellows, professors from practice, and various other categories and titles.

Tenure is costly and inflexible for schools—a lifetime marriage with a professor with almost no possibility of a divorce (except paying a ransom to purchase their departure). Even with the proposed change, there is little doubt that law schools will continue to offer tenure as an inducement to attract quality faculty. But the proportion of tenured positions within law faculties will go down.

Although one might not know it from the agonized opposition, this was not a frontal attack on academic freedom or on the quality of legal education. The proponents of the proposal, aware of the potential negative affect a reduction of tenure might have on academic expression, included language that would require law schools to put in place contractual protections for academic freedom. What motivated the proposed changes to the standards was an effort to find ways to slow the escalating cost of legal education.

SELFLESS LAW PROFESSORS ENGAGED IN PUBLIC SERVICE

AALS president Michael Olivas would have none of it, insisting in his opposition letter that it is essential to the training of competent lawyers that law schools be staffed by "career, full-time faculty" in positions with tenure.

The high quality and distinctiveness of American legal education are based largely on the work of career, full-time faculty who engage fully in the law school's teaching, scholarship, and service missions. Full-time faculty should be experts in their fields and continue to engage in scholarship that makes them even more accomplished. Given that law is fundamentally a public profession, law school faculty should perform *public service* that both models for students the *selflessness* encouraged for all lawyers, and helps fulfill the role of law schools in contributing to the improvement of law, lawyers, the legal system, and the system of justice. The scholarship and *public service* of career, full-time faculty do not merely supplement their teaching role. Both scholarship and *public service* underlie teaching and give it an authority that that teachers who merely pass on received understanding or transmit skills cannot.[5]

When repeating "career, full-time faculty," and "scholarship," Olivas was making two separate points that AALS has staunchly defended: that adjuncts should not be allowed to teach a substantial proportion of courses and that law faculties should not be filled with full-time teachers who are not scholars. A law faculty entirely filled with experienced lawyers and former judges could not produce quality lawyers because they would lack the career commitment to scholarship and legal expertise that only true academics possess.

In defense of tenure, Olivas trotted out the "we do more than train lawyers" line that academic law schools have invoked for over a century. Since law must be taught by academics, by this argument, tenure follows as a matter of course because academics require *academic* freedom. Enlisting another favorite claim, Olivas associated law professors with "public service"—thrice repeated in the above paragraph.

This is a dubious assertion. While a few professors on every law faculty engage in voluntary work for bar committees, offer pro bono services on cases, and other such activities, most do not. Law professors teach, write, serve on faculty committees, and meet with students; faculty members who engage in substantial consulting work are usually profitably compensated for it. His suggestion that law professors perform the important task of modeling "selflessness" for law students is feeble at a time when legal academics are very well compensated for what they do (as I will detail in a coming chapter). The days of the self-sacrificing law professor who gave up lucre to pursue knowledge and mold young minds are long gone. Most law professors spend limited time with students, so we do little modeling of any kind outside of the classroom.

Olivas acknowledged concerns about rising tuition but countered, "While educational cost is important, and a full and open debate about which costs are critical to a quality legal education is warranted, it is not the only consideration."[6] Of overriding importance, he reminded the ABA, is a quality legal education that trains competent lawyers. He raised the specter that the proposed changes will promote a "race to the bottom," with schools reducing their faculty expenses to cut costs.[7]

These arguments are reminiscent of the initial justifications put forth by the AALS and ABA early in the twentieth century to impose the three-year academic model of legal training, a standard that was intended at the time to drive out practitioner-taught, part-time schools that served working students. There was merit to the argument then, when the quality of instruction varied greatly among law schools, but it is implausible today. Rigorous accreditation standards will remain in place to maintain the quality of law schools. Talk of a race to the bottom is scare mongering.

What the proposals would allow is greater flexibility and variation among law schools. Schools that wish to retain their academic orientation would be free to do so, continuing a heavy commitment to research faculty; schools that prefer to deliver a legal education at lower cost by relying more heavily on adjuncts and untenured full-time professors with practice experience, and by imposing heavier teaching loads on faculty (with less research), would be free to do so. This is in tune with what Alfred Reed initially proposed: allowing differentiation within legal academia in recognition of the reality that the legal profession is differentiated.

Legal academics across the country continue to insist on the uniform model of legal education, firm in the conviction that training competent lawyers depends on law faculties predominantly staffed by scholarly professors eligible for tenure. But these essential questions are rarely addressed: At what cost? What are the consequences to society of an enormous economic barrier to becoming a lawyer?

CLINICIANS BATTLE TO PRESERVE GAINS

Another highly controversial proposed change involves removing job protections for clinical law professors. The proposal sought to erase this standard: "A law school shall afford to full time clinical faculty members a *form of security of position reasonably similar to tenure*, and noncompensatory perquisites reasonably similar to those provided other full-time faculty members."[8] The proposal also sought to abolish an official interpretation that held that clinicians were entitled to "at least a five year contract that is presumptively renewable."[9] These proposed deletions generated an outcry from the clinical community and many sympathetic colleagues on law faculties.

The original inclusion of this language in the standards and official interpretations was a hard-fought victory for clinical teachers following a decades-long campaign.[10] Even then the language was far from satisfactory for those who wanted full tenure rights. The changes were all the more offensive to clinicians for proposing to sweep away the partial progress they had made in improving their status in law schools.

In its letter opposing the proposed changes, CLEA repeated the embittered charge of clinicians about their academic-oriented colleagues: "the overwhelming capture of law school governance by faculty members whose scholarly work and teaching do not reflect a practice orientation and many of whom lack experience as a lawyer."[11] Research professors are already unfairly better treated than clinical teachers, CLEA asserted, and the proposed changes would make matters worse.

It's true, and lamentable, that clinical teachers have second-class status within many law schools. For that matter, professors who teach legal writing—an essential lawyer skill—have even lower status, third class, but have never able to muster a lobby strong enough to get protections for themselves written into the ABA standards. Clinical professors are paid less than doctrinal professors, legal writing professors are paid still less, and on many faculties neither have full voting rights on matters such as faculty hiring. Nothing is fair about any of this. The market for law professors and governance within law schools developed this way.

Fairness and sympathy, however compelling, are not reasons to include special measures for clinicians in *accreditation* standards. These measures belong in the standards only if clinicians can establish that law schools would not be able to produce competent lawyers if clinicians do not enjoy such protections. No plausible case has been made for that. CLEA gives it away when it asserts, "If the majority of doctrinal faculty are eligible for tenure, then the clinical faculty must have equivalent job security: full governance rights. . . . Only if the majority of the rest of the faculty are at-will or under short-term contracts should clinical faculty ever be consigned to this relationship to their school."[12] This is a demand for equal treatment. The vice chair of the ABA Standards Review Committee, Margaret Barry, supportive of the clinician's cause, confirmed that "the idea is to eliminate inequality between different types of law professors."[13] She did not explain why inequality among faculty bears on accreditation.

Whether a clinical professor has long-term job security does not change their daily work with students in practice settings, although it might affect the teacher's morale and sense of institutional loyalty. The many clinical teachers who now work without long-term job security—roughly 40 percent—presumably are still doing a fine job of training competent lawyers. Despite their second-class status within the faculty, the pay is good and work conditions are good enough (comfortable hours, relatively little pressure, reasonable case loads) to attract highly capable people who gladly assume the position.

Tenure for all clinicians was never in the cards because clinical programs are expensive. Doctrinal teachers can, and in many schools do, teach large classes of eighty to a hundred or so students (although many teach smaller seminars as well). Clinical classes require close supervision of each student, so the number of students per teacher is necessarily much lower, ideally no more than ten. Even law schools that champion equal status for clinical professors (about a third of clinical professors across the nation hold tenured or tenure-track positions), as my own law school Washington University does, in practice quietly get around this by hiring "staff attorneys," or "clinical fellows," or "visiting professors" to provide less costly support. This creates status differences among clinicians within a single school.

The extension of tenure to clinicians, furthermore, has an effect that is counter to their function: it prompts clinicians to engage in scholarship, traditionally the sine qua non of tenure. This is odd in several ways. The nature of the position is to train lawyers in a practice context—and clinicians are hired based on criteria tied to this function, primarily including substantial practice experience. Clinicians can be scholars, of course, but that is not what they are mainly selected for, in contrast to doctrinal faculty, for whom scholarly potential is the all-determining criterion for obtaining a position. Clinicians relentlessly criticize the emphasis on scholarship in law schools, yet now they hanker to do it themselves in order to qualify for tenure. To produce enough high-quality scholarship to earn tenure, furthermore, clinicians must be given time away from the clinics they have been hired to teach, thereby increasing the cost of the clinic—someone else must supervise the cases in their absence.

A trade-off exists between the dual agendas of clinicians: (1) to expand clinical offerings within law schools; and (2) to acquire tenure or, at least, long-term job security. Clinicians insist that the latter (status change) is necessary to achieve the former (enhance lawyer training). Clinical offerings at law schools have boomed in recent decades, as reflected in the fact that CLEA's current nine hundred–strong membership is more than double what it was in 1995. The expansion of clinics, however, would likely have been more restricted had law schools been required to attach tenure status or presumptively renewable five-year contracts to every new clinical position, given the expense and inflexibility.

One way to avoid this trade-off is to offset the expansion of (tenure-track) clinical positions with a contraction of (tenure-track) doctrinal teaching positions, but law schools have not taken this path. To the contrary, for reasons I will elaborate shortly, doctrinal positions have increased along with the growth of clinical programs.

The strident advocacy of the clinical movement was understandable, and necessary, twenty-five years ago, when clinical programs were inadequate or nonexistent at many law schools. But substantial improvements in clinical offerings have been achieved. With law schools under increasing pressure to control costs, clinicians, along with everyone else in law schools, must consider the economic implications of clinical programs and separate more sharply those work conditions they would like for themselves from what is necessary to best educate law students at an affordable cost.

THE UNEXPECTED PARALLEL BETWEEN LIBERALS TODAY AND ELITES OF YESTERYEAR

Academic freedom is critically important to the academy and tenure protects academic freedom. Clinical programs have come under pressure in recent years from state legislatures and influential interests upset at cases brought by law school clinics, posing a threat to their independence.[14] These are worthy reasons to support tenure and long-term contracts for faculty, including clinical professors and legal writing professors.

It must be paid for, however. The passion with which law professors have resisted the encroachment on tenure and have advocated job security for clinicians stands in stark contrast to our conspicuous silence about the astronomical increase in tuition that funds our operation.

Liberal law professors today would doubtless condemn the elite-dominated ABA at the turn of the twentieth century for raising the cost of legal education in a way that restricted access by the poorer classes to the profession. Economic barriers to the legal profession are once again a central issue in a fight over the regulations that govern legal education. This time liberal law professors, in the name of high-quality legal education and fairness to colleagues, are the ones staking out the higher cost position. Both then and now, arguments were couched in claims of being for the public good. One difference is that the elite bar then at least was consciously aware that they were restricting access (for what they thought were legitimate reasons), whereas law professors today apparently have blinders on that prevent them from seeing this consequence.

ANOTHER ROUND OF REGULATORY CAPTURE?

The annual AALS meeting is the largest gathering of law professors each year. The theme of the January 2012 meeting was "Academic Freedom and Academic Duty." Among the many serious issues facing contemporary law schools, the conference singled out the necessity to defend tenure privilege. The conference announcement warned about the grave threat posed by "law school accreditors considering no longer requiring a system of tenure or security of position. It is difficult to square these developments with the increased attention we at AALS have paid to our core values. Arguments for tenure include that the promise of continual employment gives faculty an incentive to work on behalf of the institution and that good faculty governance requires a tenure system."[15] These arguments, raised among ourselves, reveal that the day-to-day implications of tenure for professors are less about academic freedom, though we repeatedly cite that, than about our work environment.

Law professors were acutely aware that a battle for future conditions of employment was on, and they were mounting a fierce defense. The nigh universal protests from law faculties and AALS put the brakes on the proposed changes to the ABA accreditation standards. From a set of proposals that looked to loosen the restrictions imposed on law schools, allowing schools more flexibility in hiring professors in non-tenure-track positions, the orientation of the Standards Review committee did an apparent about-face to consider ways to further enhance the security of position for law professors.

After the term of several members on the committee expired, one of the new incoming members of the ABA Standards Review Committee was Professor Reese Hansen.[16] Hansen was the immediate past president of the AALS, the organization for law professors that led the opposition to the proposed changes. In his capacity as president of AALS, Hansen sharply criticized the proposed changes put forth by the committee.[17] Another new member of the committee, Professor Susan Kay, former president of CLEA, has been a strong advocate of tenure or its equivalent job security for clinicians. Instead of fighting these actions from the outside, now Hansen and Kay would have the far more effective position of serving on the committee that would write the standards.

This is the latest example of a long tradition in which ABA committees charged with regulating law schools are staffed with leaders from organizations that have the interests of law professors and law schools foremost in mind. Once again, the ones being regulated are writing the rules.

PART 2

About Law Professors

FOUR

Teaching Load Down, Salary Up

Law professors have always paid special attention to how much they teach and how much they are paid. Attendees at the 1910 AALS meeting discussed whether the association "should attempt to fix the salaries of teachers in law school to correspond with the salaries paid to the judges of the highest court in their respective states."[1] A 1920 AALS report urged that law professors (because they can earn more money as lawyers) must be paid on a higher scale than university professors; and it advocated that teaching loads should be no greater than "eight hours a week, and six is the better limit."[2] In 1923 the AALS Executive Committee decided to "compile annually and keep available for the use of members of the law faculties the teaching load and the actual average of salaries paid to full professors in each of the member schools."[3] A special committee recommended in 1937 that "teaching loads, tenure, and salary levels" be given "careful consideration" in determining whether schools meet AALS standards for sound educational policy.[4] These actions, precursors to the antitrust trouble mentioned in chapter 1, were justified as necessary to insure a quality legal education.

Vigorous advocacy by law professors on both fronts produced a long-term trend of pushing down teaching loads while salaries went up, with a spurt in both directions taking place in the past three decades. A push-pull dynamic has been at work. Accreditation-tied efforts to improve salaries and reduce teaching loads helped push up the folks in the bottom half, while competition among the top law schools to hire outstanding scholars helped pull up everyone in the top half. Encouraging it all was the drive to enhance scholarship and reputation.

THE DROP IN TEACHING LOADS

By the early 1920s, the "better" law schools had established a standard course load of *six* hours a week (twelve a year).[5] A survey of law schools in 1934 found that the typical full-time law professor taught *eight* hours a week (sixteen a year).[6] This basic pattern held for decades. A survey of ABA-accredited schools in 1941 divided schools into three categories: professors at larger, wealthier schools taught an average of 6.71 hours a week; at less wealthy schools with smaller faculties, the teaching load was 7.65 hours per week; at the smallest schools with limited resources, the teaching load was 8.66 hours per week.[7] A comprehensive 1961 report by AALS found that the average teaching load among law professors generally was 7.54 teaching hours per week.[8] It did not break down schools by group, but added that the "average of minimum teaching hours" per week was 5.96 and the "average of maximum teaching hours" per week was 8.84.[9] Deans of law schools taught an average of 3.84 hours per week, while assistant deans taught an average of 5.03 hours.[10]

At the cusp of the modern era of legal academia, judging from these sources, it appears that professors at wealthier ("national") law schools taught about twelve classroom hours a year, the average professor taught fifteen hours a year, and professors with the heaviest loads taught sixteen hours a year. Professors at schools with small faculties had the most arduous classroom duties, sometimes teaching nine credits of three different subjects in the same semester.[11]

AALS consistently maintained that teaching loads in excess of eight hours a semester did not allow professors sufficient time for their scholarly duties.[12] The 1961 report recommended that an eight-hour maximum (or ten hours for repeated courses) be made into a binding requirement for AALS membership.[13] To further facilitate scholarship, the report recommended that schools provide occasional relief from teaching for research projects, which fewer than half of the schools allowed at the time.[14] The report also advocated that law schools liberally grant faculty leaves with pay for research purposes. Sixty-nine out of 111 schools did not grant sabbaticals; thirty-five schools provided leaves every seven years, and only two schools granted research leaves more frequently.[15] These recommendations were later written into the ABA accreditation standards.[16] Extending a generous package to professors, an official interpretation emphasizes that "law schools provide time for these necessary [scholarly] activities by observing limits on (i) the number of weeks a year in which a teacher teaches; (ii) the number of students in each teacher's courses; and (iii) each teacher's course-hour load."[17]

For most of the twentieth century, six classroom hours a week per semester represented the ideal load. A review of Tennessee law schools prepared by a Columbia professor in 1949 complimented Vanderbilt University Law School's highly productive faculty, explaining, "The maximum teaching load of six or seven hours makes it possible for them to engage in these [research] activities, and at the same time to keep their teaching fresh and vigorous."[18] Later in the century, however, this was no longer seen as ideal, as reflected in the 1987 remark by Professor Mary Kay Kane: "At my own school, Hastings, we have a *heavy* teaching load (12 units per year)."[19]

In the final quarter of the century, when six hours a week (twelve a year) became the average teaching load for all law professors, the collective sense of what an ideal load was moved lower. This shift in perception is in part explained by greater scholarly demands. A lighter course load can feel too heavy if professors are expected to write more than previously. (Bear in mind, though, that early mid-twentieth-century legal academic giants, people like John Henry Wigmore, Samuel Williston, Joseph Henry Beale, and Prosser, managed to be prodigious scholars under the six-hour norm at elite schools.)[20] Also contributing to the sense that six hours a week teaching is "heavy" is the gnawing awareness that more fortunate colleagues in other law schools have the luxury of teaching less.

The teaching loads of law professors around the country today are not a matter of public record but a representative picture can be gleaned from various sources. A survey conducted in 1997 of law professors hired between 1986 and 1991 found an average of 11.71 credit hours teaching, and a median and mode of twelve hours.[21] Eleven percent of law professors surveyed taught fewer than ten hours and 26 percent taught fewer than eleven hours. As the author notes, the overall numbers include clinical professors, who often have higher credit allocations, so taking doctrinal professors in isolation would show lower teaching loads.[22] Without providing concrete details, the author disclosed that "faculty members who taught at more prestigious institutions taught significantly fewer credit hours, on average, than did their colleagues at less prestigious schools; this was an important variable in explaining the variance in teaching load."[23]

Teaching hours continued to fall after the 1997 study. An informal survey conducted in 2005 found that law professors at nearly all of the top twenty-five schools (by *US News* ranking) had three-course loads, which amounted to ten hours per year or less of teaching.[24] These surveys likely overstate the actual average hours taught by law professors because they do not factor in sabbaticals and research reductions, which are liberally available at elite institutions.

The most concrete recent data on teaching load are provided by a law professor who examined confidential 2006 reports on law schools compiled by the ABA. His data reveal not only that professors at higher ranked schools teach less than do other professors, which has always been the case, but that the average load of all law professors is now below historical norms. "At the 10 highest-ranked law schools, for example, the average annual teaching load is 7.94 hours; in U.S. News's third and fourth tier, it is 11.13 hours—40% higher."[25]

HISTORICALLY LOW TEACHING LOADS, STILL TRENDING DOWN

Let's put these numbers in historical perspective. Law professors at elite law schools today teach just over half what the average law professor taught for most of the twentieth century: eight credits a year compared to fifteen credits a year. They spend a quarter to a third less time in the classroom than earlier generations of elite professors. Full-time deans of law schools in 1960 averaged a reduced teaching load that amounts to almost the same as the full load of elite professors today. As a group, law professors generally now average three to four hours less of teaching—one full course down—than the average law professor taught for most of the past century. At law schools where teaching loads are a faculty governance matter, professors voted for the reduction, awarding themselves more discretionary time.

Facilitating the production of scholarship is the justification for this across-the-board reduction in teaching by law professors. And indications are that the ratcheting down of teaching in favor of scholarship has not yet reached a bottom. A number of nonelite schools that currently have twelve-hour teaching loads (two courses per semester) offer professors the option to reduce to nine hours of teaching a year (the elite range), dropping a course in exchange for writing one additional article.[26] Set aside, for the moment, questions about whether this is a wise policy for law schools and whether a single article should be accorded the same value as a full course. Contemplate instead what this implies more generally. Should this become a trend, professors at elite schools will be in line for a further course reduction if their historically lower relative teaching burden is maintained. The 2006 study found a low range of 6.7 hours annual teaching load for full-time law professors—that's just over one class per semester or two classes a year.[27] If some professors are getting that now, others being recruited surely will seek it for themselves as well. When lateral recruits get this deal, a few existing members of the faculty will inevitably demand the same, threatening to leave if not satisfied. Professors being recruited away have been known to carry a competing job offer with a reduced load to their own dean to extract the same deal (and the same bump in salary) to remain at their existing institution.[28] This is how teaching loads come down, first for a few, then for others.

It is not surprising that individual professors and law schools would trade teaching time for more scholarship. The same development has occurred in universities generally, where professors in tenure-eligible positions also teach less than previously.[29] Academia has been called a "prestige market" with scholarship the coin of the realm: financial and professional rewards to individual professors are earned through scholarly recognition. Institutions seek to enhance their academic reputation by recruiting and enabling top scholars to conduct research.[30] This creates "an active market for faculty—a national market—in which prestige-seeking colleges and universities compete with each other to build institutional excellence."[31] The professor and the institution have an overlapping interest in freeing up time for research because scholarly production redounds to the benefit of both. "When we go to recruit a star professor," Harvard president Derek

Bok wryly remarked, "the bargaining chip is always a reduced teaching load—never a reduced research load."[32] The nonstars on faculties, the professors not being recruited away, also benefit from this process owing to pressure to accord equal treatment to members within a faculty.[33]

A *National Law Journal* article published in 1997, "Feeding Frenzy for Prof Stars," announced: "Legal education has entered the age of the free agent, in which many of the nation's premier law schools are engaged in a high stakes race for scholarly stars."[34] There has always been movement of law professors from lower-prestige to higher-prestige law schools, from higher to lower teaching loads.[35] What distinguishes the contemporary scene from earlier periods is back and forth movement of law professors between elite institutions poaching from one another, dangling less teaching and more pay as inducements.[36] (The impact of this on faculty salaries will be taken up shortly.)

THE PROBLEMATIC IMPLICATIONS OF THE REDUCTION

Although the general dynamic matched what occurred in universities, the situation at law schools has additional problematic ramifications in two ways—first, internal to each institution and, second, across institutions. Internally, universities compensated for the lowered teaching loads of its tenure-eligible professors by utilizing cheaper non-tenure-track teachers, adjuncts, and graduate students, who now collectively handle 65 percent of teaching duties. Because the emphasis of ABA standards on tenure-track faculty prevented law schools from moving as far down this path as universities went, law schools had to offset reduced teaching loads in a more costly fashion by expanding the size of the tenure-track faculty.[37]

Worse than just costly—it was an inefficient means to increase scholarship. The teaching load of the entire faculty dropped to the twelve-credit range, but not all law professors utilized the extra time to boost their scholarly production. A targeted reduction in teaching, rather than across the board, would increase scholarship at the lowest cost. The strongest predictor of scholarly production is scholarly production.[38] Giving more time to prolific scholars will result in more scholarship because writing is what they do with their time; giving more time to people who write relatively little might well be spent on nonscholarly activities because that is what they tend to do. An empirical study in 1998 of almost five hundred law professors five to ten years on the job (in their prime productive years) found that "teaching load . . . showed surprisingly little correspondence to scholarly productivity."[39] Within a range of ten to thirteen credits a year, credit hours taught showed "no significant association with the number of articles published, the likelihood of publishing in a top twenty journal, or the likelihood of publishing a book."[40]

Twelve hours a year teaching is "heavy" for a scholar who churns out research, but it is a comfortable load for a less compulsive scholar (at many law schools the norm is an unhurried pace of one substantial article every two years), and it is an embarrassingly easy load for a professor who hardly writes. Just about every law faculty has at least a few professors who write little. Law schools—law deans—have shown little stomach for eliminating this inefficiency, whether by limiting reduced loads to actively writing faculty or (where a reduced load already exists) by requiring nonproducers to teach an extra course. As a consequence of these factors, in practice the reduction in teaching loads for law professors across the land has led to more scholarship from some and more free time for others, time that is occupied in various ways—from engaging in legal practice, to writing poetry collections and novels, or simply enjoying more leisure.[41]

The second problematic ramification relates to the fact that the universe of postsecondary education is more differentiated than law schools, with vocational colleges, community colleges, liberal arts colleges, and research universities. Community colleges do not compete in the national prestige market. They do not subsidize scholarship by their professors beyond minimal levels, and they are much cheaper to attend. The median teaching load for a full-time community college professor is fifteen credit hours a semester (five courses), or ten courses a year.[42] Virtually all accredited law schools, in contrast, have adopted teaching loads that provide professors ample time for scholarship. In effect, all accredited law schools are set up like research universities. Pursuant to the unified academic model promoted by AALS and enforced by the ABA, what might have developed as the law school equivalent of community colleges has been squashed, banished to the unaccredited realm, reducing the availability of low cost options for people who wish to become lawyers.

THE RISE IN SALARIES

Throughout the twentieth century, law professors have complained about being underpaid.[43] "Law School Salaries—a Threat to Legal Education," was the title of a 1953 article by Homer Crotty, the chairman of the ABA Section on Legal Education, issuing a plea for higher law professor pay.[44] It was not enough that they were paid more than other professors, he argued, because law professors can earn more money in legal practice.[45] That is the law professor mantra. The 1961 AALS report on legal academia expressed incredulity that "only" sixty-eight law schools paid law professors on a higher scale than other university professors, while thirty-eight schools did not.[46] "If this condition continues to exist, it is quite clear that the caliber of future law faculties will be seriously endangered, since only average success at the bar will offer far more handsome rewards than the best paid positions in some of our law schools."[47] In a 1987 article arguing that law professors were underpaid, Duke professor George Christie reiterated this old argument, pointing out that young associates in law firms earn more than senior professors. "Almost every outstanding law teacher I have met would have been a very successful legal practitioner," he claimed.[48] Although a 1990 report on legal education acknowledged that median faculty salaries had "more than doubled" since 1974, it reminded readers that "the median salary is still far less than beginning associates at many major law firms."[49]

Early in the last century most law professors earned modest incomes, although all along professors at elite schools did fine, and pay improved across the board after midcentury. The best paid law professors in 1920 earned $10,000—or $112,450 in 2011 inflation adjusted terms.[50] A significant number of schools at the time paid full professors $6,000 ($67,500 inflation adjusted), and others paid worse. If pay was too low, the concern was, professors would spend excessive time on side legal practices to supplement their income. When Crotty wrote his alarmist article, the best paid professors earned $15,000, equivalent to $140,000 today; the national median law professor salary was low, $6,350 ($53,900 inflation adjusted).[51] Pay had gone up nicely by 1965, when the average salary of a full professor was $16,749 ($120,100 today); and the best paid professors did well at $30,000 ($215,200).[52] Top salary for a full professor when

Christie complained about professor pay in 1987 was over $110,000, which equals $225,700 today; the median salary was $60,000 ($123,100 inflation adjusted).

At every step, second only to medical faculty (whose pay is supplemented by clinical revenues and outside research funding), law professors earned more than other college professors, often substantially more. In 1985–86, full professors of law earned 141 percent of the average salary of full professors of English, and they maintained a sizable premium every decade through 2009–10, when full law professors earned 159 percent of English professors.[53] A recent survey found that the annual salary of full professors in law schools averages $22,000 more than engineering professors and $26,000 more than business professors, the two next highest earning categories, and $52,000 more than English professors.[54]

Yet law professors remained dissatisfied in the knowledge that they earned less successful lawyers. This convenient comparison, which might have been a legitimate concern when law professors earned less than average lawyers in the same locale, has long been a stretch.[55] Third-year associates in corporate law firms do indeed earn more than many senior law professors. Law professors as a group have sparkling credentials, it is true, and many would have been eligible for well-paying corporate law jobs.[56] But the pay comparison to financially successful lawyers is false because the kind of work necessary to earn that money is not what law professors desire. The legion of law professors who gladly fled corporate law jobs to join the academy make this very point. Associates in corporate law firms bill above two thousand hours a year, routinely working six or seven days in excess of sixty hours a week, with limited vacations. If we compare earnings per hours worked, law professors earn *far* more than do associates.

Corporate law practice or high-end torts litigation is not for everyone. Nor is it obvious, Christie's confidence aside, that a successful academic would have been a financially successful lawyer—the skill sets and character traits are not the same. Moreover, with the recent influx of PhDs onto law faculties, and given that many law professors have little practice experience (and in some cases not even a JD), it is by no means a safe assumption that the bulk of law professors would have thrived in the practice of law. In the end, law professors are academics like any other college professor, and many are secretly delighted to have escaped the rigors and tedium of legal practice. If there is an economic basis for the pay premium we enjoy, it is not that law professors could have earned more as lawyers but that their students have higher expected earnings than other students do.

LAW PROFESSORS ARE WELL PAID

More to the point, law professors have been doing swimmingly well compared to most lawyers for some time now. Things had already begun to pick up in the 1980s, when Christie grumbled about law professor pay.[57] A 1993 article, "Law Profs Poor No More," noted that law professor salaries had jumped in law schools in the preceding five years, at some schools by 50 percent or more.[58] Law professor pay has continued to rise ever since, going up another 45 percent between 1998 and 2008, according to one study, which almost certainly understates the actual increase.[59]

The tables have turned on the old professor complaint that they earn less than top judges. Chief Justice John Roberts, in his entreaty to Congress to raise the pay of federal judges, pointed out that judicial salaries are now dwarfed by that of academics at top law schools: federal district judges earn $165,200, compared to senior professors at top schools, who make $330,000, and deans, who earn $430,000 (Roberts's information came from a confidential survey of top law schools).[60] Publicly available records lend support to Roberts. In 2009, Richard Matasar, the dean at New York Law School (a nonelite school), earned a base salary of $519,000, and the four highest paid New York Law School professors ranged from a high of $376,000 to a low of $308,000.[61] At the University of Minnesota, a top public school, the two highest paid law professors in 2007 earned $356,000 and $344,500, respectively.[62] University of Texas School of Law dean Larry Sager revealed the compensation packages in play at upperelite law schools: "In our own experience, candidates whom we have wished to hire have been offered more than $400,000 a year."[63]

Even with high salaries, faculties can revolt over money. At the University of Texas, in 2010, nineteen professors earned above $300,000 in compensation (highest at $351,000), and another thirty-five professors earned between $200,000 and $300,000—the median compensation for full professors at Texas was about $280,000.[64] Between 2006 and 2011, twenty members of the faculty received one-time bonus payments ranging from $75,000 to $350,000.[65] By any measure they are well compensated. Nonetheless, a few members of the faculty were apparently upset that new recruits or people being recruited away to other schools had received better deals from Dean Sager. He was fired in the resulting tumult.[66] Implacable disputes about intrafaculty equity arise—and the overall compensation level of the entire faculty goes up as a consequence—when a law school competes for professors against schools with higher pay scales. (During Sager's five-year tenure as dean, resident tuition at Texas rose from $18,208 to $28,669.)

If Texas professors are compensated at this level, given the nature of the market it is likely that many full professors at top-five law schools are in the $300,000–$400,000 range, with some earning more. Justice Roberts had the impression that elite law professors make double the compensation of federal judges. It is probably closer to triple for the best paid professors.

The vast majority of law professors do not earn these high end sums, it must be said. But recent faculty salary surveys indicate that many full professors around the country earn as much as or more than federal judges.[67] According to information supplied by SALT, the average median salary of full-time professors in 2008–9 was $147,000 (not counting benefits).[68] This average—based on nine month's pay—substantially understates the actual earnings of law professors in two ways. First, it does not count summer research grants, which on the lower end adds $10,000, and at many schools much more, to a professor's salary.

Second, this average is also skewed downward by the fact that only a handful of the most prestigious and highest-paying schools report their salary numbers to the survey. The 2008 SALT figures include just seven of the forty highest-paying law schools in 1994–95, the last time the ABA collected salary information.[69] Based on figures provided by the four highest-paying schools that did report—Michigan ($254,500), Harvard ($252,450), Minnesota ($220,000), and Emory ($212,004)—it's reasonable to surmise, since they compete with one another for professors, that the median full professor pay at another fifteen or so uncounted peer schools likely exceeds $200,000. And these numbers do not consider additional financial perks offered by elite law schools, like subsidized housing and tuition benefits for spouses and children. The curtain opened for a glimpse of this practice when the *New York Times* reported in 2008 that New York University Law Foundation purchased a $4.2 million apartment for lease by a new law professor they had recruited away from Columbia.[70] Texas law school, also through a foundation, provides triple-figure one-time payments to some faculty in the form of forgivable loans, as mentioned above (Dean Sager received $500,000).[71]

The proliferation of summer research grants at law schools in the past several decades is indicative of the enhanced flow of money to law professors. Professors are paid for thirty-nine weeks a year; classes range from twenty-six to twenty-eight weeks; and the teaching load is six hours or less each week. There is ample already-compensated time within this schedule to produce scholarship. Yet schools now also provide additional money to professors to write during the summer.

A mercenary pay-me-to-write quality attaches to these grants. One school, for example, offers a base summer grant of $8000, plus a $6000 bonus for placement in a second- or third-tier journal (journals outside the top fifty schools in *US News*), a $10,000 bonus for placement in a first-tier journal, or a $15,000 bonus for a top-twenty placement or for producing two separate articles in first- or second-tier or peer-reviewed journals.[72] A more common practice is to offer a standard amount, say $15,000 or $20,000, half up front and half after the article is done. At top schools the summer research stipend runs in the tens of thousands of dollars (twenty-eight professors at Texas law school received summer stipends above $60,000).[73] Schools justify this as a way to boost compensation to meet the competition, to reward active writers, and to motivate people who might not otherwise write. One must wonder whether scholarship motivated in this way suffers in quality or value owing to the lack of an intrinsic desire on the part of the scholar to write.

Law professor earnings in the past generation have swept not only past judges but also past the bulk of lawyers. According to the US Bureau of Labor Statistics, in 2008 "the median annual wages of all wage-and-salaried lawyers were $110,590. The middle half of the occupation earned between $74,980 and $163,320."[74] Extrapolating from the available information, it appears that a majority of full professors at law schools across the country (when summer grants are included) are in the upper quartile of lawyer earnings. Even compared to their fellow graduates from elite law schools, full professors at law schools are doing fine. According to a Forbes survey, the median midcareer salary (sixteen years out) of graduates of Harvard Law School is $203,000, and for Yale Law School graduates (many of whom become academics) it is $159,000.[75]

Full professors at elite law schools rank in the upper 1–2 percent of American wage earners. On top of salaries, faculty get retirement benefits and, at many schools, tuition remission for children and spouses. And the wealthiest schools, as mentioned, provide subsidized housing. Conferences in attractive locales—Palm Beach, New Orleans, San Francisco, and Hawai‘i—also help pay for vacations when the family comes along.[76]

Despite all that, you can still find law professors who say, as one wrote in mid-2011, that law professor pay has lagged behind the pay of lawyers, warning that if this continues, law schools "may begin to have problems attracting and retaining faculty."[77] This old argument rings hollow in light of how well law professors are doing financially—and the unparalleled freedom we exercise. It's especially implausible given the heated competition for law professor jobs. Every year seven hundred or so candidates, many with extraordinary qualifications, sign up for an annual hiring conference, clamoring to get a foot in the professorial door, with many left disappointed.

TUITION PAYS FOR LAW PROFESSOR SALARIES

There is nothing untoward in itself that law professors make a comfortable living. Many law professors are highly credentialed, talented, hard-working individuals. Some have argued that the increase in pay legitimately allows law professors to capture a greater portion of the enhanced economic value a law degree confers on graduates.[78] (This argument is tenuous, however, at institutions where the expected economic return on the degree is low relative to cost.) In a capitalist society, when the labor market sets compensation levels, no one need apologize for what they earn.

The hard question law professors must face, however, is whether (or how much) their utilization of accreditation standards have artificially boosted their salaries in classic rent-seeking terms. Accreditation actions to bring up salaries two decades ago have had a continuing effect by lifting up base-pay levels on which subsequent raises and salaries were determined. The standards also have an effect today by limiting the extent to which law faculties can be staffed by the large available pool of smart and knowledgeable lawyers who, as adjuncts and contract professors, could more cheaply teach students to practice law.[79]

Another discomfiting observation for law professors follows on the last. The reduction of teaching loads and rise of salaries chronicled here contributed to the ramp up in tuition in several ways. Less teaching from each professor requires a greater number of (well-paid) teachers over-all. A significant amount of money goes into faculty research. Faculty expenses typically comprise half of law school budgets. The tuition that supports this enterprise had to go up. This is not to say that law professor expenses have *caused* the rise in tuition—the main cause lies elsewhere, as I will address later. But it does mean law professors cannot distance themselves from high tuition, which AALS tried to do in its opposition to proposed changes in the ABA standards.[80] As former Vanderbilt University Law School dean Edward Rubin acknowledged, there can be "little doubt that a significant proportion of these ever-increasing tuition payments support faculty research."[81] Using a general rule of thumb that 40 percent of faculty time is (or should be) devoted to scholarship, Rubin acknowledged that the faculty portion of the budget can be significantly slashed by dropping research for more teaching.[82]

One final point: the fact that law professors are doing well financially compared to the bulk of lawyers should put to rest the image we encourage that we have made a financial sacrifice to take this job or that simply being a law professor is a form of public service. AALS's assertion that law professors model "selflessness" for students is not credible. Our pay is excellent, the stress is low, the hours are whatever we want them to be, we have no boss, and our job security is nigh impregnable. [83] Our pay is far better than that of other professors in the university, and we teach less than most professors. (And unlike professors generally, who undergo a rigorous tenure process, tenure for law professors—lifetime job security—is achieved with a relatively low quantity of scholarly production and in practice is seldom denied.) Our quality of life is far better than that of lawyers, and we make more money than most lawyers. Law professors have found the sweet spot between two professions—thank you very much.

FIVE

The Cost and Consequences of Academic Pursuits

An age old rift has bedeviled law schools from their initial implantation in universities up through the present. Law students attend law school to learn how to become lawyers. Law professors are academics. The interests of the two main constituents of law schools are at odds owing to this difference in orientation.

Indications of this rift are longstanding and plentiful. An academic-oriented Columbia law professor in 1923 lamented, "The idea of the trade school is on us yet."[1] The dispute erupted in a 1937 AALS debate over the law school curriculum, with some advocating greater exposure to social science courses and others opposed.

> It is apparent that a very substantial number of member schools accept without qualification the proposition that the function of the law school is to train "lawyers to practice law" along traditional lines. On the other hand a rather vigorous minority repudiates this as the sole purpose and insists that the function is to train lawyers for public service. It is said in support of this proposition that legal education should be placed on a plane above trade school practices and objectives and that therefore the situation calls for a broader educational base and a technique which will insure a legal education of a deeper and broader sort.[2]

Four decades ago, Thomas Bergin memorably captured a schizophrenic tension that law professors continue to struggle to straddle: "The pure academic, if asked what the chief aim of legal education should be, will typically reply that it is to add to man's understanding of the meaning of law and its role in society. . . . The pure Hessian-trainer has one answer only: the purpose of legal education is to prepare law students for practice at the Bar."[3]

LAW PROFESSORS BECOME SCHOLARS ABOVE ALL ELSE

By the closing decades of the twentieth century the academic side was decisively dominant. A prominent academic insisted in 1985 that "law professors are not paid to train lawyers, but to study the law and to teach their students what they happen to discover."[4] In a 2010 letter, outgoing AALS president Reese Hansen repeated the old rationalization for the academic model: "Lawyers are not 'produced' or even 'trained' by law schools. What lawyers must ultimately deliver is judgment."[5] To acquire such judgment, he argued, students must be taught by scholarly professors. Among contemporary legal academics, anyone who maintains that law schools should focus on training lawyers for practice risks being branded an anti-intellectual.

Throughout this period, detractors have scorched law schools for doing a poor job of training lawyers. This criticism was leveled in the first Carnegie report on legal academia (in 1921) and in the last Carnegie report (in 2007).[6] Writing early in the twentieth century, Alfred Reed reported that "the prevailing attitude of the profession has always been that even a complete law school course is inadequate preparation for admission to the bar, and that a certain amount of practical office work should therefore be required in addition."[7] Late in the twentieth century, an ABA report on legal education noted that "surveys understandably indicate that practicing lawyers believe that their law school training left them deficient in skills that they were forced to acquire after graduation."[8]

Complaints are not just that law schools are failing at training lawyers but, additionally, that the scholarly output of legal academics has become utterly detached from the law. "What the academy is doing, as far as I can tell," said Chief Justice Roberts in 2011, "is largely of no use or interest to people who actually practice law."[9] This was the latest in a string of disdainful comments by judges about professorial writing, tracing back two decades to an article by federal judge (and former law professor) Harry Edwards, "The Growing Disjunction between Legal Education and the

Legal Profession."[10] And not only judges have this view: "Practitioners tend to view much academic scholarship as increasingly irrelevant to their day-to-day concerns, particularly when compared with the great treatises of an earlier era."[11]

Concerns about scholarly irrelevance are heightened by a study of 385,000 law review articles, which found that 40 percent are never cited in other articles and almost 80 percent are cited fewer than ten times (counting self-citations by an author).[12] Volumes of material are being written by law professors that appear to leave little or no trace. Even law professors have expressed skepticism about the value of these truckloads of scholarly output.[13] "American legal scholarship today is dead—totally dead, deader than at any time in the past thirty years," according to Pierre Schlag, himself a prolific scholar.[14] Legal scholarship is being produced at a greater clip than ever before, but hardly any of it matters, he says. There is useful doctrinal work to be done, but most professors don't engage in it because it is unexciting and not considered scholarly. Riding one intellectual fad after another, law professors are spinning wheels going nowhere. Another critic of scholarship estimated that, at top law schools, the cost of a single law review article, counting reduced teaching and summer research grants, comes to $100,000.[15] This estimate, based upon contestable assumptions, was no doubt selected for its shock value, but the point remains that the amount of money that supports scholarship comes to a kingly sum.

Egghead academics are easy targets for bashing, and the critical comments indulge in exaggeration.[16] Assertions by judges that they pay no attention to law reviews are overblown, as demonstrated by a recent study going back sixty years, which found that federal courts continue to cite law reviews at a steady rate.[17] Many law professors have written articles and books on legal problems and issues revolving around statutes, cases, and regulations.

What *is* correct in these complaints is that the scholarship of earlier generations of legal academics mainly involved the analysis of legal doctrine. Law professors would synthesize areas of the law and write on legal problems in close dialogue with and helpful to lawyers and judges. That is no longer highly regarded scholarly work.[18] Doctrinal articles tend not to be published in elite journals, and professors who wish to build a scholarly reputation and be hired by elite law schools do not write them. Theory has scholarly cachet. Interdisciplinary and empirical studies of law are especially popular at the moment. Theories of constitutional interpretation, normative arguments about what the law should be, legal philosophy, critical race theory, sociological studies of law, legal history, economic analysis of law, quantitative studies of judging—these and other perspectives on and *about* law are what occupy legal academics. Most of this is not immediately relevant to the daily tasks of judges and lawyers, although it may have direct and indirect benefits for the legal system more generally.[19]

Much of the research produced by law professors is standard academic fare, indistinguishable from scholarship one finds in political science, history, economics, and women's studies departments, for example, except that law professors focus on law-related matters. Contemporary law faculties, especially at elite institutions, have become mini-universities, staffed by professors with advance training in economics, history, political science, philosophy, sociology, or psychology. A number of law schools conduct annual seminars to train law faculty in empirical research methodology; University of California Berkeley School of Law offers a joint degree program in law and the social sciences; Vanderbilt and University of Chicago Law School offer JD/PhDs in law and economics. Faculty speakers and workshops bounce from one academic field to the next—and law professors in the audience are expected to have the competence to engage with a range of specialized fields.

Citation patterns in other academic fields are similar to those in law, with the lion's share of citations going to a small percentage of articles while many are never cited at all.[20] In every field only a few scholars produce work that stands out, although all are contributing to the total body of information. Scholars in other fields are not beholden to the instrumental dictates of others, and neither are law professors. There is no obligation to produce scholarship that is useful for judges and lawyers—although law professors are best positioned, with subject matter expertise and the luxury of time, to provide this essential service to the legal system. Most professors in most academic fields, like law professors, write for each other.

Think of law professors as members of the "legal studies" department of a university. This way of looking at things helps make sense of the current trend of law schools hiring professors with PhDs in subjects other than law, many with no legal experience at all.[21] At the top thirteen schools, nearly one-third of the faculty have PhDs, as do one-fifth of the professors at schools ranked fourteenth through twenty-sixth; a combined total of sixty-six faculty members at the top twenty-six law schools have PhDs *without* a law degree.[22] Years of additional schooling in other fields pull these professors away from legal knowledge and legal practices, the kind of information their students expect to acquire in law school.

An increasing proportion of new law professors are now hired after spending a year or two as fellows or visiting assistant professors on law faculties. From just a handful a decade ago, dozens of these programs have sprouted across the country.[23] Visiting assistant professors teach courses at a fraction of the cost of professors, providing cheap labor for law schools. They are sold as transitional positions for people who wish to secure tenure-track jobs, giving them an opportunity to spend a year on research and get the feel of an academic setting. Thus, in place of the additional experience they could have obtained as a lawyer, candidates invest a year or two grooming themselves for the professoriate. These programs indirectly make it harder for people from practice (those who cannot afford the pay cut or family disruption to assume a visiting assistant professor spot) to secure law professor positions because they are competing head-to-head against candidates with a polished "academic" look and more publications coming in.

A sampling of forty law schools found that tenure-track professors (excluding skills teachers) hired in the past decade have a median of three years of legal practice; at top schools, the median practice experience of new hires is one year.[24] Another study found that the "number of years of practice experience was negatively predictive, with those having more years of experience less likely to be hired at a higher-ranking law school."[25] For decades law faculties have been staffed predominantly by graduates from elite law schools with limited practice experience.[26] A veteran member of the ABA Section on Legal Education who conducted numerous accreditation inspections of law schools protested, over fifty years ago, that "there are a lot of men trying to teach law who do not have any conception of what lawyers actually do in practice." "Some teachers are interested only in research and writing."[27]

Law professors *do not* teach in legal studies departments but in law schools. That is why persistent complaints arise about the excessive academic orientation of the faculty. Law professors—and the PhDs on law faculties—are paid substantially more than they would earn had they worked in legal studies departments. Students matriculate to gain entry to the practice of law and expect to learn the skills that will enable them to succeed as lawyers. It is questionable whether a professor with little or no practice experience is ideally suited to train students for legal practice. A scholar who specializes in the economic analysis (or history or philosophy) of property law, to give an example, does not necessarily know how to negotiate or draft a commercial real estate transaction or what to do if the deal goes bad.

In the 1990s, prodded by withering criticisms from the bar, law schools finally began to significantly boost skills-training courses. New clinics were added and additional clinical professors were hired, now totaling nearly fourteen hundred full-time clinical faculty across the country.[28] Many law schools also hired full-time professors to teach legal research and writing courses. These additions to the faculty allowed law schools to respond to objections about inadequate training of students for legal practice while letting the bulk of professors to continue blissfully with their scholarly engagements—solving the problem of not providing skills training by hiring other people to take care of it.

Critics were not appeased.[29] A "best practices" manifesto for law schools put out in 2007 by the Clinical Legal Education Association (the organization of clinical professors) asserted that "law schools are not fully committed to preparing students for practice."[30] "Most law school graduates are not sufficiently competent to provide legal services to clients or even to perform the work expected of them in large firms."[31] What is needed to train students adequately for practice, clinicians repeatedly assert, is to integrate skills training throughout the curriculum and to make clinical courses mandatory for students in the third year.

This is infeasible financially under the current model, which allocates such large amounts of faculty time to scholarship. Owing to the intensive supervision involved in clinics, a class of two hundred students split over two semesters requires ten full-time clinical faculty, supplemented by adjuncts.[32] Schools can afford to increase clinical staffs up to these levels only by shifting some faculty currently engaging in research to serve instead as clinical professors (although many have limited practice experience). Ironically, the pressure is going in the opposite direction: so compelling is the prestige of scholarship and the desire for tenure that clinical professors and legal writing professors are now, at a number of law schools, provided with time and money to produce scholarship.[33] Drawn by its gravitation pull, the designated and avowed Hessian trainers on law faculties are themselves morphing into scholars.

The greater attention law schools gave to skills training during this period was a sidelight to the real action. Scholarly pursuits elevated to ever higher heights. A 1999 article by Northwestern law professor James Lindgren, "Fifty Ways to Promote Scholarship," revealed the measures top schools were taking and served as a blueprint for those who wished to get in the game. Lindgren proposed generous research leaves, reduced teaching loads, higher raises to productive scholars, summer research grants that amount to 25 percent of total pay, and hiring more promising and proven scholars.[34] To lessen the need for courses, he also proposed cutting back on the credits students needed for graduation.[35] Many law schools created a new position, associate dean for faculty research, also suggested by Lindgren, dedicated to raising faculty scholarship.[36]

Scholarship fever swept through law schools. Feeding this was the fact that the heaviest weighted factor in the US News rankings, 25 percent of the total, is the reputation rating among academics. Law schools sent out brochures, derisively dubbed "law porn," extolling newly hired scholars and lists of articles and books produced by its faculty. Juicing the momentum, productive scholars within law faculties pressed hard for this agenda, which raised their status within faculties and sent more rewards their way; whatever made writing easier and more valued enhanced the career prospects of scholars. Entering the twenty-first century, the competitive drive for scholarship by individual professors and law schools was on full blast—a major factor in institutional policy and the overall budget.

WHO PAYS FOR KNOWLEDGE PRODUCTION, AND IN WHAT AMOUNT

I should pause for a moment to answer the rumble, if not roar, of protest likely to emanate from legal scholars who have read these passages as an attack on the value of scholarship. Academic institutions are dedicated to the development of knowledge and have an essential place in society. As the author of six legal theory books, it is not my view that scholarly work with no immediate pay-off is worthless (although that might be the case in given instances). Knowledge is a valuable public good that our society must encourage. Nothing I say here questions that.

Rather, what we must do, I argue, is more critically examine the cost of the legal scholarship frenzy. We must inquire whether it is appropriate that law students are forced to pay for the production of scholarship at current levels and to the same extent at law schools across the board. Not all law schools and not all law professors must be oriented toward research. Especially at lower-ranked schools where graduates have a lower expected income, the students should not be made to bear a costly burden for faculty research. Had I been required to teach one more course every year of my career I might have written four books instead of six and, perhaps, a dozen fewer articles and book chapters. That still leaves plenty of scholarly output. One can be committed to the value of legal scholarship while accepting that, on balance, society would not suffer if the mountain of writing now coming out of law faculties is cut down to a less extravagant size.

SIX

More Professors, More Revenue Needed

LAW FACULTIES GROW

"**H**LS Expansions to Continue with Curricular Reforms and Faculty Hiring," read a 2006 headline about more additions to an already much expanded Harvard law faculty.[1] The University of Illinois College of Law adopted a strategic plan that same year to increase its faculty from thirty-nine to forty-five in five years.[2] "Cornell Law School Announces Major Expansion in Permanent Faculty," was a 2008 headline.[3] An internal Cornell faculty document detailed, "We have increased the tenure-track faculty over twenty percent, from 34 in 2003 to 42 in July, 2009, with a target of 45."[4] The University of Miami School of Law announced in 2009 a university-approved plan to "add significantly to the size of the faculty," proposing to hire seventeen new law faculty in the near future.[5] Notre Dame Law School's dean told students at a town hall meeting in 2010 that the faculty would increase by 25 percent in coming years.[6]

Law faculties have been growing for some time now owing to a combination of factors: to handle larger numbers of students, to make up for reduced teaching loads, to add more scholars, to add clinical and legal writing teachers, and to lower faculty-student ratios (a factor on *US News* rankings). AALS tallied 7,421 full-time law faculty in 1990–91. The number has increased every year since, reaching 10,965 in 2008–9.[7] A portion of this overall increase is attributable to twenty-five newly accredited law schools during this period, but much of it is from individual faculties getting larger. Student-faculty ratios have plummeted as a result. At the largest law schools, the ratio was cut almost in half, from 27.3 students per faculty in 1989–90, to 15.3 in 2009–10; at midsized schools over this period it dropped from 25 to 14.4.[8]

Although it is frequently suggested that this reduction is beneficial to students, and it does result in more seminars with smaller enrollments, the reality is that students do not necessarily gain more interaction with professors from having more of them around. Student face time takes away from scholarship, which is what professors are rewarded for. Additional law professors can simply result in more faculty offices with closed doors.

THE ECONOMIC CONSEQUENCES OF SIZING UP

An iron law governs law school finances: expenses must be paid for by the number of students multiplied by tuition. Schools with large endowments are also ruled by this law, albeit enjoying a margin of flexibility. To pay for an expansion of the faculty, a law school *must* increase the number of students and tuition, in some combination. The grip of this iron law was reflected in a memo to the provost from the Cornell law faculty, which proposed to fund its expansion by cutting staff positions, trimming library acquisitions, eliminating a "popular but expensive study abroad program," and "increasing the size of our entering JD class and LLM class by 5 students each."[9] Tuition hikes were left unstated in the memo because tuition always goes up. A choice like this, sacrificing personnel and popular programs to hire more professors, shows the preeminence professors accord to faculty reputation.

Many law schools have made the same choice: grow the faculty, bring in more students—JDs, transfers, and LLMs—and raise tuition. Schools with large faculties are processing students on a massive scale. In 2010, 644 JDs graduated from Georgetown, 577 from Harvard, 513 from George Washington, 483 from New York University, 479 from Fordham, and 433 from Columbia.[10] Bigness is not limited to top-ranked schools: in 2010, Florida Coastal School of Law enrolled an enormous first-year class of 808 students, New York Law School enrolled 641, the John Marshall Law School (Chicago) enrolled 539, and Suffolk University Law School enrolled 531.[11] Thomas M. Cooley Law School was in a zone unto itself with 1,583 first-year students. Streams of graduates facing daunting employment odds are being pumped out by law schools during the throes of a wrenching cutback in legal hiring.

LLM programs, masters degrees in law that take a year to complete, are the new growth area for harvesting additional bodies. They have existed for a hundred years, but were marginal for most of this time.[12] They generate free money for law schools because the students who enroll fill empty seats in already existing JD courses. Almost three hundred programs now exist. International students usually sign up for basic legal subjects (several states permit international students with LLMs to sit for the bar); American JDs who enroll in LLM programs, often graduates of lower-ranked schools seeking to burnish their credentials at higher-ranked schools, specialize in areas such as tax law, intellectual property, banking, bankruptcy, and environmental law. Most law graduates do not pursue LLMs because it is unnecessary—one can take all the same courses and practice in any of these fields with a JD. In 2010, New York University had 552 LLM students and Georgetown had 394—both graduating a total of over a thousand students (JD and LLMs combined); Harvard had 151 LLMs and George Washington had 175—both graduating about 700 students; Columbia (230 LLMs) and Fordham (162 LLMs) awarded around 650 degrees.[13] The total number of LLM students across the country has increased by 65 percent in the past decade, to 5,212 LLM degrees in 2010, and rising.[14] International LLM students are increasingly tapped by US law schools for bodies to fill seats.

Because the roster of full-time faculty is difficult to trim, once expansion takes place it creates a voracious need for revenue that dictates law school policies in fundamental ways. Even when applications fall, law schools are under economic pressure to take in students to meet expenses. Twice this pattern has played out in the past two decades, once in the early 1990s and again recently.[15] From a peak of nearly 100,000 total applicants in 1991, the number declined every year until it reached a low of 71,726 applicants in 1998.[16] First-year JD enrollment during this period fluctuated up and down within a narrow range, from a high of 44,050 to a low of 42,186, not dropping to match the severe contraction in the applicant pool. When the number of applicants began to rise in 1998, climbing quickly back up again to 100,000 applicants by 2004, first-year JD enrollment shot up in sync. Thus law schools (in the aggregate) exhibited a one-way ratchet, holding enrollment totals steady when the number of appli-

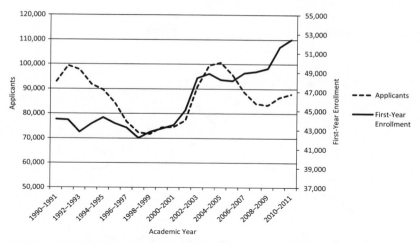

Fig. 6.1. Applicants and first-year enrollment. Source: Law School Admission Council and American Bar Association, *Official Guide to ABA-Approved Law Schools* ([Newtown, PA]: ABA-LSAC, 2011).

cants went down but going up when it rose. Throughout this period, remember, law faculties were expanding and tuition increased every year.

Recent events make the point more powerfully. After reaching a peak of 100,600 applicants in 2004, the number rapidly dropped four years in a row, to a low of 83,371 applicants in 2008. When the recession hit, college graduates seeking escape from the dismal job market turned to law school—and applicants went up again by 3,200 in 2009, and another 1,300 in 2010. This two-year bump proved temporary, however, as the number of applicants turned down again by 11 percent in 2011. The crucial point, as figure 6.1 shows, is that even as the number of applicants plummeted between 2004 and 2008, first-year JD enrollment remained at the higher plateau of around 48,000–49,000 students, and actually rose during the drop. Then, when the number of applicants went up for two successive years, enrollment turned up again to surpass 52,000 entering students. (The most recent downturn is not shown in the figure because final statistics are not available.) Figure 6.1 shows that law schools, which fatten up when more students apply, do not noticeably slim down in response to a decline in applicants. JD enrollment increases understate matters because law schools have also taken in greater numbers of LLM students.

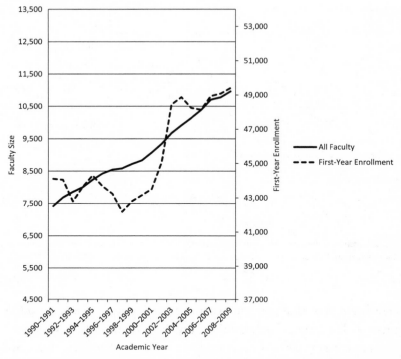

Fig. 6.2. Faculty size and first-year enrollment. Sources: for first-year enrollment:, see Law School Admission Council and American Bar Association, *Official Guide to ABA-Approved Law Schools* ([Newtown, PA]: ABA-LSAC, 2011); for faculty size, see Association of American Law Schools, *Statistical Report on Law School Faculty And Candidates for Law Faculty Positions*, http://www.aals .org/statistics/2002-03/index.html.

Law schools have recently enrolled record numbers of students, increasing each year at a time when lawyers were being laid off and many current law school graduates could not find jobs. When asked to explain this, law schools said they were merely responding to an increase in demand for a legal education.[17]

Law faculties like to think they have a say in admissions policies as a matter of faculty governance, but this is mostly a delusion. Admissions policies are ruled by the need for revenue to cover expenses. Consider figure 6.2, which juxtaposes first-year enrollment numbers against the increase in faculty size over the same period. The steady climb of faculty roughly coincides with the jagged upward climb of enrollment. These matching upward slopes partially reflect newly accredited law schools coming on line, proportionally adding professors and students to the to-tal. But it also reflects law faculties getting larger and JD enrollment going up to pay for it—adding LLMs to the total would sharpen the upward angle of the enrollment rise.

The ramp-up in faculty and students, furthermore, coincided with a ramp-up in the size of administrations to manage more programs and more people in the building, with more associate deans and personnel in career services offices, library staffs, and information technology offices. From 1996 to 2010, the number of full-time deans and administrators (excluding librarians) increased from 3,028 to 4,091, producing a ratio of about one administrator (associate deans, assistant deans, etc.) to every two-and-a-half full-time professors—although some of this increase is due to title inflation for jobs that previously were not considered "dean."[18]

TRAPPED BY SIZE

Law schools are financially trapped by what they have become: top-heavy institutions with scholars teaching few classes (writing a lot) and clini-cians teaching few students. The perpetual "more" of recent decades—cre-ating more time for writing, hiring more scholars and more skills-training teachers, and spreading more money around—severely constrains law schools going forward. Law schools have a limited capacity to adjust to a drop in applications or poor employment prospects for its graduates.

Why have they put themselves in this position? Law schools frequently cite an improved student-faculty ratio as the reason for expansion. That is not it. Competition for better placement in US News rankings has contrib-uted, apparently under the assumption that growing the faculty pays off in an improved reputation. That is mistaken. Reputation is sticky and facul-ties at peer schools are interchangeable. Professors who are added in an expansion intangibly meld to an existing perception. Faculties competing this way size up together, providing no individual school a comparative reputation gain.[19]

There is something deeper here than ranking competition: the "Harvard effect." At the turn of the millennium Harvard decided to embark on a major expansion. In Spring 2001 it had eighty full-time faculty—a decade later it had 119.[20] That increase alone exceeds the entire size of a number of law faculties. Often credited to Elena Kagan, the expansion began shortly before she was appointed dean, though she carried it through magnificently with a stream of big name hires. Elite law schools followed suit, and others outside of that group did as well. Emulating schools were not directly *competing* with Harvard (only Yale has that distinction). Harvard set a new definition of what it meant to be an elite school: "elite" law schools (and those striving for this status) expand their faculty as a conspicuous display of intellectual wealth. Elites stockpile scholarly talent.

While Harvard has the financial heft to pull it off, most law schools do not. The need for revenue kicked in.

PART 3

The US News *Ranking Effect*

SEVEN

The Ranking Made Us Do It

A BAD YEAR FOR LAW SCHOOLS

The year got off to a dismal start for law schools when, in early January 2011, the *New York Times* published a sensational exposé, "Is Law School a Losing Game?"[1] In a multipage report, David Segal splayed open for public consumption the rampant practice of law schools reporting misleading employment data. The legal market was in the midst of a severe recession. Yet miraculously, ninety-seven of the top one hundred law schools, as well as a majority of the bottom hundred, claimed that more than 90 percent of their graduates were employed within nine months of graduation.[2] Dozens of law schools posted eye-popping employment rates of 98–100 percent; and several dozen law schools posted midrange salary numbers claiming that recent graduates earned up to $160,000 a year. Judging from these numbers, going to law school was a smart move that paid off handsomely, especially at a time when so many recent college graduates were unemployed.

Segal disclosed, however, that law schools have been doctoring their employment figures for years, using a variety of fudges to jimmy them up. Several strategies did the trick. When obtaining employment information, law schools asked their graduates whether they have jobs of *any* kind—not just lawyer jobs. Law schools graduates who were employed in a position outside of the legal field, like a grocery clerk, would be identified as "employed" in "business and industry." This provides a nice lift to the employment numbers because most graduates must have a job of some kind to pay their bills. In another combination of moves, schools left out any graduates who were "not seeking employment" or were pursuing further education (like enrolling in LLM programs or completing a joint degree); and because US News automatically treated 25 percent of graduates whose status was unknown as "employed," law schools made less of an effort to get answers from graduates they suspected were unemployed (successful graduates are pleased to report jobs).[3] Finally, law schools offered unemployed graduates temporary jobs—as research assistants or interns at ten dollars an hour—which expired after the period covered by the survey, thus counting them as "employed" when it mattered. As for salary numbers, law schools artfully crafted categories ("private full-time legal employment") and used selective reporting to elevate amounts, prominently displaying high-income figures that reflected only a small percentage of the class.

These techniques spread through law schools over time. In the 1997 US News ranking, almost all of the top twenty-five schools had placement rates in the ninetieth percentile range (the highest was 97.1 percent); the majority of the schools ranked twenty-six to fifty were in the eightieth percentile range; schools below the top fifty were scattered around the seventies and eighties (flagship state schools that dominated local legal markets were in the nineties), and a dozen schools listed placement rates below 70 percent.[4] That was a plausible distribution. In ensuing years placement rates began to drift up at law schools across the board. By the mid-2000s, nearly every law school in the top hundred advertised employments rates in the 90th percentile range, as did many schools ranked lower.[5] Some of this rise is attributable to a healthy job market for law graduates, but that does not explain such high figures across the board. Goosing the numbers evidently had become pervasive.

It was widely known, at least among law school administrators and professors who were paying attention, that advertised employment numbers were inflated. They rationalized that since most law schools were doing it, it wasn't wrong, and any school that did not boost numbers would suffer next to competitor schools that engaged in the practice. Few people inside or outside of law schools complained about or criticized the artificially high reported employment rates. The extent of the inflation was not readily apparent.

That changed when waves of lawyer layoffs plowed through the bar in 2008 and 2009, leaving no doubt that the job market was terrible.[6]

The percentage of graduates who obtained jobs as lawyers (among those whose jobs status was known) declined every year—from a high of 76.9 percent in 2007, to 74.7 percent in 2008, 70.6 percent in 2009, and 68.4 percent in 2010.[7] The percentage of part-time jobs rose significantly, from a norm of 5 percent or less, to 11 percent in 2009.[8] One in five jobs obtained by the class of 2010 were temporary, double the number in 2007.[9] The only employment category to show gains was "academic" jobs for law graduates, which reached an all time high—the result of law schools putting more unemployed graduates on their payroll with part-time jobs (to keep up faltering employment numbers).[10]

An association that collects employment information on recent law graduates, National Association for Law Placement, concluded that only 64 percent of 2010 graduates (whose job status was known) had found full-time lawyer jobs, and the "aggregate starting private practice salaries fell an astonishing 20% for this class."[11] An analysis factoring in the thousands of lawyers laid off estimated that only 19,397 lawyer jobs were available annually from 2008 to 2010—law schools produce more than two times that number of graduates each year.[12] There was less than one job opening for every two new lawyers. By all indications, this was the worst job market in decades. Defying this reality, many law schools continued to report employments rates for graduates above the ninetieth percentile. The disparity between this cheery picture and the ongoing carnage in the legal job market was too great to go unnoticed.

Not all law schools used every technique for manipulating the employment figures and some massaged the numbers more ruthlessly than others, but most schools did some of it, including elite law schools. (Northwestern University Law School pioneered the "hire your unemployed" technique.) Through these devices, the bulk of law schools across the country were able to certify that nine out of ten of their graduates landed employment, with many scoring high salaries.

Legal educators are unapologetic about their use of these expediencies, having a ready justification for each. Legal academics insist, for instance, that lots of graduates don't practice law yet still use the degree to advance their careers in "business." To fixate only on lawyer jobs would understate successful outcomes. And putting unemployed grads temporarily on the law school payroll extends them a helping hand in difficult times.[13] The reported employment numbers, they say, are truthful—not fabricated—and comply with reporting guidelines acceptable to the ABA.

This is "truthiness" in the technical sense that lawyers are infamous for, but it wasn't honest. As legal educators know, prospective students who saw claims of "98 percent employed 9 months after graduation" would naturally assume that meant *lawyer* jobs at decent pay. That is the primary career law schools are selling.

Skeptical prospective students who conducted a diligent investigation into the employment numbers would have realized that something didn't add up. Many schools advertised employment rates that exceeded their bar pass rates, which implies that not all the jobs were lawyer jobs, although a person reading the information would have to draw the connection on his or her own. Unwary students—and why should they think that law schools were substantially distorting the employment numbers?—would have been fooled. Segal called out law schools for the deception.

Public scandal hit again a month after Segal's article when the new dean at Villanova University School of Law, John Gotanda, let it be known that the previous administration had submitted falsely inflated LSAT numbers to the ABA and *US News* for several years, reporting a 162 when it was actually 159.[14] This was not creative accounting or truthiness—but flat-out lying, which was rewarded with a higher rank for the school. After its actual median was counted, Villanova tumbled in rank from sixty-seven to eighty-four.

Embarrassing blows to law schools kept coming month after month. In March, US Senator Barbara Boxer sent a letter to ABA president Stephen Zack demanding that the ABA implement reforms to halt the deceptive reporting practices of law schools. "Most students reasonably expect to obtain post-graduation employment," Boxer sternly wrote, "that will allow them to pay off their student loan debts, and rely on this information [provided by law schools]—which may be false at worst and misleading at best—to inform their decision."[15]

In April, Segal published a follow-up piece in the *New York Times* likening the scholarship policies of many law schools to "bait and switch" schemes.[16] To attract students, law schools offered sizable scholarships for three years, contingent after the first year on maintaining a minimum qualifying grade point average (GPA), a B average, for instance. This would not seem like much to be concerned about for prospective students, most of whom got high grades in college. What students were not told clearly enough is that many of their classmates, at some schools more than half the class, were offered similar deals, and first-year grading is done on a curve that strictly limits the number of students who receive Bs and above.

To see how this snare works, say that 50 percent of the class comes in with a scholarship, but at the end of the first year only 30 percent of the class achieves a B average. In an arrangement like this, four out of ten scholarship students would lose their scholarships for the second and third year, ending up paying tens of thousands of dollars more for law school than they had planned.[17] Had students realized the magnitude of the risk, they might have decided instead to attend a higher-ranked school, paying full price all the way but obtaining better job opportunities on graduation. Law school officials defended the arrangement as an appropriate allocation of scholarships and insisted that students knew the conditions. Students who lost out were devastated and felt deceived because they were not specifically told that a significant number of students yearly forfeited scholarships. (Eighty-five percent of law schools outside the top fifty, and about half of the top fifty, attach contingencies of this sort to their scholarship offers.)[18]

The assault on law schools escalated in May, when a group of graduates filed a class action lawsuit charging Thomas Jefferson School of Law with fraud and deceptive business practices, misinforming prospective students about job placement rates. Similar lawsuits were soon filed against Thomas Cooley Law School and New York Law School,[19] and a dozen additional law schools were sued several months later, with more suits reportedly to follow. [20]

In July, a second US Senator, Charles Grassley, ranking member on the Judiciary Committee, sent a letter to the president of the ABA raising concerns about law school scholarship practices, the overproducing of law graduates during a bleak job market, and the risk that growing numbers of students might default on federally backed student loans, costing taxpayers a great deal of money.[21] The prospect of closer scrutiny by the Senate of the law school situation was implicit in the list of thirty-one questions set forth in the letter, with a demand for a prompt response.

In September a second law school was exposed for reporting false numbers. Illinois law school advertised an LSAT median of 168, when in fact it was 163.[22] After further investigation, it was revealed that Illinois had reported false LSAT and/or GPA medians to the ABA six times in the preceding ten years, as well as false acceptance numbers (substantially boosting their selectivity rate).[23] This was not the first time Illinois had been caught for questionable reporting. In 2005 Illinois inflated the amount it spent on students (a factor in the ranking) by reporting to *US News* the estimated fair market value of electronic legal research subscriptions to Westlaw and Lexis, claiming to have spent $8.78 million instead of the $100,000 it actually paid for those services.[24]

With the news about Illinois coming on the heels of the disclosure of Villanova's false LSAT numbers, the obvious question was how many other law schools have been doing the same. "It really makes you wonder," said Sarah Zearfoss, assistant dean for admissions at University of Michigan Law School. "There have been schools that my colleagues and I thought were cheating, because we knew enough about their applicant pools that their numbers didn't seem credible. Maybe they really weren't credible."[25] Law School Admission Council (LSAC), an organization that processes law school applications and enrollment on behalf of law schools, has accurate LSAT/GPA medians of every accredited law school in its database and could easily monitor the scores submitted by law schools. When asked whether LSAC would do this, President Daniel Bernstine resisted: "That's just not something we have done historically, and I don't see why we would. We are not in the reporting business."[26] What is peculiar about this whole affair is that the ABA and LSAC jointly publish the *Official Guide to ABA-Approved Law Schools*. The ABA asks law schools to supply their annual LSAT/GPA medians for inclusion in the guide, when LSAC could provide this information directly to the ABA free from error or deception. The ABA has thus created an arrangement that allows law schools to report false scores with impunity.[27]

In October Senate scrutiny shifted from talk to action, when Senator Tom Coburn and Senator Boxer jointly directed the inspector general of the Department of Education to conduct an investigation into law schools.[28] The senators sought this report as a prelude to possible reforms of the Higher Education Act to rectify the problematic situation with law schools.

Finally moved to act by all the negative attention, the ABA Section on Legal Education met the call for greater transparency by approving new rules that would require law schools to provide prospective students with more clear and accurate information about the employment results of recent graduates, although questions still remained.[29] By taking so long to deal with the problem, the ABA's action had the appearance of being forced, an attempt to head off Senate scrutiny rather than a genuine embracing of reform.[30] ABA officials continued to deny the seriousness and pervasiveness of the problem, insisting that "the number of institutions that fail to report employment data accurately is small."[31]

Throughout this period, a relentless stream of invective was directed at law schools by a "scamblog" movement, two dozen active blogs by recent law graduates who dedicate themselves to exposing "the law school scam."[32] They warn readers that law schools lie about employment statistics and that the fate of many graduates is huge debt with no job. Law professors and deans are painted as profiteers who make money by selling a false product. The most popular of these blogs, with over 400,000 visits, is *Third Tier Reality*, where the author, Nando, weekly posts a detailed profile of a law school.[33] Prominently displayed at the head of each profile is a shot of an excrement-filled toilet—a play on the phrase "third-tier toilet" or "TTT"—followed by information about tuition, expenses, ranking, job prospects, and dean and professor pay. In profanity laced attacks, Nando ridicules the employment numbers posted by each school, exposing the tricks used to pump them up. He concludes each profile with a blunt warning to prospective students to stay way.

An uproar erupted when a law professor joined the scamblog movement with an anonymous blog, *Inside the Law School Scam*, presenting a series of posts contending that law professors did hardly any preparation for class, knew little about the practice of law, and produced reams of worthless scholarship. He argued that attending law school is a bad idea for most students, costing too much for a dubious economic return.[34] The author, who later outed himself as Colorado law professor Paul Campos, was excoriated by law professors for indulging in sweeping exaggerations.

Critics of law schools praised him for candidly raising issues that the legal academy was doing its best to ignore.

THE GRIP OF *US NEWS* OVER LAW SCHOOLS

Law schools have always presented themselves as the upstanding conscience of the legal profession—always. How could this deflating series of events happen? Segal explains: "The problem, as many professors have noted, is structural. A school that does not aggressively manage its ranking will founder."[35] When called to account for their conduct, legal educators point the finger at the *US News* ranking system. Once a few law schools began to use questionable techniques to squeeze up their score in the factors that went into the ranking, others risked being punished with a lower rank if they did not follow suit.

The rankings have law schools by the throat. No question. From 1990, when *US News* began to issue a systematic annual ranking, its influence over law schools has grown enormously. Deceptive reporting practices are just a part of its pervasive impact.[36] Multiple deans have resigned after a drop in rank. Schools have altered their admissions formula to maximize their ranking. The internal composition of the student body has changed in multiple ways at law schools as a result of the ranking. Schools have shifted scholarships away from financially needy students owing to the ranking. Tens of thousands of dollars are spent on promotional material by law schools hoping to improve their ranking. Faculties have formed committees and plotted strategies to chart a rise in the rankings. The fact that reputation among academics is the most heavily weighted factor in the ranking—25 percent of the score—turbocharged the market for lateral hires, boosting professor pay at the high end. The Government Accounting Office issued a report to Congress concluding that competition among law schools over the ranking is a major contributor to the increase in tuition.[37]

Each spring, when the new annual ranking is announced, law professors and students across the nation apprehensively await their fate. A few schools are elated at a jump, a few are dejected at an unexpected slide, and everyone else is relieved to have avoided a devastating fall—at least until next time around. Because schools are tightly bunched together in their raw scores, minor fluctuations have outsized consequences. On average, about two-thirds of law schools experience a change in rank from the previous year. This absurdly high rate puts every school on edge.[38] Dropping a tier is especially dreaded, like going off a cliff.

The annual pronouncement of the surviving rump of a defunct magazine thus mercilessly lords over legal academia—an amazing state of affairs when you think about it. Colleges and other professional schools are subject to competing rankings so no single ranking system dominates to the same extent that law schools dance to the tune of *US News*.

The *US News* ranking gets its inordinate power because students choosing between law schools attach preeminent weight to the ranking. Students are sensible to consider rank (although its significance diminishes the further one gets from the top), alongside location and scholarship offers, because legal employers view rank as an indicator of student quality.[39] The largest 250 corporate law firms hire heavily from the top schools.[40] Law is an obsessively credential-focused profession. Every justice on the current Supreme Court attended top-five law schools (Harvard, Yale, Columbia), and Harvard and Yale together produce a substantial proportion of the law professors across the country.[41]

A statistical analysis of the influence of the ranking on student's decisions confirmed what law schools already knew: "Ranks affect how many students apply to a school, how many of those applicants have exceptionally high LSAT scores, the percentage of applicants who are accepted, and the percentage of accepted students who matriculate."[42] This influence shows up most dramatically when schools experience sharp movements up or down in the rankings or shifts between tiers. After a significant movement, the number and quality of applications will change from the previous year to match the shift in rank.[43]

Legal educators endlessly gripe that the *US News* ranking is bunk, poking holes in every aspect of its construction and methodology.[44] Here is just one example of an egregious flaw: the reputation rating by practitioners, which carries significant weight in the final score, is based on a survey *US News* sends to 750 law partners asking them to rate all the law schools across the country (on the questionable assumption that they know about the quality of particular law schools). The response rate typically is low. Consequently, the opinions of two hundred or so lawyers determines 15 percent of the final score each year.[45] (Fewer than 120 responses were received in 2010, not enough to be credible, which forced *US News* to shift to an average of two years.) Complaints about the flaws in the ranking, however, have no apparent effect.

For an illustration of its impact, take Emory University School of Law, which fell from twenty-two to thirty in the 2012 ranking, a devastating plunge. From a spot close to the coveted top twenty, the school was dumped into the thirties. Whatever statistical input produced the drop must have had no connection with the quality of the school because nothing meaningful had changed in a single year.[46] The dean resigned.

Immediately, Emory's situation changed *because* of the fall. Emory ranked thirtieth will attract an aggregate pile of applications with a median LSAT perhaps a point or two lower than Emory did when it was ranked twenty-second.[47] LSAT median is all important and a single point shift matters because schools are separated by fractions in the raw scores that underlie the ranking.[48] Previously, Emory competed on an even basis for students against schools like Boston University—tied with Emory at twenty-second—offering a roughly similar scholarship to entice students. After the drop, however, it must offer higher amounts if it hopes to win students away in a head-to-head competition. Students from the Northeast, a pool Emory draws heavily from, would be reluctant to choose the thirtieth-ranked school over twenty-second in the absence of significant financial inducement. And that might not be enough to appease risk-averse students worried about a further slide by Emory. As a consequence of the drop, Emory faces the prospect of a dual financial hit, increasing its scholarship budget as well as enrolling fewer students to stave off a drop in its LSAT median.

In this manner, the ranking creates its own reality. An initial fall precipitates further downward pressure that is costly and must be reversed immediately before becoming self-perpetuating.[49] Schools ranked fiftieth attract applications from students who fit that LSAT/GPA profile range—likewise at hundredth or at tenth. With new crops of applicants arriving each year, a school's current rank is what counts, in combination with general reputation and strength in the local legal market. A bit of shuffling between spots occurs, but the top fourteen law schools in 1990 have remained the top fourteen up through the present, hence the phrase "T-14," although in 2011 Texas joined the club in a tie for fourteenth. Their rank, in a self-reinforcing fashion, secures their rank by drawing the best applications and by enhancing their elite reputation.[50] Schools ranked in the twenties and thirties, particularly ones that draw nationally, constantly jostle with cohorts in a tight competition for students and position. In this race, any school that stumbles is run over. Further down the chain, schools worry about their rank relative to local competitors at their range. Only schools at the lowest level are free to ignore *US News*, helpless to alter their fate because the ranking has condemned them to the basement.

That is why law schools loath the ranking and many do whatever they can—including cross the ethical line—to maximize their rank. Questionable reporting practices and gaming happened early on and has never let up. In the 1995 ranking issue, *US News* named twenty-nine schools that had "disturbing discrepancies," supplying it with higher LSAT scores than they had reported to the ABA.[51] The magazine also noted that, according to a firm that surveys legal salaries, salary figures reported by some schools "seem a bit high." AALS president Dale Whitman, in his 2002 presidential address, "Do the Right Thing," implored schools to stop gaming for ranking purposes. His criticism of six strategies schools were using did not halt them and probably his disclosure of these tactics to an attentive audience of legal educators did more to help spread them.[52] An article in the *New York Times* in 2005 revealed a host of dubious moves law schools were making to manipulate their scores.[53] A month after the 2010 ranking came out, *US News* discovered that Brooklyn Law School had improperly failed to report the (lower) LSAT median of their part-time students; the administration called it a "mistake."[54] The multiple years of false reporting by Villanova and Illinois in the mid-2000s were not mistakes.

This will not stop. And its consequences go beyond superficial gaming. Real changes have occurred in law schools as a result, with manifold consequences. Law schools closely monitor each factor counted in the ranking and strive to raise their score by any means available.[55] The most heavily weighted factor is the reputation rating of a school based on the surveys *US News* sends to academics (25 percent) and practitioners (15 percent). A school cannot directly affect its reputation, but the effort to elevate reputation has fueled the hiring of star laterals and a profusion of promotional material. The second heaviest factor in the ranking, student selectivity (LSAT, GPA, acceptance rate), 25 percent of the overall score, can be shaped by law schools; the effort to boost this score has warped law schools in several ways, which I'll elaborate in the next chapter. Placement success comes next in weight, at 20 percent, which is behind the dubious reporting practices of law schools mentioned earlier. The final category, totaling 15 percent, covers resources for students: library expenditures, student-faculty ratio, other spending on students, and volumes in the library. To raise scores in this category, law schools spend more money per student (or use accounting tricks to claim higher expenditures)—yet another factor pushing up the spiraling cost of a legal education.

The "Investigative Report: University of Illinois College of Law Class Profile Reporting"—an investigation ordered by the university's legal counsel and ethics office after its false reporting was exposed—provides a behind-the-scenes look at the extraordinary extent to which the ranking can consume a school. The stated goal of the 2006 five-year strategic plan was to move from its current twenty-fifth ranking to its former perch in the top twenty.[56] Each proposed action in the plan begins with a statement of how much the target item counts in the *US News* ranking and what can be done to increase the score. The plan noted that the academic reputation rating is the most heavily weighted variable. To improve this score the faculty would expand from thirty-nine to forty-five; to retain faculty, professor pay would have to be increased to match the compensation level of peer law schools.[57] Student credentials also count heavily, the plan noted, so it set 168 LSAT and 3.7 GPA medians as its goal. To accomplish this, the law school would hold down class size, increase scholarships to "buy high-end students," and actively recruit higher-tuition-paying out-of-state students.[58] In addition, the law school "launched an aggressive national Transfer Program that attracts and enrolls transfer students from other institutions in the 2L [second] year and that helps to offset the loss of tuition revenue that is entailed by recruiting a smaller incoming class."[59] Next, the plan observed that "the other significant remaining obstacle to our ability to climb the rankings hierarchy" is the rate of employment on graduation, which also counts heavily in the ranking.[60] Unfortunately, the released document stops there, withholding the plan's strategies for increasing the employment rate (the conspicuous cutoff of the released document at this point is suspicious).

Administrators utilized a calculator that a professor had constructed that duplicates the ranking methodology to determine whether "a 165/3.8 LSAT/GPA combination was preferable to a 167/3.6 combination" as the best way to raise their score.[61] The calculator made projections on how many places the school would improve in the rank given different LSAT/GPA combinations. They collected extensive data on peer schools, estimating the raw scores of competitors on items measured in the ranking and devising tailored strategies to leap over schools in its proximity (Indiana especially).[62] As a part of its initiative, the law school developed a program that granted admission to University of Illinois students with high GPAs without requiring that they take the LSAT exam. The administrator in charge of the program confided that it enabled him to "trap about 20 of the little bastards with high GPA's that count and no LSAT score to count against my median."[63] When hearing of the plan, a correspondent admiringly responded, "That is clever. Jack up the GPA without risking the low LSAT. . . . nice gaming the system."[64]

This was the setting in which Illinois's false reporting took place. Each year, the admissions dean falsified the LSAT, GPA, and acceptance rate just enough to meet the targets. The institutional commitment to improve its rank paid off, at least temporarily, with Illinois rising from twenty-fifth to twenty-first during this period, until sliding back to twenty-third. Although the "Investigative Report" placed the entire blame for the false reporting on the admissions dean, it also makes clear that the institutional obsession with achieving ranking benchmarks had warped internal policies.

This is not just about Illinois. Law schools across the country pay very close attention to the ranking and many follow Illinois-like strategies (false reporting aside) to boost their raw scores. These strategies have had sweeping effects on the schools—several of which are taken up in the next chapter. That educational institutions are under the thumb of the ranking to such an extreme degree is stunning.

A common refrain among legal educators is that they cannot be blamed for the unfortunate and unintended consequences of "structural" factors that govern legal academia. What they mean by this is that law schools operate in an environment in which schools compete intensely against one another for students. Since students rely heavily on the *US*

News rankings in their decision, schools are forced to maximize their rank to succeed in the competition. Law schools are helpless to do otherwise as long as these conditions hold. The students want the ranking to be high because it adds value to their credential. The alumni want the ranking to be high for the same reason and as a matter of personal pride. No law school administrator likes posting misleading employment numbers or putting out scholarship offers that trap unwary students, but once a few less scrupulous schools used these techniques to advance their position in the ranking, other schools inevitably followed. That is how it spread. As Indiana law professor Bill Henderson put it in the *Times* article that initially brought scrutiny to these practices, "Enron-type accounting standards have become the norm [among law schools]. Every time I look at this data, I feel dirty."[65]

The structural explanation for why honorable law school administrators ended up taking disreputable actions for ranking purposes helps explain the developments of the past two decades. A conscientious dean who refused to engage in questionable number reporting or any of the other dubious practices risked not just her continued tenure as dean but the standing of her institution, which would pay the price for her scruples by looking worse than competitor institutions that were being less forthright. When serving as interim dean in 1998, after I learned (to my astonishment) from a professor at Northwestern that the school was putting its unemployed graduates temporarily on their payroll to boost their employment rate artificially, I immediately did the same—well aware that it was a bogus move.

Recognizing the structural forces that impelled us down this path does not cleanse us of responsibility. It is too convenient to assert that we collectively found ourselves in a bad place owing to structural factors but that no one did anything wrong personally, other than a couple of atypical cheaters who outright lied. Legal educators made choices every step of the way. Neither administrators nor professors stood up to say "Stop. That may be permissible under the rules but it's not right."

EIGHT

Detrimental Developments in Legal Academia

US News ranking competition has wrought profound detrimental changes. The loss of moral credibility suffered by law schools for the reasons laid out in the preceding chapter is the damage most apparent on the surface. Additional injurious developments have occurred that are less visible but no less significant. The *US News* ranking metric became a template that law schools across the country rigorously adhered to—in combination with the ABA accreditation formula—in a way that had a homogenizing influence on the student body, on the faculty, and across law schools, dampening innovation and diversity. Law schools have devised admissions policies and allocated resources in accordance with this metric. We became what the ranking counted.

Several crucial developments revolve around efforts at LSAT profile shaping. Median LSAT is the most heavily weighted individual score (12.5 percent) that law schools can directly affect in terms of their ranking. It is also the only uniform measure of the quality of students (grades are unreliable comparators owing to varying degrees of grade inflation among majors and colleges), with a signaling effect to legal employers of the caliber of graduates.[1] Consequently, a student's LSAT score is the most important factor, above any other consideration, in admissions. A high LSAT score is money in the pocket for students because law schools strategically utilize scholarship awards to raise or maintain their median LSAT. Law schools have used two additional strategies to massage their LSAT averages—strategies involving part-time programs and transfer students. These two strategies plus the efforts just mentioned to manipulate LSAT medians have produced contortions with serious ramifications.

THE PART-TIME PROGRAM DANCE

Part-time programs have been an element of the law school scene since the late nineteenth century, when law schools in large urban areas ran night classes to serve working students. More recently, before things were altered owing to the ranking, such students were typically older than full-time students, had been out of college for a few years, had lower scores on the LSAT (less time to prepare for the test, rusty from being out of school), and bore family responsibilities. Evening students enrolled in one or two fewer courses each semester than did full-time students and took four years to graduate. Part-time programs run on a separate admissions track from full time. Recognizing these differences in purpose and student profile, *US News* originally did not count part-time students in a school's median.

Law schools began to treat part-time programs as a loophole. It was irresistibly easy. A number of students with LSAT scores below the median were denied admission to the full-time program but given the good news that they could take a seat in the evening program instead; after the first year, these students could take a summer course and be permitted to transfer into the second-year day class, still graduating within three years. (A variant of this enrolls the student in one less course each semester, hence qualifying as "part time," but still attending the same day classes with the rest of the students.) The ostensible reason provided by the school for this treatment was concern, in view of the student's lower LSAT score, that a full course load might be too heavy; starting in the evening would allow the student time to adjust to the rigors of law school. That explanation was hooey. The real reason was that placing the student in the part-time program allowed the school to enroll the student, securing tuition without hurting its LSAT median.

A price was paid for this by the students. Because they had to take courses after the first year to catch up, they would not be able to work at summer legal jobs, a traditional way to build resumes and gain experience. Students put in this position, furthermore, may have found it stigmatizing, since everyone understood what it was about. In law schools where significant numbers of African American and Latino students—who on average have lower LSAT scores than do whites and Asians—were placed into part-time programs, perceptions were further affected by racial over-tones.[2] Genuine evening students, on their end, were disgruntled at being forced to compete on the same curve with students who didn't share the disadvantage of juggling the demands of school with full-time jobs and family obligations.

It is not known how many law schools used part-time programs in this fashion or on what scale. But there is no doubt that it was taking place. Philip Closius presided as dean over a spectacular rise by Toledo law school from the fourth to the second tier in a few years; thereafter he was hired as dean at Baltimore law school, sparking another rapid rise. His golden strategy, Closius admitted in a 2008 *Wall Street Journal* article about law school manipulation, involved massively shifting bodies from the full-time program to the part time.[3] Note the flip in proportion of students at Toledo: in 1993 (pregaming), it enrolled 177 full-time students and seventy-four part-time; in 2007, it enrolled seventy-six full time and 127 part time.[4] Few schools were as blatant as Toledo, but the *Wall Street Journal* article identified eighteen law schools up and down the hierarchy that would likely fall in rank if the LSAT scores of part-time students were counted.

Prodded by complaints of rampant gaming, *US News* closed this loophole in 2009 by including part-time numbers in the LSAT median. Ensuing events at two law schools—George Washington (GW) and Brook-lyn—demonstrate the extent to which law schools are whipsawed by the ranking.

The first year *US News* counted part-time LSAT medians, GW imme-diately fell in rank from twenty to twenty-eight. That hurt. In 2008, their full-time program enrolled 426 students and part time had 124 students; the median LSAT of the part-time students was three points lower (165 median full time; 162 part time).[5] Before the rule change, schools could take large numbers of students with lower medians without harming their score because part-timers were not counted; after the change their scores did count (*US News* never explained what precipitated GW's fall in rank, so other factors may have contributed). GW has since regained its former rank, but now with a different make up: the full-time program is bigger than it was (489 students) and the part-time program has shrunk dramat-ically (from 124 to thirty-four students); the gap in the medians increased

(167 median full time, 162 part time), but that matters less because the part-time class is so much smaller.

Brooklyn avoided GW's fate only by failing to disclose its part-time numbers, as mentioned above. When exposing its breach, *US News* director of research Robert Morse stated that Brooklyn's rank would have been lower had they properly reported the numbers. Like GW, Brooklyn's class now looks different from prior to the rule change. The part-time class is much smaller than it used to be (190 then, sixty-nine today) and the full-time class much bigger (303 then, 417 today); in addition, the drop off in LSAT median between full and part time was reduced from four points to two (163/159 then, 163/161today).

Neither school will confirm it, but it is apparent that the changes made at both were in reaction to the shift in how *US News* treated part-time students. And although it might seem like a good thing that this avenue for gaming has been closed, the fix has harmful consequences of its own. Part-time evening programs have long served as an alternative path to the bar for working people. (Former Chief Justice Warren Burger of the US Supreme Court attended night school in Minneapolis while working full time.) Because these students typically come in with lower LSAT scores, now that these scores are counted schools will incur a penalty if they let in too many. Schools committed to creating a diverse class face the same dilemma with African American and Latino students, who score less on average than whites do on the LSAT.[6]

Whereas previously a more rounded view of applicants was considered—background, work experience, hardships overcome, strong letters of recommendation, future contribution to the community—admissions decisions have homogenized around their LSAT/GPA profile—LSAT above all else because that is what the ranking counts.[7] Taken to a narrow extreme, ability to do well on a standardized test now serves as *the* key to entry.

THE UBIQUITOUS TRANSFER PHENOMENON

Another way the *US News* ranking has changed the face of legal academia is the transfer phenomenon. Transfers were once rare in legal academia, limited to the occasional student who switched schools midstream for family or relocation reasons. Taking transfer students rubs against the classic conceit that a law school inculcates in students its own stamp though lengthy immersion. Central to this process is the uniquely demanding first year—a legendary ordeal involving sleep-deprived hours of study, daily classroom grilling, and intense pressure over a two-week series of three-to-four-hour exams. First year is *the* year, which not only trains students in legal reasoning but also cements bonds among classmates. A transfer also ill-fits two essential law school opportunities: coveted positions on law journals are earned through first-year grades and a writing competition; employers visit a law school's career services office early in the fall of the second year to interview selected students based on their first-year performance.

Law schools have long been reticent about transfers for these reasons. Transfer students are anathema to traditionalists, tainted by their back door entry and devoid of first-year stories to tell.

That was before the *US News* ranking. Now transfers are sweeping across law schools, with about 5 percent of students moving annually.[8] A clear sign of its growing significance is that, for the first time, four years ago the ABA began to publish transfer numbers (with a several-year lag) on the statistical profile page it puts out on each law school. In 2008, the most recent year with publicly available records, every accredited law school in America but one saw transfers; and at almost every law school, the transfer door swung in both directions: outgoing students departed for a better school, just as incoming students came in to a better school. It is an annual reshuffle of students up, always up, the law school ladder.

The *US News* ranking formula does not take any account of transfers. Because their LSAT scores don't matter—like part-time students before the recent rule change—it did not take long before law schools turned to transfer students as a source of "LSAT free" money, filling empty seats. (The same status holds for LLM students, mentioned in chapter 6.)

Remarkably, a sign of how crazy things have gotten, even students at top-fifteen schools transfer up in the law school hierarchy. In the four years on record, as many as ten students have transferred up in a given year from Michigan, Duke, and Northwestern, and a greater number have left

Cornell and Georgetown. Immune are only Yale, Harvard, and Stanford, which welcome a good number of these transfers. Forty thousand law students from around the country lust after a seat at top-fourteen schools, but apparently a degree from those schools was not enough for many who had it. An elite-drenched environment like legal academia (with most of the professors from Harvard/Yale/Columbia), and the legal profession more generally, gives folks below the absolute pinnacle the sense that they have fallen short.

Transfer students are all about revenue. This phenomenon starts at the top. Schools try to strike the best balance between improving or maintaining their median LSAT and harvesting revenue. The awarding of scholarships aside, the most direct way for a school to bump up its LSAT median is to shrink the first-year class, lopping off the group of students with the lowest scores. (This was the Illinois plan mentioned earlier.) That sacrifices revenue. At a school satisfied with its LSAT median but hungry for more revenue, taking more first-year students is a risky move that endangers the median. As LSAT-invisible revenue payers, transfer students are the perfect solution to both situations. They bring in revenue with no downside beyond some institutional inconvenience.

Among elite law schools, the undisputed champions of cashing in on transfers are Georgetown (net student gain of 87, 87, 81, and 71 in 2005–2008, respectively) and Columbia (39, 54, 62, and 72 in those same years). The other industry blue bloods are not shy about it either. Almost all the elite schools bring in transfers each year in significant numbers—one to two dozen at Yale, Stanford, Penn, and Chicago (in 2008, adding from 8 to 13 percent to their classes); two to three dozen at Harvard, Michigan, Berkeley; three to four dozen at NYU and Northwestern. (Gaining a leg up in the transfer grab, Northwestern sent "conditional admittance" letters to a bunch of students denied initial admission, informing them that they will be admitted as transfers if they meet a specified class rank in their first year elsewhere.)[9] Virginia swings up and down. Only Duke, Cornell, and Texas consistently net around ten or fewer students—the gain of the first two depressed by the significant number of students they lose.

Once schools at the top absorb transfers in real numbers, the process inevitably cascades. Schools being drained take transfers from schools lower in the chain, and so on down. That's why virtually every school in the country sees transfers in or out, and in most cases in both directions. This is already having an impact in ways that cannot be seen on the surface.

An illuminating snapshot can be taken from the latest published statistics (keep in mind that what follows is just for one year, 2008, and things are fluid). When measured in terms of the percentage that incoming transfers constitute of the second-year class—which tells you the proportion of new bodies in the group that will graduate two years later—Rutgers School of Law—Camden is number one at nearly 23 percent of the class, and Columbia is second at 21 percent. One out of five Columbia law school graduates in 2010 did their first year elsewhere.

Flagship state schools are big players in the transfer market, placing eight schools among the top twelve in percentage terms. In 2008, transfers composed a significant portion of the second-year class of Rutgers—Camden (22.71 percent), Buffalo (19.52 percent), Florida State (18.44 percent), Minnesota (18.14 percent), Arizona State (17.03 percent), Berkeley (16.79 percent), UCLA (15.59 percent), and Utah (14.29 percent). This tells you how state schools are compensating for reductions in funding from legislatures: raising revenue from transfers in a way that does not damage their median LSAT. With strength in the local legal market and relatively lower tuition for residents, leading state schools, even those not among the national elite, are attractive destinations for transfers.

When deciding to where they should transfer—only students who do well in the first year have a chance—ranking alone is not determinative. Whether a law school is in a strong legal market (the strongest are New York, Washington, DC, Los Angeles, and Chicago) and its comparative standing among other law schools within that market bear on whether transferring will pay off with improved employment opportunities. Loyola Marymount in Los Angeles (net +37) and Cardozo (net +20) in New York, for example, both ranked around fifty, reap a significant number of transfers because they are the best nonelite schools (hence a realistic destination for lower-down students) in large legal markets. Schools in weaker legal markets will be less desirable destinations for prospective transfers than their high rank might otherwise indicate. Another consideration is expense: transfer students usually pay full sticker price, giving up scholarships they might have had at their original school, which can amount to tens of thousands of dollars more out of pocket after a move.

On the receiving end, law schools will take transfers who they evaluate can perform reasonably well among the existing student body. This assessment is a function of how well a student did in the first year and the quality of the school they came from relative to the quality of the school they are seeking to transfer to. Students who rank in the top 5–10 percent of the first-year class are strongly preferred; law schools, at least in the ideal, will not admit as transfers even top students from schools too far beneath their standing. These two factors are inversely related: the further down the school of origin is from the taking school, the higher in the class the student must be. But law schools have different tolerance levels on both criteria. From the outside, one cannot tell whether a high number of transfer admissions reflects the popularity of a school as a transfer destination or lax standards on the part of the school (gorging its desire for revenue).

A few observations will reveal crucial dynamics at play. GW took in a large amount (+51) of transfers and lost a sizable amount (−24). In revenue terms the school did well, achieving a net gain of twenty-seven tuition payers. But class composition is less positive. GW exchanged a significant chunk of their best students for a passel of successful students from lower-down schools. With a whopping seventy-five people switching places, this has a transformative effect on the class (albeit hidden from view), stripped of many of its most outstanding performers. UCLA (+46, −9) and Washington University (+46, −12) also leveraged their top-twenty prestige to yield a slew of transfers. Other schools in this rank-range participated at a more modest level. USC (net +15), Vanderbilt (net +10), and Notre Dame (net +12) took in fewer transfers and lost only a handful. Illinois, Boston University, and Boston College roughly broke even with fifteen or fewer in and out. Transfers out from these schools are swept up in a talent suck to the top.

What happens at the cluster of law schools ranked from about fifteen to twenty-five has vital implications for the entire market. If more law schools in the top fifteen begin to take transfers on a scale approaching Columbia's, students from law schools ranked in the second group (fifteen to twenty-five) will serve as their prime draft pool. Schools in this category will be stripped of a painful number of their better students, à la GW, and will have to take in more students to make up for the financial hit.

Even if the top fifteen maintain their current transfer patterns, schools in the fifteen-to-twenty-five range can, on their own, ramp up their transfer numbers to the levels of GW, UCLA, and Washington University. Either of these scenarios would ramify through the remaining 175 law schools. Every transfer student taken, remember, is a loss elsewhere, which losing schools would try to make up by taking transfers of their own. In this fashion, each transfer at the top can multiply several times down the ladder. The logic of the situation leans toward escalation because schools that currently moderate their transfer numbers are leaving money—transfer bodies—on the table to be grabbed by their more aggressive cohorts.

This is a perilously unstable arrangement. No law school entirely controls its own fate. Every school is subject to the consequences of decisions made by higher-ups as well as decisions by competitor schools in the same rank group. At most schools in the country, the transfer numbers are at a relatively low level, around ten in, ten out, often in both directions. This is, however, still a relatively early stage in the transfer phenomenon, with law schools feeling things out. The 2008 numbers cited above may already be obsolete. Akin to what occurred with puffed-up employment numbers, it appears that equilibrium will only be reached, if at all, when most law schools across the board have maxed out their relative net transfer capacity in the market.

And then there are the losers—literally not pejoratively. Two law schools, Cooley and Florida Coastal, incorporate transfers out as a component of their economic model. These schools feed on students with rock-bottom LSAT scores who have little chance of obtaining initial entry elsewhere. Many students come in hoping to do well enough to transfer to a better school after the first year. For this to work financially, these schools must take in a large number of students, anticipating massive attrition at the end of the first year (transfers out, quitting, failing out). Unlike most law schools, which count on three years of tuition, these institutions are willing to take one. In 2008, Cooley law school lost 188 transfers out, but it had 1,903 entering students. On a less gargantuan scale, Florida Coastal lost seventy-eight transfers out from a total class of 573. Ramping up in size, in 2010 they took in 808 JD students. These schools will be okay financially as long as their first-year enrollment holds up.

Other large losers may be in trouble. Ave Maria saw twenty-seven students leave a class of 127. Whittier lost twenty-eight students from a class of 156 (four transferred in). Ave Maria, Whittier, Thomas Jefferson, Detroit Mercy, Phoenix, and Widener (Wilmington) all suffered net losses of more than 10 percent of their class. Syracuse and Florida A&M were nearly 10 percent down. Valparaiso and St. Thomas (Minnesota) were down 8.5 percent. New England lost 8 percent, and Catholic was close to that. Hofstra, Oklahoma City, and Dayton suffered net losses of more than 7 percent.

These are serious financial blows, as well as the exodus of many of their best students. Each student who leaves represents two years of tuition, discounted for scholarships, gone up in smoke. Few businesses could sustain revenue losses on this order without undergoing changes in how they operate. But law schools in this position have limited options. They can increase scholarship offers to dissuade students from heading out. That would take away money needed for the next year's entering class, however, and many students will depart for greener pastures anyway. Alternatively, these schools can take in more transfers themselves—although their position in the transfer market is weak. Some schools might be pushed involuntarily toward the Cooley model of enrolling greater numbers of first years in anticipation of significant transfer losses. Challenges lie ahead for schools that find themselves in this position.

The list above should be unsettling for law schools up and down the chain. Most net losers in 2008 were in the bottom tiers of the ranking.[10] But Catholic, Hofstra, and Syracuse are in the top hundred—and the first two are located in two of the strongest legal markets in the country (though Hofstra is at an inconvenient distance from New York City). A school can be vulnerable to, or protected from, significant transfer losses for a host of reasons.

Nothing insures that the transfer market will remain at the level it is now, around 5 percent of students moving annually. A few factors dampen the process. In particular, students eligible to transfer will go from an established position at the top of their existing school to starting all over at a new school, and many (those who had scholarships) will pay more out of pocket after the move. Law schools are constrained by the number and quality of applicants, limiting themselves to students who are on a par with their existing class and who won't be a high risk to fail the bar exam after graduation. But no one is looking over their shoulders, and when revenue demands become compelling enough law schools may reach deeper down into the pool of transfer applicants than would be ideal.

The transfer phenomenon is yet another demonstration of the mind-boggling power the ranking holds over law schools. A bunch of folks in a magazine office brainstorming about what they will chose to count (first-year LSAT median) and not count (transfers) set in motion a phenomenon that is reshaping the internal composition of law schools as well as the relationship among law schools, placing some schools in financial jeopardy. The contours of a $5 billion educational industry are being carved by a self-appointed maker of lists, which are sold for a profit.

Squelching the transfer market would be easy. If *US News* decides that henceforth it will incorporate the LSAT scores of transfers into its ranking, the attractiveness of transfers as sources of revenue will instantly plummet. A law professor, in a recent issue of the *Journal of Legal Education*, vehemently argued that *US News* should make this change. The process is unfair to law schools that lose students, he complained. Students who transfer ungratefully take the benefit of their one-year education and run. Schools deprived of their best students by "poachers" are left with a degraded classroom experience and have lost the professional accomplishments (and future donations) of transfer students who would have gone on to become high-achieving alumni had they remained. "The school of initial matriculation has made an investment," he wrote, "which deserves some type of protection in order to encourage it."[11]

It is understandable that net loser schools are desperate to find ways to prevent transfers from disembarking in painful numbers, but this is a decidedly one-sided argument. The quid pro quo from students for that one year was the tuition they paid (even if reduced by a scholarship), their LSAT scores, and whatever positive benefit their presence brought to the class at the time. After all, law professors who are successful seldom hesitate to skedaddle off to a higher-ranked place that comes calling for their services, so why should successful students who have the opportunity to make the same move be artificially constricted? Professors with a genuine commitment to students ought to encourage them to take advantage of opportunities that will improve their career prospects (after thoroughly considering the costs and consequences), regardless of whether their departure is a loss for the school.

Allowing transfers to remain LSAT-free for ranking purposes, furthermore, has the redeeming benefit of partially ameliorating a distortion caused by the ranking itself. Law schools myopically focus on LSAT scores when deciding who to admit to the first-year class because the ranking penalizes them for not doing so. LSAT scores are predictions based on a narrow set of test-taking skills. In general terms it has predictive validity, but there is a great deal of variance (up and down) between LSAT scores and actual law school grades. Transfer students have *proven* that they can perform at a high level. The LSAT underpredicted their ability in the sense that top students at any of the schools ranked between fifteen and thirty would do fine, and some would excel at any of the top-fifteen schools. And so on down the hierarchy. The transfer mechanism is an avenue to correct the heavy overemphasis on LSAT scores by law schools.

Whatever the folks in the ranking-methodology room at *US News* decide to do with transfers, there is no doubt that law schools will roll over and sit up on command.

THE EXPLOSION AND REDIRECTION OF SCHOLARSHIPS AND ITS CONSEQUENCES

The ABA reported that in 2009–10 law schools collectively awarded $899,506,281 in scholarships.[12] Scholarships have exploded—increasing by $362,851,399 since 2004–5—commensurate with the rise in tuition. Judging from the recent rate of increase, law schools likely awarded in excess of $1 *billion* in scholarships in 2011–12.

Many law students get tuition breaks.[13] The percentage of students with scholarships ranges from a low of 2.4 percent of the entering class at Atlanta's John Marshall, to a high of 88.6 percent at Drexel.[14] Most schools have between 25 percent and 60 percent of entering JD students on scholarships. The dollar amount of the scholarships law schools offer are determined by the particular dynamics of the group of schools they compete against for the same pool of students. (John Marshall apparently monopolizes the bottom of the Atlanta law student market.) Full-tuition scholarships are seldom handed out, and many law schools do not award any, but it is not unusual for 25 percent or so of the students to have scholarships in the amount of half or more of the tuition.

Law school seats are like airline seats, with students paying different prices to sit in the same room. As a gross generalization, roughly half of the students (usually those with LSAT scores below the school's median) pay full price and the remainder are discounted at different rates. High LSAT–high GPA students get the best financial packages, and so on down from there, with LSAT score counting the most. Savvy applicants can sometimes bid up awards before closing the deal by bringing in higher offers from competitor schools at the same level; law schools, which keep close track of what competitors are bidding, try to nail the price point that will reel in a student without offering a dollar more than necessary. Applicants can find out what scholarship amounts law schools have offered others in the class with a similar profile on a popular prelaw website, Law School Numbers.[15]

Across the country, in 2010–11, a total of 69,466 JD students (47 percent of all JD students) received scholarships.[16] A billion dollars in total scholarships delivers remissions to a lot of people. The discount price in many law schools—the effective amount paid across the class—is perhaps as much as 20 percent or more below the listed tuition. This seeming piece of good news, however, masks a dark underside.

Prior to the dominance of the ranking, most scholarship money was parceled out according to the financial need of students. Not anymore. At law schools across the country the awarding of scholarships has switched heavily away from need-based to merit-based criteria. It happened quickly.[17] In 1994–95, 58 percent of aid was need based and 42 percent was merit based; by 1999–2000 the proportions had flipped, with 44 percent need based and 56 percent merit based. Between 2005 and 2010, despite an overall increase in the number of students enrolled, the number of students receiving need-based scholarships dropped by three thousand (17,610 receiving need aid), while the number of students receiving merit scholarships increased by 12,500 (60,010 received merit based); in 2010, law schools awarded $143,361,001 in need-based scholarships, and $757,691,508 in merit-based scholarships.[18]

The law school chase to "purchase" LSAT scores to shape medians uses up scholarship budgets, leaving far less money (except at the wealthiest schools) to provide financial assistance to students with limited resources.[19] Law deans bemoan this shift and blame it on the ranking.[20] Universities, caught up in their own prestige competition, have moved heavily into merit-based scholarships for undergraduates as well, but they have retained a substantial need-based component.[21] Among law schools today only Harvard, Yale, and Stanford offer wholly or primarily need-based scholarships.

Financially challenged students face a double hit. Not only is scant need-based assistance available, they are at a disadvantage under the merit-based distribution of funds. "Many administrators feel that the LSAT, more than other admissions criteria, favors the wealthy because of their backgrounds, their educational experience, and their test-preparation courses."[22] To the extent that this bears out, wealthy students have a better chance to maximize their LSAT score, thereby seizing a greater share of financial assistance.

Owing to the relationship between LSAT scores, grades, and jobs, the current system of awarding merit scholarships produces a perverse result. Students who score below the median LSAT of a given school (other than Harvard, Yale, and Stanford) are almost invariably the ones who pay the most tuition because, to put it in blunt terms, their score has no value to a school. (The main exceptions to this are African American and Latino students who obtain merit scholarships at lower relative scores.) And while there is much variance, those with higher LSAT scores on the whole tend to get better law school grades.[23] Students with the best grades, especially in the first year, secure the best paying jobs out of law school. Consequently, generalizing the interaction of these factors, the bottom half of the class subsidizes the education of the top half of the class. The students in line for the worst paying jobs thus provide financial assistance to their classmates who will land the best paying jobs upon graduation. No one would intentionally design this financing scheme, which is indefensible on its own terms, but that is how it works in practice. Every class has a few students with below median LSAT scores who earn excellent grades, and high LSAT scorers who do poorly, but in general the expected relationship holds.

Law schools have in effect constructed a reverse–Robin Hood arrangement, redistributing resources between students, making the (likely) poorer future graduates help pick up the tab for the (likely) wealthier future graduates. Seen in this light, the tuition discount price has malign consequences. A fairer way to charge students would drop tuition across the board to the discount price, eliminating merit aid entirely, retaining scholarship funds only for need-based assistance. The cross subsidy between students would end, and everyone would share equally in the benefit, paying 20–30 percent lower tuition.

There is no chance this will happen. Any school that implements it on its own will disarm unilaterally, robbing itself of the ability to shape its LSAT profile with finely tuned differential pricing. Competitor schools would swoop in to buy away a swath of the top half of the class by offering discounts below the stated tuition. It would be easy pickings. As long as the rankings operate the way they do—placing a premium on LSAT scores—scholarships will be used to shape the class and the reverse–Robin Hood subsidy will remain.

THE CONSOLIDATION OF THE ELITE

Yet another negative development with considerable consequences lurks within this arrangement.

In 2010, tuition at Yale was $50,750, plus $19,700 in estimated living expenses. About 40 percent of the incoming students paid full price. Using numbers from the prior year, nearly 24 percent received a remission of half or more of tuition, 35 percent received less than half, and no student received a full-tuition scholarship. At Harvard about half of the JD students paid full price; tuition was $46,616, with estimated living expenses of $23,484. It handed out twenty-four full-tuition or more than full-tuition scholarships. At Stanford 40 percent of the students paid full price; tuition was $46,581, plus $24,581 in living expenses. It awarded eleven scholarships at or above full tuition. At Columbia tuition was $50,428 and living expenses $21,700. Half of the students received scholarships, including forty-five at full tuition or more. The top schools, with some variation, distribute scholarships roughly along these lines: 40–60 percent of the students pay full fare, 20–30 percent get a discount of half or more, 20–30 percent get less than half off, and a dozen or so students enjoy full scholarships.

The key dynamic involves students who are made to pay full fare. Typically, they will be in the bottom half of the LSAT/GPA profile of students admitted to the JD class at any particular school. The highest-ranked schools have students with the highest LSAT/GPA combination—with LSAT numbers steadily falling as you travel down the ranking. For example, an applicant with a 171 LSAT would have placed below the median of the class at Columbia, but in the top quartile at Michigan, Penn, Berkeley, Virginia, Duke, and so on.[24]

An applicant in this position would be confronted with a tough choice: go to Columbia and pay full price ($50,428), or attend a lower-down school, say Duke ($47,722), with a tuition discount of half or more; Columbia at $150,000 tuition over three years or Duke at $70,000. When you add in projected expenses, the final price would be $210,000 for a degree at Columbia versus $120,000 for a degree at Duke.

Applicants from wealthy families who can help financially wouldn't hesitate to go to Columbia. But applicants from middle-class families—with parents who are school teachers, middle management, small business owners, solo practitioner lawyers (parents who exhausted their resources helping their child make it through college with less debt)—will find the Duke offer hard to turn down.

I use Columbia as the example rather than Harvard, Yale, and Stanford because, as previously mentioned, the latter three, uniquely among law schools, provide scholarships wholly or predominantly on a need rather than merit basis. Once admitted, a student with a bottom-quartile LSAT at Harvard, Yale, and Stanford would be eligible for a grant on the same terms as a top-quartile student. Yet the same economic dilemma would exist for a person with limited economic means because the amount of need-based aid provided would not necessarily offset the merit-based scholarship offered by a school like Duke. Harvard, Yale, and Stanford typically require students to be responsible for a base amount each year ($33,000 at Stanford, $38,800 at Yale), plus an additional amount that parents and spouses are theoretically capable of contributing (based on income formulas)—only above that figure does the school begin to provide need-based aid.[25] In 2010, Harvard graduates had an average debt of $115,000, Stanford graduates had $104,000, and Yale grads had $99,000.[26] These are much higher debt levels than a student with a full-tuition scholarship at Duke would carry.

This might not seem like a major concern because a student who goes to Duke will have an outstanding career anyway. That is correct as far as it goes, but there is more. Law is a highly elitist, credential-oriented profession. Consider that in the history of the US Supreme Court, seventeen justices attended Harvard, ten attended Yale, and seven attended Columbia; no other law school counts more than three; Duke has none. [27] It is far easier to land elite clerkships, choice positions in the Department of Justice, and a law professor job coming out of top-five schools.[28] Although a Duke degree is an elite credential that opens many doors, the difference in career opportunities compared to Harvard, Yale, Stanford, or Columbia is not negligible.

Imagining a choice between Columbia and Duke is misleading in that the downside does not seem so bad. But the phenomenon goes much further. Versions of this same choice play out all the way down the law school hierarchy, often with more dramatic differences at stake. Applicants at the bottom LSAT quartile point (166–68), who would be required to pay full price at Michigan, Penn, Cornell, Duke, and Northwestern, would get substantial tuition reductions to attend any school ranked twentieth or higher. Pay full tuition at Vanderbilt or attend Iowa, North Carolina, Emory, etc., at a big discount? Frequently the pertinent choice will be between local alternatives. An applicant who scores 165 on the LSAT would be in the bottom 25 percent of the class at UCLA but in the upper 25 percent at Loyola Marymount. Pay full tuition at the former or get more than half-off at the latter? In all of these examples, the disparity in career opportunities entailed in the choice is considerable.

Applicants from families with money would attend the better school without hesitation. Applicants from middle-class families will be faced with the agonizing decision of whether taking on mountainous debt will be worth the advantages gained from going to the higher-ranked school. Some will make the leap to the higher school. When making this choice, they are placing a bet that they will land a corporate law upon graduation to pay off the loan (regardless of whether that is a job they desire). Some applicants with modest means will, reluctantly, select the lower school at a discount. They can go on to have stellar legal careers anyway, but the higher school would have laid an easier path with better opportunities.

In this manner, the tuition-scholarship relationship to the higher-versus-lower-school choice constitutes an allocation matrix that uniformly funnels wealthy applicants to the higher school, securing the attendant advantages, while people with less financial means divide between higher and lower. Multiply this out by tens of thousands of like decisions each year and the effect is large.

A generation ago, a middle-class aspirant to a legal career would not have been forced to make this choice. But current and future generations must face it. And it seems that an inevitable consequence of the pricing structure of law schools—as a greater proportion of middle class and poor select the lower option in the law school hierarchy for financial reasons—is that more and more elite legal positions will be in the hands of the wealthy. This cannot be laid on the *US News* ranking. But the ways law schools have reacted to the ranking are bringing in their wake troublesome implications for society and the legal system.

Legal academia has always manifested a wealth effect, showing up a century ago in the debates over whether law school should be two years or three. A study of the graduating class of 2000 found that, "across the spectrum of law schools, there is a lopsided concentration of law students toward the high end of the socioeconomic spectrum, which becomes more lopsided with the eliteness of the law school."[29] Top-ten law schools had the highest concentration of students from the top decile of socioeconomic households (57 percent), while the bottom hundred law schools had the lowest concentration from the top socioeconomic decile (27 percent).[30]

If the tuition-scholarship relationship continues to operate in the manner I suggest, the already-present wealth concentration in law schools will strengthen over time. Subsequent to the class examined in the study, average tuition at private law schools went up by another $15,000.

Elite law schools tend to have a lower percentage of graduates with debt compared to the lowest-ranked law schools, another indication of a wealth effect. Although Yale charges the highest tuition, only 73 percent of its graduates in 2010 had law school debt, one of the lowest rates in the country.[31] At today's prices, substantial financial resources are required to leave law school without debt. At Northwestern only 69 percent of the class had debt; 77 percent at Columbia; 80 percent at NYU and Cornell; and 81 percent at Stanford. (Harvard did not disclose its figure.) Contrast those with the percentage of the class in debt at some of the lowest-ranked schools: Thomas Jefferson (95 percent); Touro (94 percent); Atlanta's John Marshall (96 percent); New York Law School (93 percent); Oklahoma City (99 percent); and Florida Coastal (91 percent).

A wealth effect also shows up in undergraduate colleges.[32] Both manifestations are reflections of the growing separation between rich and poor in America and the hollowing out of the middle class.[33] What is special about legal academia is not the wealth-effect phenomenon but, rather, its broader consequences: law has a central role in American society, and graduates of elite law schools secure an outsized proportion of top legal positions.

PART IV

The Broken Economic Model

NINE

Rising Tuition, Rising Debt

Twenty-five years ago Dean John Kramer of Tulane University Law School sounded an alarm about rising law school tuition in an article titled "Will Legal Education Remain Affordable, by Whom, and How?"

> Law schools for the last twenty years have been testing the elasticity of demand for their product. As tuition has increased year after year, outpacing even the rate of inflation, law schools have been pressing toward the point where significant numbers of college graduates may decide that it makes good economic sense to seek less expensive forms of graduate education or forgo additional credentials altogether.[1]

In the previous decade, average tuition had increased nearly 200 percent at public law schools and 179 percent at private law schools.[2] Kramer worried about the rising debt of law graduates and suggested that in coming years many would struggle financially. If the rise in tuition continued at the same pace, Kramer predicted, future generations of law school "seats may be filled almost exclusively by the sons and daughters of rich and upper middle class white families and a handful of black and brown students from relatively impoverished backgrounds who receive substantial grants."[3] The remaining seats would be taken up by students who take out large loans to finance their education, graduating to become lawyers compelled by the "single-minded objective of milking the profession for all it is worth in order to be able to pay retrospectively for their legal education."[4]

It was a prophetic essay—a standing rebuke to later generations of legal academics who were warned about the consequences of their trajectory.

Kramer was spectacularly off, however, about testing the limits of elasticity of demand. At the time he wrote, Harvard Law School's tuition was $11,135. Today its tuition is $46,616, more than double the price then in inflation adjusted dollars—yet Harvard has no trouble filling its seats.

Rising tuition directly results in rising debt.[5] A series of articles in the mid-1990s warned about the record levels of debt carried by law students.[6] Law graduates had the worst loan default record among professional students.[7] By the late 1990s, it appeared to be nearing crisis proportions. "Student debt has quadrupled in the past 10 years," wrote the *National Jurist* in a special issue on law student debt, "dropping the average recent graduate's standard of living by 33 percent. Graduates at some schools now have a lower standard of living than they did when they were students."[8]

TUITION COMPARED TO INFLATION

Oblivious to these concerns, law school tuition continued its meteoric rise. When Kramer issued his warning, in 1987, average tuition and fees for a resident at public law schools was $2,398. It was $7,367 in 1999, when the *National Jurist* published its article about the debt burden. Ten years later, in 2009, average tuition for state residents at public law schools had more than doubled to $18,472. Tuition has gone up every year since Kramer's article, averaging a 10 percent increase at public schools *each* year—during a period in which inflation averaged slightly more than 3 percent per year. Average tuition at private law schools also went up *every* year, by large amounts, though the percentage was lower because it started at a higher base. At private law schools, average tuition in 1987 was $8,911; in 1999 it was $20,709; in 2009 it was $35,743.[9] Tuition at private law schools has increased by $15,000 (on average) in just the past ten years.

Taking the entire span from 1985 through 2009, resident tuition at public law schools increased by a staggering 820 percent—from $2,006 to $18,472 (nonresident tuition increased by 543 percent, from $4,724 to $30,413)—while tuition at private law schools went up by 375 percent—from $7,526 to $35,743. These increases far outstripped the rate of inflation. Had tuition increases merely kept pace with inflation, average resident tuition at public law schools would only be $3,945 today, less than a fourth of what it is, and average private school tuition would be $14,800, less than half of what it is. Law school would still be affordable if the schools had not extracted such a large premium over inflation.

The stunning pace and size of the increase can be observed through the prime mover: Yale. Tuition at Yale Law School was $12,450 in 1987; in 1999 it was $26,950; in 2010 it was $50,750.[10] That is an increase of nearly $24,000, close to doubling in just over a decade. Factoring in projected living expenses ($19,700), Yale students without scholarships who commenced their legal studies in 2010 will pay more than $200,000 to obtain their law degrees. If the recent rate of increase continues, in ten years tuition at Yale Law School will be $70,000.[11] That might sound impossible, but ten years ago many would have scoffed at the suggestion that tuition at Yale would be $50,000 today.

Another way to get a concrete sense of the increase is to compare it to income from summer jobs. Law students in the seventies and early eighties who worked at corporate law firms during the summer could earn enough to cover the following year's tuition and perhaps some living expenses. This helped keep down the level of debt. Despite the dramatic increase in starting associate pay at corporate law firms that occurred in the early 2000s, the best-paying summer jobs today, which few students land, generate enough income for a student to pay half, at most, of one year's tuition at a top school.

THE RISING DEBT BURDEN IN CONCRETE TERMS

Student debt has ballooned in conjunction with tuition, inevitably, since law students typically borrow to finance their legal educations. The average combined debt (undergraduate and law school) of law school graduates in the mid-1980s was $15,676.[12] The average debt of law graduates was $47,000 in 1999.[13] In 2010, according to numbers complied by the ABA, average law school debt alone was $68,827 for graduates from public schools and $106,249 at private schools—this is on top of whatever undergraduate debt they might have accumulated.[14] A nonprofit organization that tracks students loans across all categories finds that 88.60 percent of law students overall borrow money to finance their legal education; the average cumulative law school debt of these borrowers is $80,081; and the average combined debt of undergraduate and law schools loans is $92,937.[15] That estimate is likely far too low. According to numbers the law schools supplied to *US News*, the overall average law school debt of the graduating class of 2010 was $98,500, before adding undergraduate debt.[16] Average college debt for graduates of the class of 2010 (with nearly two-thirds of students in debt) was $25,250.[17] The two averages combined totals nearly $124,000. Keep in mind that, under current law, student loans cannot be discharged in bankruptcy.

These averages, high as they appear, understate the magnitude of the debt burden of many graduates because those with lower debt dilute the heavy borrowers. A list of the twenty-two law schools in 2010 with the highest average debt (of students who had debt) among graduates reveals the heavy burden borne by many law graduates.[18]

1. California Western: $145,621 (88 percent of the class in debt)
2. Thomas Jefferson: $137,352 (95 percent)
3. Southwestern: $136,569 (79 percent)
4. American: $136,121 (84 percent)
5. Catholic (DC): $134,133 (91 percent)
6. Golden Gate: $132,895 (89 percent)
7. Northwestern: $132,685 (69 percent)
8. Loyola Marymount: $132,267 (85 percent)
9. Charleston: $128,571 (84 percent)
10. Pacific (McGeorge): $128,495 (93 percent)
11. Chicago: $127,997 (84 percent)
12. Vermont: $127,914 (93 percent)
13. Columbia: $126,945 (77 percent)
14. Cornell: $126,000 (80 percent)
15. John Marshall: $125,806 (74 percent)
16. Touro: $125,481 (94 percent)
17. New York University: $125,169 (80 percent)
18. Pepperdine: $125,114 (82 percent)
19. San Francisco: $124,982 (76 percent)
20. Albany: $124,271 (88 percent)
21. Roger Williams: $123,338 (88 percent)
22. Atlanta's John Marshall: $123,025 (96 percent)

Overall, in 2010, graduates of eighty-eight law schools, private and public, carried an average law school debt exceeding $100,000 (most within a range from 80 to 95 percent of the class in debt). A nationwide survey of law students in 2010 found that almost one-third expected to graduate with a debt of more than $120,000.[19]

How much income would be required to manage the monthly payments on a debt that size? An often-repeated rule of thumb offered by student debt advisers is that "debt should never exceed starting salary."[20] For many law graduates that counsel is hopelessly out of reach, given that in 2010 the average debt was nearly $100,000 while the average salary was $77,000. Debt payments cannot be too high relative to income because other major expenses must be covered as well: federal and state taxes, rent or mortgage, transportation, food and clothing, insurance, retirement savings, etc. Although economists offer different estimates of manageable monthly debt payments, there appears to be a consensus that 10 percent of income is manageable, 15 percent is problematic, "and the payment-to-income ratio should *never* exceed 18 to 20 percent."[21] Staying beneath that strict upper limit will not be possible for many law graduates.

Let's assume that a newly minted twenty-five-year-old graduate—we'll call her Sarah—wishes to pay her $120,000 debt off in the standard ten-year term, and let's assume a consolidated loan rate of 7.25 percent (this combines the two types of available government loans, Stafford [6.8 percent] and GradPlus loans[7.9 percent]). Her monthly loan payment will be $1,400. A student loan information site, FinAid, advises Sarah "that you will need an annual salary of at least $169,057.20 to be able to afford to repay this loan." That would keep the loan payment at the recommended 10 percent of her gross salary. She might manage to make debt payments as high as 15 percent of her gross monthly income, which would require an annual salary of $112,000, but FinAid advises that she might experience "financial difficulty."[22] If Sarah earned $85,000, the loan payment would consume 20 percent of her gross monthly income, putting her at the upper limit.

Now consider that the class of 2010 earned a median salary of $63,000.[23] A simple calculation shows why Sarah would be in trouble if that was her salary. Assuming taxes (federal, state, social security, Medicare) took

30 percent of her pay, Sarah would have $3,675 in net monthly income. Subtracting her loan payment of $1,400 and rent of $1,500 leaves Sarah with $775 a month to spend on all of her remaining expenses: food, transportation, cell phone bill, and so on. It's not doable. Sarah the new lawyer would be forced to enter a reduced loan payment program, the implications of which will be taken up shortly.

TWO SEPARATE UNIVERSES OF PAY: TOP CORPORATE LAW JOBS VERSUS THE REST

Students from elite law schools have a solid chance of securing corporate law jobs that pay a salary sufficient to comfortably manage $120,000 debt. In 2010, 27 percent of law graduates (down from 30 percent in 2009) secured employment at the nation's 250 largest corporate law firms (by revenue), known as the NLJ 250.[24] The benchmark for starting associate pay at these firms is $160,000—though many NLJ 250 firms, especially those outside of New York and Los Angeles, offer lower starting pay. Top-fifteen law schools send 30–60 percent or more of their graduates to NLJ 250 firms each year, reaching a high in the 70 percent range before the recession. But the percentage of graduates securing these positions rapidly falls the further down the law school ranking one goes. The top sixteen- to twenty-five-ranked law schools place between 20 and 30 percent of their graduates at these firms. Outside the top twenty-five, about 10 percent of graduates place in NLJ 250 firms. To offer a few examples, Tulane, Temple, North Carolina, Minnesota, Ohio State—all well regarded law schools— placed 10–12 percent of their graduates in NLJ 250 firms in 2010. Outside the top fifty or so ranked law schools, particularly those not located in major legal markets, most place fewer than 5 percent, and in some cases none, of their graduates in these coveted jobs.

Starting pay for new law graduates falls into a distinctive pattern called a bimodal distribution, with two earnings clusters separated by a large gap of about $100,000. For the class of 2010, nearly half of law graduates earned between $40,000 and $65,000.[25] This is the left peak in figure 9.1. *Among those who reported their salaries,* nearly 20 percent of law graduates earned around $160,000—the narrower right peak, made up of top-

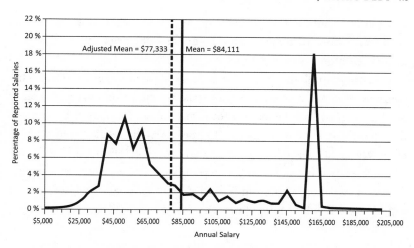

Fig. 9.1. The NALP graph illustrates the bimodal salary distribution recent law school graduates experience. Few graduates actually earn the adjusted average pay of $77,333. Half of all graduates earn between $40,000 and $65,000, while nearly 20 percent of graduates land corporate jobs paying $160,000. © NALP 2011. Modified after www.nalp.org.

paying corporate law jobs. (Approximately 10 percent of 2010 graduates overall landed these salaries.)[26] In the long, flat valley between these two peaks are scattered most of the remaining graduates. The adjusted average pay for the class of 2010, $77,333, sounds like an attractive amount, but few graduates actually earned that amount. (The mean is adjusted downward because the majority of graduates in lower paying jobs do not report their salaries, which misleadingly skews the calculated average upward.)

This bimodal pay distribution has existed for over a decade.[27] Thanks to a feverish bout of hiring competition for top law school talent, starting pay for associates at corporate law firms shot up in the early 2000s.[28] This created the peak that is pulled off far to the right, representing much higher earnings. The 50 percent or so of law graduates in the lower-earning cluster pay saw no real wage gains because hiring competition only affected the top end. With fresh crops of law graduates each year supplying more new lawyers than available openings, there is little economic pressure to increase wages in the bottom half of the job market. The current legal recession has increased the size of the low-earning left peak and reduced that of the high-earning right peak, but the basic bimodal distribution continues to persist. At the average debt of $98,500, only graduates whose earnings approach the far right peak can comfortably make their monthly loan payments.

One might think that over time the debt payments of graduates will become easier to manage because compensation will increase over the course of a legal career. That will be true for some, but not for many. According to the US Bureau of Labor Statistics, "In May 2008, the median annual wages of all wage-and-salaried lawyers were $110,590. The middle half of the occupation earned between $74,980 and $163,320."[29] These numbers suggest that, at least among "wage-and-salaried lawyers," many will continue to experience difficulty paying down a $120,000 loan well into their careers.

THE HIGH PERCENTAGE OF GRADUATES WHO DO NOT OBTAIN JOBS AS LAWYERS

That is not the worst of the situation. A significant number of law graduates in recent years do not land jobs as lawyers. For the class of 2009 at thirty law schools, only 50 percent or fewer of the graduates obtained jobs as lawyers; at nearly ninety law schools, one-third or more of graduates did not land jobs as lawyers (both figures are based on nine months after graduation). While 2009 was not a good year for legal employment, 2010 was even worse (among a total 42,854 graduates, only 28,167 obtained jobs as lawyers), and 2011 will also be poor.[30]

Figure 9.2 plots the percentage of the 2009 class that obtained lawyer jobs against law school by rank (fourth-tier schools have no rank, so they are indicated after the line in alphabetical order). As one would expect, the top schools tend to have the highest rates of graduates who obtain jobs as lawyers (in the 90 percent range), but the further down the ranking one goes the lower the percentage of the class that obtains jobs as lawyers.

Following is a list of law schools with the lowest percentage of the 2009 class (nine months after graduation) that obtained a job requiring a JD—this includes private law firm jobs, government legal positions, public interest legal positions, judicial clerkships, and in-house legal positions.

University of DC, 26 percent
Western State, 28 percent

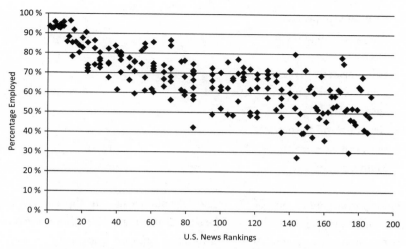

Fig. 9.2. Grads employed at nine months with job requiring a JD (2009). The data points reflected on these graphs were made by combining two employment statistics categories: "Graduates known to be employed at nine months after graduation" and "Bar admission required." These statistics can be found with an online subscription to U.S News Best Law Schools, *2011 Rankings*, http://gradschools.usnews.rankingsandreviews.com/best-graduate-schools/top-law-schools/law-rankings.

NC Central, 36 percent

Florida A&M, 38 percent

Ave Maria, 40 percent

Barry, 40 percent

Western New England, 40 percent

Capital, 43 percent

Touro, 44 percent

Appalachian, 45 percent

Northern Illinois, 46 percent

Cooley, 46 percent

Ohio Northern, 46 percent

Texas Wesleyan, 47 percent

Liberty, 48 percent

CUNY, 48 percent

Arkansas, 48 percent

Whittier, 48 percent

Pace, 49 percent

Quinnipiac, 49 percent

La Verne, 49 percent

Chapman, 49 percent

Michigan State, 49 percent

Valparaiso, 50 percent

Atlanta's John Marshall, 50 percent

Santa Clara, 50 percent

New England, 50 percent

Vermont, 50 percent

Maine, 50 percent

A 2009 graduate of one of these law schools had a coin-flip chance, at best, of landing a job as a lawyer. The situation at many law schools is even worse than these dismal numbers indicate because a growing proportion of lawyer jobs are part-time positions (fewer than thirty-five hours a week). At Golden Gate law school, for example, 53 percent of the class got jobs as lawyers, which is bad enough, but 42 percent of *these* jobs were part time.

These employment figures are taken nine months after graduation. Graduates who persevered may have later found lawyer jobs, although they will have been out of law for many months and would shortly be competing with a new crop of graduates. There is no solid information on what happens to them. They must at some point take a job, any job, to cover loan payments and bills.

When confronted with these numbers, law schools respond that the dismal job placement rate is a recent phenomenon, a product of the current recession, suggesting that things were fine before, and all will be well again when the legal market rebounds. It's wrong to isolate on and condemn law schools, they say, for results that merely reflect a historically bad time in our economy for jobs of all kinds.

The problem with this response is that it is not true.

While it is correct that the recession exacerbated matters, at many law schools the low rate of placement in lawyer jobs predates the recession. Figure 9.3 plots the year before the recession, 2007 (*circles*), alongside 2009 (*diamonds*). Although the placement rate in lawyer jobs was indeed higher in 2007, prior to the implosion of the legal market that nailed the

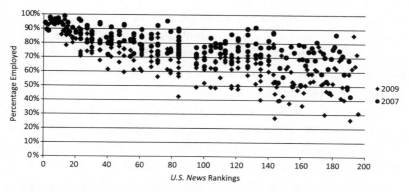

Fig. 9.3. Grads employed at nine months with job requiring JD (2007, 2009). Source: U.S News Best Law Schools, *2011 Rankings*, http://grad-schools.usnews.rankingsandreviews.com/best-graduate-schools/top-law-schools/law-rankings.

class of 2009, the same basic pattern held. A significant percentage of graduates at many law schools outside the top fifty did not obtain jobs as lawyers. This is telling because 2007 was a boom year—the peak before the crash.

Data on rates of employment across law schools tell us that this pattern extends at least as far back as 2001 (a change in data collection by NALP, the association that tracks this information in conjunction with law schools, precludes comparisons with earlier periods). The percentages of graduates who obtained jobs as lawyers in those years were: 68.3 percent (2001); 67 percent (2002); 65.5 percent (2003); 65.1 percent (2004); 66.7 percent (2005); 68.3 percent (2006); 70.7 percent (2007); 67.2 percent (2008); 62.5 percent (2009).[31] Data from the Bureau of Labor Statistics also indicate a significant oversupply of law graduates to lawyer jobs in this period. The bureau estimates that from 2000 to 2010 the economy created 123,000 new lawyer jobs; departures from the legal profession over ten years added another 151,400 openings.[32] Combining the two, there were about 275,000 job openings for lawyers during a period in which law schools produced more than 400,000 new graduates.[33] Throughout these years, it bears repeating, a majority of law schools listed on their *US News* profile employment rates ranging from the high 80 percent range to the high 90 percent range.

On a fairly consistent basis, these data indicate, about *one-third of law graduates in the past decade* have not obtained jobs as lawyers, and figure 9.3 suggests that this is disproportionately the case at the lowest-ranked law schools. The poor job placement in lawyer positions is not a product of the current legal recession.

There is every reason to believe that graduates of lower-ranked law schools, if they had the chance, would gladly take lawyer jobs in the same 90 percentile range that occurs at elite law schools. More than 90 percent of law graduates sit for the bar exam, an investment of time and money after graduation that indicates a desire to at least be eligible to work as a lawyer.[34] Evidently degrees from low-ranked law schools do not put their graduates in a strong position to land lawyer jobs.

Law schools frequently assert—and have said so for decades—that graduates who do not obtain jobs as lawyers often successfully use their law degree to advance their careers in other ways, usually citing the same examples of graduates who obtain jobs in accounting firms and as Federal Bureau of Investigation agents. Even if that happens in selected instances, it cannot account for the large numbers of graduates who fail to get lawyer jobs.

Twenty years ago, or even as recently as ten years ago, when the debt load was more bearable, a law graduate who did not land a job as a lawyer might still have come out okay financially. In those days it was not uncommon to see police officers, or midlevel corporate managers or government officials, attend law school (often part time) as a way to advance in their existing careers. There also were young people who came to law school intending to enhance their opportunities in business. But annual tuition was much lower then. With private law school tuition now ranging from $30,000 to $50,000, fewer of these people come to law school today. It makes much less economic sense to invest so much time and money in a legal education as a means to enhance a nonlegal career, especially for midcareer people who have fewer years of future earnings to recoup the cost.

Legal educators who reflexively recite the old line that law degrees pay dividends for graduates who don't become lawyers fail to appreciate the changing economic calculus wrought by a doubling and tripling of tuition in a few decades.

THE NEGATIVE IMPLICATIONS OF INCOME-BASED REPAYMENT

The worst combination for a law school is to have graduates with high average debt, a low rate of success in obtaining a lawyer job, and a high chance of landing in the lower-paying category of the bimodal distribution of pay. That is the current situation at many expensive lower-ranked law schools.

Heavily indebted graduates of these law schools, as well as many from law schools higher up in the hierarchy, will by necessity elect an extended loan repayment period of up to thirty years. If Sarah, with her $120,000 debt, chose the thirty-year plan, her monthly debt payment would drop to $800, which she could manage on her $63,000 income. On this schedule, the debt will be closed when Sarah is fifty-five years of age, and she will have paid up nearly $300,000 in total. Law graduates understandably are reluctant to sign up for extended repayment, and law school financial aid counselors consider it inadvisable.[35] In addition to increasing the cost of their legal education through the greater accumulation of interest, debtors will still be making loan payments well into middle age, when also likely paying down a mortgage, saving for their children's college, and setting aside money for their own retirement.

Another alternative for Sarah is to enroll in Income Based Repayment (IBR)—a federal program that allows students who qualify to pay lower monthly amounts and forgives the unpaid balance after twenty-five years.[36] For graduates in public-service jobs, the terms are the same but forgiveness occurs after ten years.

The monthly loan payment of a person on IBR will be 15 percent (10 percent for debtors eligible in 2014) of the difference between her adjusted gross income and 150 percent of poverty guidelines. The Department of Education provides a sample calculation: "For example, 150 percent of the 2009 HHS [Health and Human Services] poverty guidelines for a family of three is $27,465. If your AGI [adjusted gross income] was $40,000, the difference would be $12,535. Fifteen percent of that is $1,880; dividing this amount by 12 results in a monthly IBR payment amount of $157."[37] A graduate is eligible for IBR—which only applies to federal loans, not private loans—if the monthly repayment amount under the standard ten-year repayment plan exceeds the amount that would be required under IBR.

Many thousands of recent law graduates will be eligible for this program. To see why, assume that a graduate with a family of three, we'll call him Bob, obtains a job that pays $63,000.[38] The monthly loan payment under IBR for a graduate with a family of three is $444.[39] If Bob has $120,000 in law school debt, like Sarah, his monthly loan payment of $1,400 is far above the IBR payment.[40] If Bob has $100,000 in debt his monthly payment is $1,200, again far above IBR. Bob's monthly loan payment if he has $60,000 in debt is $700, still above IBR. At any of these debt levels Bob would qualify for IBR. On an income of $63,000, only graduates (having a family of three) with debt below $40,000 will *not* qualify for IBR. We know many recent graduates will qualify for IBR because $63,000 is the median salary for the class of 2010 and about two-thirds of law graduates have debt of $60,000 or higher.[41]

Or take Mr. Average law grad (with a family of three) for the class of 2010, with the average law school debt of $98,500, earning the average lawyer salary of $77,300.[42] His standard monthly loan payment would be $1,150, about $500 dollars above the IBR payment amount ($623). Even if Mr. Average was single with no dependants he would qualify for IBR by a substantial margin. (This calculation, it bears recalling, omits Mr. Average's $25,000 college debt, which would push his total above $120,000, raising his monthly payments accordingly.)

Owing to the substantial debt levels prevalent today, even law graduates who secure relatively well-paying jobs may qualify for IBR. By almost any measure, a starting job with a salary of $100,000 is a very successful outcome. But not when you factor in debt. If Bob has a debt of $100,000 and lands a $100,000 job, he would *still* qualify for IBR because the standard monthly loan payment due ($1,200) exceeds the IBR payment ($906).[43] He would be prudent to forgo IBR and make the standard payments, but something is out of whack when a person earning $100,000 is potentially in financial hardship.

Nearly 90 percent of law graduates in 2010 had debt, and average debt for the class was nearly $100,000[44] Data provided by NALP indicates that only about 15 percent of law graduates in 2010 obtained salaries in excess of $100,000.[45] Based on the numbers provided above it is reasonable to speculate that perhaps as many as half or more of the graduates of the class of 2010 qualify for IBR. That such a high proportion of graduates might qualify is indicative of a serious problem with the economics of legal education.

Income Based Repayment is "designed for those for whom standard repayment would be a *great hardship*" owing to a combination of high student debt and income insufficient to bear that debt.[46] When the program was created, estimates were that it would be used by perhaps 15–30 percent of borrowers.[47] Among recent law school graduates (the classes of 2009, 2010, and 2011) the percent eligible for IBR is likely much higher. Not all law graduates who are eligible for IBR will enroll in the program, but many will have no choice.

An educational sector, or an individual school, that systematically produces a high IBR rate among graduates is signaling that the debt level is too high relative to the earning opportunities provided. This would hold regardless of whether we are speaking of culinary institutes or law schools.

Although IBR throws a lifeline to law graduates with high debt, saving them from struggling to make payments or defaulting on the loan, it is not ideal. The loan balance will continue to grow by the amount of the underpayment, plus interest (although the government will pay the interest for the first three years). If at some later point a graduate's earnings rise enough to afford the standard ten-year payment rate, the debtor will ultimately pay much more interest before finally closing the books on the debt. Negative amortization at these debt levels can quickly increase the size of the loan balance, making it all the harder to put an end to it.

The loan balance forgiveness aspect of IBR—currently twenty-five years, twenty years for those who are eligible in 2014 (assuming this program is not gutted in deficit reduction efforts)—might sound like a good deal. (Under current rules, however, it appears that the discharge of the loan balance is a benefit that the debtor must pay taxes on, although this would not apply to the public-service version.) It will certainly be a relief to individuals when it finally happens, freed at last from a weighty financial and psychological burden. Yet it will mean, in effect, that for the bulk of their legal careers they will have labored under a degree of financial hardship.[48] This will adversely affect people in the program in other ways as well. Credit might be denied or the cost of credit for the debtor might be higher because the all important FICO credit-worthiness score, which affects interest rates for individual borrowers on mortgages and other major loans, takes into consideration the size of a person's total debt and the rate at which it is being paid down. The IBR albatross may even affect matters like finding a marriage partner and how couples arrange their economic affairs.

A hundred law schools have loan forgiveness programs, but only a handful of them, those at the wealthiest schools, are meaningful. For the rest, the amounts forgiven typically are small, providing little relief to heavily indebted graduates.[49] A few federal and state programs offer debt repayment/forgiveness help for qualifying employees, but only selected positions enjoy this benefit and it is contingent on funding.

The best way for law graduates to obtain relief is though the Public Service Loan Forgiveness Program, which is similar to IBR except that the remaining debt balance is wiped out after ten years for anyone employed full time in a "public service" position.[50] This is an excellent deal, which retires the loan in the same time it would take to pay it off under the standard plan. Public-service jobs are broadly defined to include all government positions (municipal, state, federal), as well as legal aid positions and positions at nonprofit organizations. Competition for these positions is keen—it is the final hope of a reasonable escape from debt for the multitude of heavily indebted graduates who do not secure corporate law jobs.

LAW SCHOOLS THAT PRODUCE DUBIOUS ECONOMIC RESULTS

A sizable segment of law schools—low-ranked schools with a high percentage of graduates bearing high debt—produce highly questionable results year in and year out. A significant percent of their graduates do not obtain lawyer jobs, and those that do tend to land low-paid jobs that do not produce an income commensurate to the level of debt.

Thomas Jefferson School of Law serves as a useful illustration.[51] The average debt of the class of 2010 was $137,352 (95 percent graduated with debt). Only seventy-three of the 211 graduates landed jobs as lawyers within nine months after graduation. The highest salaries were obtained by graduates who landed jobs as attorneys in private law firms (fifty-five students out of a class of 221). Their earnings breakdown by quartile is $47,500 (twenty-fifth percentile); $65,000 (median); $77,500 (seventy-fifth percentile). (Only twelve graduates working as attorneys reported their salaries so the numbers for the entire group are almost certainly lower.)

Assume a 2010 Thomas Jefferson graduate with average debt—again let's call her Sarah (unmarried with no dependants). Sarah was one of the lucky 25 percent of the class who landed jobs as attorneys in private firms, and she was doubly blessed, compared to her classmates, to have landed one of the best-paying jobs, earning $77,500. Unfortunately, on her $137,000 debt, the standard monthly loan payment is $1,600 (her IBR monthly payment would be $765). The standard loan payment would constitute nearly 25 percent of her gross pay, beyond the recommended strict upper limit of 20 percent.

Assume, conservatively, that Sarah pays 30 percent in taxes (federal, state, city, social security, Medicare), leaving her with a net monthly paycheck of$4,500. After paying her $1,200 rent (in San Diego) and $1,600 loan payment, Sarah would be left with $1,700 in disposable income to cover food, clothing, transportation, insurance, cell phone and cable bills, and a host of other expenses. With financial discipline, Sarah will be okay.

However, the startling point is that, judging from the numbers supplied, Sarah was more successful in employment terms than 90 percent of her classmates at Thomas Jefferson. Excluding the 5 percent of the class who did not have debt, there is a real possibility (on the assumption that most graduates had debt around the average) that the bulk of the Thomas Jefferson class of 2010 qualifies for IBR. That is so because a graduate with the average debt would have to earn at least $145,000 in order not to qualify. Using the same calculations applied to Sarah, a Thomas Jefferson graduate with average debt who earned a salary of $65,000 (the listed median for private practice) would be left with $1000 to spend each month after rent and loan payments are subtracted. This person would likely enroll in IBR.

It bears repeating, to put this discussion in the proper perspective, that only a third of the class obtained jobs as lawyers, and the salary figures are unrepresentative anyway because most graduates did not report salaries. The numbers I use for these calculations are likely inflated and do not cover the entire class. What the real jobs-and-earnings picture is for the class as a whole cannot be gleaned from the information provided, but the fate of many graduates is worse than the scenarios I set forth. The most telling information provided by Thomas Jefferson is that the bulk of their graduates in "private practice" are in firms with two to ten attorneys—which are the lowest-salaried law firm positions coming out of school (above only solo practice, which a number of graduates also entered).[52] According to Thomas Jefferson, the median salary for this group is $50,000. A graduate with average debt earning this salary would have $100 left over after making her rent and loan payments.

This is not just about dubious economic results for graduates. The debt of Thomas Jefferson graduates from the years 2008, 2009, 2010, and 2011 combined was over $100 million. (How many students with positive outcomes did this money buy?) The 2010 graduating class of Cooley law school alone had an aggregate debt of $91 million. Add up the law schools similarly situated, multiply this over coming years, and the magnitude of the problem comes into view. Nearly all of this debt is covered by the federal government, and a significant proportion of it will not be repaid.

Loan default rates of law graduates are relatively low so far (below 2 percent), but this is an illusion.[53] A debtor on IBR does not show as a default even if her monthly loan payment under the formula is zero. Debtors in IBR whose loan balances are actually growing in size will nonetheless remain in good standing. Thus IBR conceals the full extent of underperforming loans. Once a debtor falls behind on a large debt the compounding effect kicks in to make it hard to catch up even if her salary improves. A potentially huge sum of money due on law school debt ultimately will be written off by the government as either uncollectable or forgiven through the operation of IBR.[54] Law school graduates of the class of 2010 had a combined debt exceeding 3.6 billion dollars.[55] This is just *one* year—and average debt levels among law graduates are rising.

Predictably, legal educators have now incorporated IBR into their sales pitch. A law professor asserted in a national law magazine in 2011 that owing to the benefits of IBR law school debt is not that bad. "After 25 years, any remaining loan balance is forgiven. . . . Moreover, the loan forgiveness aspects of these plans are essentially back-end scholarships."[56] This is a cavalier way to speak about the fate of graduates who spend the bulk of their professional careers in a program designed to help people in financial hardship. What law schools portray as a "back-end scholarship" the graduates will experience as a life-crimping financial ball and chain. From the standpoint of the national fisc, it is worrisome when law schools try to induce naïve students to enter law school by telling them that they won't really have to pay back the scary loan amounts if things don't work out.

TEN

Why Tuition Has Gone Up So Quickly

The set of reasons listed below—most of which have been mentioned in earlier chapters—are those commonly cited as the main causes of the relentless upward march of law school tuition.

1. Law faculties have grown owing to reduced teaching loads to facilitate research and the expansion of clinical programs and legal writing staff. The former resulted from an increased emphasis on scholarly production and competition to attract scholars. *US News*, by heavily weighting academic reputation, fueled the competition for scholarly professors and encouraged the expansion of faculty by rewarding low student-faculty ratios with a better score. ABA accreditation precluded law schools from relying more heavily on cheaper adjuncts to make up for the reduced teaching loads by tenure-track professors. The expansion of clinical faculty was prompted by longstanding complaints from the bar that law schools produce graduates ill-prepared for the practice of law. Administrative staffs have expanded as well, to provide more services and handle greater numbers of faculty and students in the building.

2. Law professor pay has increased significantly in the past three decades, at the high end owing to competition over star professors, now with salaries exceeding $300,000, and at the low end pushed up by accreditation efforts to increase professor compensation.

3. The jump in starting pay at corporate law firms that occurred in the early 2000s, owing to the dot.com salary competition for lawyers—going from $70,000s to $130,000s in a few years—had two

consequences for rising tuition.[1] The high corporate law salary numbers helped draw more applicants to law school (increasing from 75,000 in 2000, to 100,000 in 2004) because they believed the sparkling financial return justified the constantly increasing price.[2] The greater demand for law degrees (more applicants) made it easier for law schools to raise tuition. Law professors, on their end, could argue that they were underpaid compared to new graduates and the quality of law professors would decline if pay lagged too far behind; this encouraged larger raises (no. 2 above), which was paid for through tuition increases.

4. A substantial sum is expended to support research, including reduced teaching loads and sabbaticals, summer research grants, funds for research assistants and book purchases, travel funds to attend conferences, funds to sponsor conferences, and the subsidy of multiple journals.

5. Merit scholarships to attract desirable students have increased enormously, fueled by the *US News* focus on LSAT/GPA profiles. Law schools now allocate about a billion dollars to scholarships, which have increased every year along with tuition. A significant portion of the annual tuition increase is cycled back to students as scholarships in what amounts to a redistribution from one segment of the student body to another.

6. Some universities treat law schools as "cash cows," siphoning away 15–30 percent of law school tuition revenue (in isolated instances more).[3] This varies by school and does not exist everywhere. Some of this money pays for expenses generated by the law school (security, power, building maintenance, administrative handling of pay), while some subsidizes other university programs and activities. Revenue hungry universities strongly encourage, and some will insist, on hikes in law school tuition.

7. Public law schools have raised tuition in recent years to make up for reduced funding from legislatures.

A handful of secondary factors are also assigned a share of the blame: (8) ABA-accreditation standards impose costs by requiring substantial library collections and fancy facilities for law schools. (9)Technology is expensive and information technology staffs have expanded. (10) Beyond the ways mentioned above, *US News*–ranking competition encourages more spending per student because that counts in the score.

There is something to each of these factors. But we must be careful not to misapprehend effect for cause—mistaking what law schools have spent their stream of tuition dollars on for the reasons tuition rose. An observation from two decades ago, when law schools had already made their leap into the current high-cost model, suggests that the relationship between expenditures and revenue runs the other way.

Law schools were enjoying good times in 1990, according to the annual report of the ABA Consultant on Legal Education. Over a hundred law schools had "new or substantially renovated" facilities. "The size of faculties increased." "Median faculty salaries more than doubled" since 1974. "Administrative staffing increased," taking over admissions and placement tasks previously performed by faculty. "Library staffs increased as did their salaries, and new technologies of word processing and computers were introduced." All of this was taking place, it bears noting, *before US News* began to exert its malign influence on law schools.

Why were law schools enjoying an all-around uplift? The report explains: "These and similar improvements were made possible in large measure by increases in [class] size, and increases in tuition that would have been unthinkable in earlier times."[4] The number of applicants to law school had surpassed 90,000 for the first time. Enrollment at law schools had increased for the fourth year in a row. Tuition had increased by 250 percent for public schools and 140 percent for private schools in a single decade. The things law schools spent their money on in 1990—more faculty, higher pay, more administrators, nicer buildings—did not *cause* tuition to rise. Law schools were able to do all these things *because* they were flush with money.

TUITION PRICING AT LAW SCHOOLS AND UNIVERSITIES

To understand why law school tuition has increased by so much one must recognize that tuition at undergraduate four-year institutions, private and public, has gone up rapidly as well. Figure 10.1 shows the respective average tuition increases of private four-year undergraduate institutions and

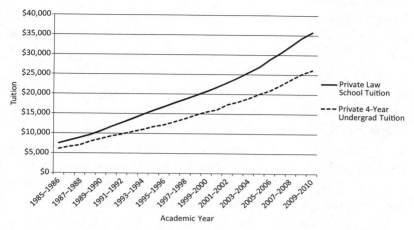

Fig. 10.1. Private school tuition: four-year undergrad vs. law school. Sources: "Law School Tuition, 1985-2009, http://www.americanbar.org/content/dam/aba/migrated/legaled/statistics/charts/ stats_5.authcheckdam.pdf; College Entrance Examination Board, *Trends in Student Aid*, 2010 (Washington, DC: College Board, 2010).

private law schools. Law school tuition started out higher and rose at a higher rate than private undergraduate institutions, which makes the current law school price tag even more painful, but both went up a lot.

Increases in university tuition, like law school tuition, far outpaced the rate of inflation. From 1985 to 2009, tuition increased by 327 percent at private undergraduate institutions and by 375 percent at private law schools. Tuition at public schools, undergraduate and law, has increased during this period by even higher percentages than at private schools because they started at much lower amounts (specific percentage comparisons cannot be provided owing to insufficient information about the proportion of resident and nonresident tuition payers). It is no wonder, given these increases, that total student debt (undergraduate and graduate combined) has increased overall by 511 percent since 1999, with many observers calling it the next debt bubble primed to burst.[5]

Universities and law schools, when responding to the chorus of complaints, insist that tuition has risen rapidly through no fault of their own. They blame the rapidly rising costs of educating students—citing various university or law school versions of the factors listed above.[6] Tuition pricing patterns, however, suggest that the explanation lies elsewhere.

For both universities and law schools, tuition at the most prestigious private institutions cluster together a level or two higher than tuition at the less prestigious schools. (Public schools are harder to compare owing to variations in levels of public support.) Elite private *universities* and colleges are priced in the high-thirty to low-forty thousand dollar range, while nonelite private schools are in the high-twenty to low-thirty thousand range. Elite private *law schools* cluster in the mid-forty to fifty thousand dollar range (as do elite public law schools), while nonelites are priced a level below, in the low-to mid-thirty thousand dollar range. (This pattern does not hold for nonelite law schools in major legal markets, which are priced in the elite range for reasons explained shortly.)

This pattern exists without regard to the size of the institution or its location, factors that should produce differences in the actual costs of running an institution. Tuition is almost identical at Amherst College ($40,862), a small elite liberal arts college in bucolic western Massachusetts, and the University of Pennsylvania ($40,514), a large, elite university in urban Philadelphia. "Why would it cost almost exactly the same to operate any two institutions as complex as a university?" asked Henry Riggs, the former president of Harvey Mudd College.[7] His answer: It doesn't. "Pricing is a marketing, not a cost accounting decision." "Tuition in the private higher-education industry is a classic example of price leadership—the 'top players' define the sticker price and all others follow suit."

Tuition varies in relation to prestige—not costs—because the perceived value of the education affects how much students (and their parents) are willing to pay for it. As long as a sufficient pool of purchasers of higher education continue to believe that degrees from elite institutions provide the best opportunities, elite schools can, and will, raise their prices. Nonelite schools raise tuition as well, keeping a price separation one level below, to pick up the remaining demand for higher education.

DEMAND AND PRICE

Now we have the answer: Law schools have raised their tuition to obscene levels because they can. Demand for law degrees seems, until recently, to be largely impervious to price. Apparent insensitivity to price hikes invited further tuition increases.

Elite law schools charge $10,000–$15,000 higher than nonelite schools do because demand for their credentials is greater. But even nonelite schools can charge hefty tuition because demand for law degrees is strong enough to support it. Nonelite schools in New York, Los Angeles, DC, Chicago, and San Francisco, owing to their proximity to a large number of well-paying legal employers, can charge a premium that puts them in the elite tuition range. Accreditation restrictions help protect the price level of third- and fourth-tier schools by keeping out lower-priced competitors. Any new law school aiming to become accredited can set its price in the low-thirty-thousand dollar range (as John Marshall in Atlanta has done) because that's the going rate for a low-ranked accredited school.

Economists will roll their eyes at the obviousness of the point: tuition has gone up as a function of demand. The list of factors law schools recite as causes of tuition increases are better understood, instead, as how law schools have spent the oodles of money they have been able to extract through tuition increases that willing students lined up to pay. Had tuition increases noticeably inhibited demand, it would not have increased as much. With less revenue to spread around, law schools would not have reduced teaching loads that much, hired that many more clinicians, bumped up pay as much, allocated so much to research, given as much to the university, and so on.

The workings of the connection between prestige, price, and demand can be seen in the differential pricing system that law schools and prospective students create. This is a full-fledged market in which law schools compete with one another for students with desirable LSAT/GPA medians while savvy prospective students try to get law schools to reduce the price (bidding up scholarship offers). The student must decide whether it is worth it to pay the higher price at a more prestigious institution or the scholarship-discounted price at a lower-ranked one. As mentioned earlier, students with LSAT scores in the bottom half at Columbia would be in the top quartile at Duke. Every student who chooses the lower-ranked school is saying that the enhanced value of a credential from the higher school is not worth the higher price. When a law school has trouble attracting sufficient numbers of full-tuition-paying students (the bottom half of the class at many law schools pay full fare), it has priced itself beyond what demand for its credential will bear. A law school in this position will be forced to offer tuition discounts much deeper into the class, thereby implementing an unannounced tuition reduction.

The ultimate explanation for why law school costs so much today is that two generations of law students have been *willing* and *able* to plunk down whatever law schools charged. There was no economic reason not to increase tuition so long as this continued. Because in a prestige market, price signals value—some schools have increased price precisely to signal higher value.[8] Schools that choose to moderate their tuition increases risk diminishing their perceived prestige if tuition falls below peer schools. Competition for ranking all but forced schools to increase tuition as long as others were going up: a school that charged less than what the market would bear would leave tuition dollars on the table that its competitors would seize and spend to their advantage (more scholarships for students, more funds to attract star professors). When asked to explain why his law school had raised tuition by 77 percent in the past seven years, Dean Philip Closius of Baltimore candidly admitted, "The only thing that justifies it is, so is everyone else in the law school world."[9] Cutting to the core, that is the tawdry truth of the matter.

THE RESPONSIBILITY OF THE ELITE LAW SCHOOLS

This is the place to call to account Yale, Harvard, Stanford, Columbia, Chicago, NYU, and so forth—the überelite law schools—for their responsibility in the rise of tuition nationwide. These super elites are the price leaders who set the market price, enabling all the other schools to rise beneath their wings. Had they exercised greater restraint, all other law schools would have remained lower as well.

As *the* acknowledged prestige leader, Yale played an inordinate role when it ramped up tuition by $24,000 in just over a decade. Imagine what would be the case if Yale had increased tuition by only $14,000 during this period (still exceeding inflation). Yale would be priced at $40,000 today. Tuition at the other top schools would also cluster around $40,000 (tuition at Columbia, e.g., would not be $50,000 if Yale cost $40,000). And tuition all the way down the law school hierarchy would be $10,000 cheaper than it is now. Having less revenue to spend, the Yale faculty would be smaller and full-professor pay would be arrayed below $300,000 rather than above, but otherwise not too much would be different. It would still be on top, with outstanding professors and students. Yale students would still receive terrific educations. Law faculties nationwide would be smaller and professors more modestly but still comfortably compensated (closer to our university brethren). Average student debt levels would be much lower.

I am not laying moral blame on Yale and the other überelite, but merely pointing out the broader consequences of their actions. This is a straightforward causal argument about how pricing operates in a prestige market.

Taken in isolation, what these schools have done can be justified. Yale and Harvard distribute financial aid on an exclusively need basis, which in effect makes the students from higher socioeconomic classes help defray the costs of those from lower (in contrast to the reverse–Robin Hood merit-scholarship arrangement at virtually all other law schools in which the bottom half of the class subsidizes the top). Law schools at the very top also have generous loan-forgiveness programs that provide genuine relief to their graduates in financial distress. The economic value conferred by a degree from a top law school handily exceeds current prices. They have exercised restraint in the sense that they could charge even more and still fill their class. And students at elite institutions are taught by the leading lights in law.

Pointing to these factors, professors at top-five institutions may insist that their high pay is well deserved and their students receive an excellent return. They have every right (and intention) to continue to raise tuition under these conditions, they may say, and cannot be blamed for economic harms that other law schools might inflict on their own benighted students.

This response is persuasive if the external ramifications of the actions of elite law schools are not something their professors need to consider. When tallying up the adverse implications of rising tuition and seeking ways to slow it, as this book aims to do, moral blameworthiness is beside the point—the causal connection to social harm is what matters.

The mantra of progressives is social justice. Key aspects of social justice are equal opportunity and access to law. Most law professors on elite faculties, including at Yale, are progressives. When raising tuition without restraint, elite law schools, *and all the rest of us following along,* collectively worked against social justice by erecting an enormous economic barrier to access to a legal career. Students from middle-class and poor families frightened by the specter of taking on insurmountable debt will increasingly forgo law school. Current law graduates are compelled by their debt to seek corporate law jobs that many do not otherwise desire. Our tuition-scholarship matrix helps the wealthy consolidate their grip on elite legal positions.

Law professors at elite law schools and across the country who see these as unfortunate developments can help by resisting tuition increases and reducing costs. That will entail some personal sacrifice and inconvenience. It is another hard choice for us to make within the structural conditions that propel legal academia forward.

ELEVEN

Is Law School Worth the Cost?

Tens of thousands of people apply to law school each year because it is an avenue to a desirable career. There is prestige attached to the status of a lawyer. Lawyers are smart professionals who wear suits. Most lawyers earn a comfortable living, and very successful ones become wealthy. Many lawyers play leading roles in advising or managing corporations. Many public figures are lawyers. One can do good things as a lawyer—support a cause, work in public service, prosecute criminals, become a politician, serve as a judge, become a high-level government official, advocate for the poor, defend the unjustly accused. Lawyers are pillars of the community. A broad cultural mythology about lawyers—simultaneously loathed, admired, envied, and feared—runs through American society, built up in history, fiction, and popular television and movies. There are also more base reasons as to why people end up in law: it is the fallback profession of choice for people who lack the aptitude to become a doctor, and it is seen as the safer career path for risk-averse folks who lack the derring-do of an entrepreneur or the hustle of a salesman. The belief that law school is a solid choice is bolstered by the general article of faith in American society that education is good—the more the better.

Two roughly distinguishable types come through the doors, at least according to conventional wisdom. For the bulk of students, law school was *the* destination all along. Something implanted this goal in the student early on: having a lawyer parent, doing well in high school debate, winning a mock trial contest, following a famous trial or popular law drama on television, or being raised by a parent who defines success as a professional career (doctor, lawyer, engineer, in that order).[1] Whatever it is, that student was on the path toward law school for some time, picking a college major with law school in mind (majoring in political science, history, sociology, prelaw, etc.), without a fallback plan. For the second group of students, law school was on the horizon of possibilities but they were never entirely committed to the notion of becoming a lawyer. As the end of college neared, or after a year or two in a less than satisfying job, the law school option loomed larger as a possibility, less for its own attractions than for dissatisfaction with other options.

Law schools see plenty of both types. As students, the two types are not obviously distinguishable. Both types can do well in law school—or not. After they leave, students who thought law was a calling might discover that being a lawyer is less than they expected, and students who fell into a legal career might find it rewarding. We have no information about their eventual careers or long-term satisfaction. These groups are separated only by degrees of shading. In the end, the main difference is that the first group was headed toward law school all along, while circumstances put the second group into the seats.

This distinction helps provide a partial explanation of the cyclical rise and fall of the number of applicants to law school. Law school has traditionally been thought of as a safe harbor in a poor economy. For recent college graduates who cannot find jobs, or people who have been laid off, spending three years in law school is perceived to be a good way to wait out a recession and retool to reenter the job market with a new set of opportunities. As I will show in chapter 13, the number of applicants to law school tends to rise when the overall rate of unemployment rises and fall when the job market improves. This correlation—which has remained strong until recently—suggests that the core demand for law school (the group that intended to go to law school along) is added to in bad economic times by people prompted into law school for lack of economic opportunities (the second group). Both groups expect to come out of law school with a decent standard of living.

FIGURING OUT THE ECONOMIC RETURN ON A LAW DEGREE

When deciding whether to make the leap into law school, prospective students assume that though the price of entry to the profession is high it will pay off in the long run through a career of higher earnings. This is also what legal educators assume, as articulated by George Washington Law School dean Paul Berman:

> A legal education prepares students for a lifetime, not just the first year out. And for most students, that means a career of 50 years or more. . . .
>
> Thus, if one is doing a cost-benefit analysis of legal education (which itself is only a crude measure that ignores the intrinsic value of education in personal, intellectual, spiritual, and emotional growth), that cost-benefit analysis needs to include career trajectories over a much larger time span. And while I recognize that recent grads feel particularly pinched in trying to make loan payments, I still believe that the relevant factor in thinking about whether getting a legal education is "worth it," requires a longer time horizon than we usually see in discussions of this kind. For example, even if a graduate's income increased only $25,000 per year as a result of having a law degree rather than not having it, the graduate would have recovered his or her investment in only about a decade. The non-economic benefits, while harder to quantify, only adds to the benefit side of the ratio, leading, I believe, to the clear conclusion that coming to law school—even one with a high tuition—is an investment that will pay life-long benefits.[2]

This encapsulates the basic reasoning of buyers and sellers of legal education—and there is evidence to support it.

A much-trumpeted study issued by the Census Bureau in 2002 confirmed that education produces a "big payoff," which increases with each level of attainment, the biggest boost of all going to professional degrees.[3] A 2011 follow-up study by Pew reinforced these findings. Graduates with professional degrees (lumping together medical degrees and law degrees), it estimated, average $1.2 million more in life earnings than workers with bachelor's degrees.[4] When estimating the value of a law degree, Pew subtracted lost earnings of $96,000 for three years in law school (the typical annual earnings of recent social science graduates is $32,000), and another $75,000 for the cost of law school. The report, unfortunately, was unable to provide a separate breakdown for lawyer's earnings, and the authors acknowledged that the $1.2 million figure is skewed upward by the higher salaries of doctors. Nonetheless, they concluded that it was reasonable to assume that the life earnings from a law degree "far exceeds" the cost (out of pocket and opportunity) of acquiring it.[5]

Another recent study, by the Georgetown Center on Education and the Workplace, came to the same conclusion (although with different numbers): "No matter how you cut it, more education pays. . . . The 33 percent of Bachelor's degree holders that continue on to graduate and professional schools have even more prosperous futures ahead."[6] This study estimates the average lifetime earnings of lawyers and judges at $4,032,000. That's far above elementary school teachers ($2,292,000), accountants ($2,422,000), and managers ($3,094,000) with bachelor's degrees; compared to other professional degree holders, lawyers earn the same as dentists ($4,032,000), but less than pharmacists ($4,420,000) and doctors ($6,172,000).[7]

Law school appears to pay off quite nicely. The reports, however, add several notes of caution to this optimistic picture. The Pew report acknowledged that tuition varies greatly, and the higher price of private colleges eats into gains.[8] This alters the picture significantly because the $75,000 estimate it used for the out-of-pocket cost of law school (tuition and living expenses) is too low for all private schools and dozens of public schools. Nonscholarship students at private law schools will pay double that, at least, and as much as $200,000 at a number of schools. A more accurate estimate of the cost of law school at these institutions (including lost wages) is closer to $300,000.

Furthermore, the reports note, the average lifetime earnings calculated are not representative of the prospects for everyone. Both studies projected lifetime earnings based on forty-year careers of full-time work. As they recognize, only about half of men work this long and a "small share" of women do; people work fewer years because of illness, temporary unemployment, early retirement, et cetera.[9] Projected earnings for professional women are 25 percent lower than for men owing to pay differentials and because women tend to be out of the workplace for longer periods (usually for child rearing).[10]

Dean Berman's back-of-the-envelope figuring of the worth of attending law school, we know from this, is too optimistic in projecting a fifty-year return.[11] Female law students in particular would be prudent to anticipate a much shorter career span. A study tracking the careers of lawyers found that "women are far more likely than men to be unemployed or to work part-time."[12]

Anyone thinking about the economic return on a law degree, furthermore, must consider the chance of being laid off, or of not landing a lawyer job at all, both of which are genuine possibilities. As indicated earlier, about a third of graduates in the past decade have not secured jobs as lawyers within nine months after graduation. The Bureau of Labor Statistics projects about 25,000 openings for lawyers each year through 2018 (new positions and replacements for departures), while in recent years law schools have annually produced about 45,000 new graduates.[13] Comparisons to the expected earnings of dentists and doctors cannot be taken straightforwardly. Nearly all the students who complete those educational programs can count on landing in that professional category with its attendant economic return whereas law students, owing to the oversupply of such graduates, cannot assume that they will become a lawyer to begin with. To put the point another way, when viewed *ex ante*, a medical degree translates into doctor earnings, whereas a law degree (based on past rates) secures a two-thirds chance of obtaining lawyer earnings—at top schools nearly 100 percent, and at bottom schools below 50 percent.

One caveat that both reports emphasize has particular significance when trying to estimate the return on a law degree: "There is wide variation in earnings within educational levels, which means that the highest earners of a lower educational level earn more than the typical worker at a higher level of education attainment."[14] A well-paid manager, for instance, earns more than a low-paid lawyer. Pew calculated that the mean annual wage of a worker with a bachelor's degree (over a lifetime) is $71,912.[15] The midcareer median salary of workers with a bachelor's in political science—a common major for law students—is $77,300.[16] These figures approximate the twenty-fifth percentile wage of all wage-earning and salaried lawyers, according to the Bureau of Labor Statistics.

Lawyers who end up in the bottom quartile of lawyer earnings, in hindsight, could have saved the money they spent on law school and earned the same amount with a bachelor's degree in business, engineering, social science, science, or computers. The holders of these degrees have average or above-average earnings for workers with bachelor's degrees (liberal arts degrees have earnings a bit below average, and education degrees have significantly lower earnings than other bachelor's degree).[17] Law students are a smart and motivated bunch so it is reasonable to assume that they would have gotten the average earnings of their fellow bachelor's degree holders.

Hindsight is too late, though. An analysis by a prospective student of whether attending law school is financially worthwhile (setting aside the noneconomic gains of being a lawyer) must be made *before* deciding to attend.[18] This *ex ante* analysis must discount the desired economic results by the chance a person has of obtaining those results when graduating from a particular law school. Much of this is shrouded in uncertainty.

ESTIMATING THE ODDS THAT A LAW DEGREE WILL PAY OFF

A prospective student can make a rough reckoning of the odds of landing in the bottom quartile of lawyer earnings by thinking about two factors: corporate law hiring patterns and the bimodal distribution of pay. As indicated earlier, outside the top twenty or so law schools only the top 10 percent of the class have a chance of landing NLJ 250 jobs. At lower-ranked schools only the top 5 percent have a chance. Most of the remaining graduates will either land in the lower mound of lawyer pay, with starting salaries between $40,000 and $65,000, or they will not get a lawyer job at all. The lowest-paid positions (excluding solo practice) are in firms of two to ten lawyers. The earnings of lawyers in this range will increase modestly—about ten years out, average earnings peak and remain flat thereafter—but many in these positions will end up in the bottom quartile of lawyer earnings.[19]

This projection is consistent with the findings of two studies that tracked the earnings of lawyers over time. An extensive study of lawyers in Chicago found that the initial job a graduate obtains has career-determining consequences: those who obtain corporate legal positions tend to remain in the higher-earning track that services institutional clients, while those who do not initially obtain these positions tend to have lower earnings, serving individual clients and occupying lower-paid government positions.[20] The bar breaks out into two distinct hemispheres, with little career movement between them. Lawyers in the corporate law-firm hemisphere had mostly graduated from prestigious law schools and were doing well financially; lawyers in the hemisphere of small firms and local government jobs graduated from lower-ranked local law schools and the median income of these lawyers had declined in real terms in the previous twenty years.[21] Although the study ended in the mid-1990s, the stark division it found within the profession remains.

An ongoing study sponsored by the ABA, *After the JD*, follows the careers of several thousand graduates of the class of 2000. The latest snapshot was taken in 2007, after seven years in practice, when lawyers are entering strong earning years. (This was completed just before the recession nailed the legal market.) The study found that graduates of top-ten law schools had average earnings of $162,000 (including bonuses), far above all other groups; graduates from law schools ranked eleventh to fiftieth averaged $107,000–$108,000; graduates from the fifty-first- to hundredth-ranked schools, as well as from third-tier schools (roughly the next fifty), averaged $92,000; and fourth-tier graduates averaged $83,000.[22] (These figures, keep in mind, are based on people who responded to the survey and thus do not represent the overall picture of law graduates.)

At top-ten schools it doesn't matter how low a student graduates in the class—all have earnings above $120,000. Outside the top-ten law schools, however, grades are significant, with top-ranked students earning the most and bottom students earning much less, in the $60,000–$70,000 range.

After the JD findings reinforce common knowledge: graduates from top schools are placing well and "graduates of less prestigious schools who performed very well in law school were also employed in some of the most lucrative settings."[23] "Lawyers graduating from law schools in the middle and lower tiers of the law school status hierarchy were more likely to work in smaller firms, in state and local government, and in the business sector, where salaries tend to be somewhat lower."[24] The fiftieth percentile earnings of state and local government lawyers seven years out ranged between $60,000 and $70,000; for solo lawyers the fiftieth percentile was $80,000, and for firms of two to twenty lawyers, it was $90,000.

These are decent sounding sums—until one considers debt. For anyone with $100,000 debt, all of the average earnings listed above for lawyers seven years after graduation, top-ten schools aside, would qualify for IBR.[25] This tells us that at current average debt levels lawyers will have trouble managing their loan payments well into their careers. Owing to the public-service income-based repayment program, only government and public-service lawyers need not worry (as long as they reach the ten years of service necessary to qualify for debt forgiveness).

Debt also worsens the already tough road for brave (or desperate) law graduates who hang out a shingle—typically the lowest earners of all. Finding paying clients who will entrust their case to a fresh-faced rookie is hard enough. The more immediate hurdle is setting up a work space. Sharing an office reduces cost, but there is still some rent to pay. This is on top of normal living expenses. For graduates in this position, sending in the monthly loan check will be practically impossible. Those who enter IBR will be required to pay nothing, or very little, until their business gets off the ground, which may take years.

When legal educators insist that it is a mistake to focus too much on starting salaries out of law school, insisting that the degree pays off over a long career, they fail to appreciate the concrete impact of debt. Starting salary matters mightily because it is crucial to make loan payments right out of the box. Once in IBR, it is not easy to exit because large debt quickly becomes massive when not paid down on the ten-year schedule. If the initial job a law graduate obtains is insufficient to cover the monthly loan payments, the debt will be a career-long financial yoke, adversely affecting every aspect of their lives, from buying a house, to raising children, to saving for retirement. Not paying down the loan on schedule also increases the cost of law school by adding to the amount paid back in the end, reducing the economic return of the degree.

The *After the JD* study confirmed another well-known phenomenon. There is a high level of lawyer mobility, with more than 60 percent of lawyers switching jobs at least once within the first seven years.[26] After a few years a significant number of graduates depart the best-paying jobs. "Megafirms," the study found, "are a temporary holding place for many new graduates, and as they build their careers they scatter into a range of settings both within and outside of the private sector."[27] Lawyers who leave corporate law firms often take pay cuts. When calculating long-term economic return, it is false to assume that pay for lawyers continues to rise over time.

For any prospective law student trying to figure out the likely economic return on a degree, especially a student who borrows $100,000 or more to finance their legal education, it comes to this: What is one's chance of landing a NLJ 250 job? This is a crass and reductionist observation that ignores the noneconomic benefits of obtaining a legal education. It also ignores the multitude of other rewarding settings in which one could be a lawyer or use the law degree in worthwhile ways. Liberal law professors, especially, will be rankled at the suggestion that the key consideration for a prospective law student is to aim at getting a corporate law job.

This is what high tuition has wrought, however. In an age of $100,000-plus debt, people ignore the bottom-line financial reality at their peril. Only prospective students unalterably committed to public-service work after law school can eschew the NLJ 250 route because, if they are fortunate enough to land one of these jobs, their unpaid debt will forgiven after ten years. Competition for public-service law jobs is approaching that of NLJ 250 jobs. Aside from the innate attractions of the work, it is the best way to get out from under a mountain of debt for anyone who does not land a corporate law job.

IMPEDIMENTS TO SOUND CHOICES BY PROSPECTIVE STUDENTS

Prospective law students are impeded in three ways from making sound decisions about whether, and where, to attend law school. The first impediment is that the information required to think about the long-term return on a law degree is not readily available and a lot of uncertainties shroud the issue. There are a variety of ways to figure out economic return, none simple or incontestable. Legal educators have limited knowledge about this, and prospective students have even less.

The second impediment is a well-recognized bane of rational decision making: the influence of optimism bias.[28] Students may know that only one out of ten (or one out of twenty) students at their school land the top-paying jobs but some of them will think that their personal chance is better than 10 percent. Law students are high achievers, accustomed to doing well with effort. They assume that this reliable path to past success will pay off again without fully realizing—until they sit in the class and look around—that everyone else in the room is just as smart and hard working. Only after arrival do the long odds of success sink in—and then it is too late.

The third impediment is that most law schools post misleading and incomplete information about the employment outcomes of their graduates. Even people whose judgment is clouded by optimism bias would turn away if they knew the true magnitude of the economic risk they take at certain law schools. There is a difference between foolishly optimistic and completely irrational, and few law students are the latter.

TWELVE

Warning Signs for Students

The inflated employment and salary rates posted by law schools helped artificially prop up demand. In the 2011 *US News* ranking, five law schools listed 100 percent employment rates. All but two of the top one hundred schools listed employment above 90 percent (the two laggards were at 89.2 percent and 89.6 percent). A majority of third- and fourth-tier schools also listed employment in the 90 percent range. Many law schools listed sparkling salary figures, often surpassing the magical $100,000 mark. Employment data posted by schools in the 2012 rankings have come down, but a substantial majority of law schools still list employment rates in the 80 and 90 percent range. Law schools put the same attractive salary numbers on their websites.

It is an elaborately constructed mirage. Most law schools were not lying. They did not need to. A false image could be created through the subtle construction of categories and partial information to paint an alluringly rosy picture. When seeing "Private Law Firm Median Salary (full time): $140,000," for example, few readers would realize that only 25 percent of the class landed those positions and only half of the people in these jobs reported their salaries. Unusual skill and skepticism on the part of a prospective student would be required to see through these numbers. Legal educators insist that law school is well worth the cost, while withholding the very information a prospective student would need to make a sound evaluation.

UNRELIABLE SALARY NUMBERS

South Texas College of Law, in the 2012 *US News* ranking, lists its earnings quartiles for full-time private-sector jobs as follows: $75,000 (twenty-fifth percentile), $92,500 (median), $160,000 (seventy-fifth percentile). That looks great. However, only 5 percent of the people employed in the private sector provided salary information. What this means is that those numbers reflect perhaps a dozen graduates out of a class of 376. A savvy prospective student would be able to discern that these salary numbers are extremely unrepresentative, but only if she paid a subscription fee to *US News* to gain access to the full data (the reporting percentage is not indicated in the magazine). Unsuspecting readers would be fooled into thinking that good money was to be had coming out of this school.

South Texas is the most egregious example, but misleading number reporting is rampant, especially among (but not limited to) lower-ranked schools. Law schools post salaries taken from graduates who report their salaries; if a significant percentage of graduates do not tell the law school how much they earn, the advertised numbers will present a distorted picture of the salaries for the class as a whole. That is because most graduates in high-paying jobs (happily) report their salaries while those in low-paying jobs tend to not report their salaries When a school's reporting rate is 5 percent, as it was for South Texas, that means the salaries of 95 percent of employed graduates have not been factored into the figures displayed by the school—adding those missing salaries would produce entirely different (undoubtedly lower) numbers. The lower the reporting rate, the less reliable and more inflated are the salary figures posted by schools. Below is a partial list of law schools that advertise salaries in the latest *US News* ranking based on very low reporting rates, shown here as a percentage of the group with private full-time jobs.

South Texas, 5 percent
Florida A&M, 9 percent
St. Mary's, 9 percent
Mississippi College, 10 percent
Ohio Northern, 13 percent
Roger Williams, 13 percent

Florida International, 14 percent

Tulsa, 14 percent

Thomas Jefferson, 17 percent

Gonzaga, 19 percent

Atlanta's John Marshall, 20 percent

Touro, 21 percent

Detroit Mercy, 24 percent

California Western, 25 percent

Seattle, 25 percent

Stetson, 25 percent

Florida Coastal, 28 percent

New York Law School, 28 percent

Southern Illinois, 28 percent

Cleveland-Marshall, 29 percent

Hamline, 29 percent

Loyola Chicago, 29 percent

Southwestern, 30 percent

Widener, 30 percent

Drake, 32 percent

Baltimore, 32 percent

Miami, 32 percent

John Marshall, 33 percent

Pace, 33 percent

Capital, 34 percent

Hofstra, 34 percent

Missouri, 34 percent

This list goes on. Nearly seventy law schools post salary figures taken from half or fewer of the people with private full-time jobs.

Law schools complain that it is unfair to blame them for low salary reporting rates: it is not their fault that students do not provide this information. But that is not the primary explanation for what is going on. Grounds for skepticism lie in the results shown in figure 12.1, which plots response rate against law school rank. A strong downward drift is evident, with the top schools having uniformly high response rates and the lower-ranked schools having lower rates (with exceptions to be mentioned). Why

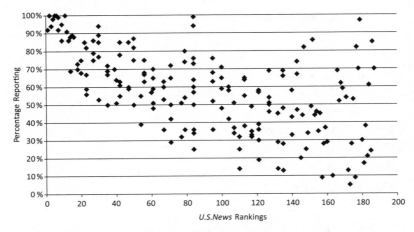

Fig. 12.1. Percentage reporting full-time private-sector salary (2009). Source: "Class of 2009 *U.S. News* Employment Summary Data," Law School Transparency, http://www.lawschooltransparency .com/2011/04/class-of-2009-u-s-news-data/.

would this pattern exist? It makes sense that employment rates (see fig. 9.2) would show a downward drift because fewer graduates from lower-down schools are getting jobs as lawyers. But figure 12.1 relates exclusively to graduates who *have* jobs. In response to the law school's survey (calls, e-mails, letters), the graduates say "Yes, employed in a private firm," but then fail to answer the "How much do you earn?" question. The further one goes down the ranking, the greater the proportion of graduates who do not disclose their salary. Why?

There are two obvious explanations. Greater numbers of students at lower schools are too embarrassed or resentful to state their earnings. That is a part of it. Another part is that law schools with low reporting rates are not trying very hard to get this information. Salary breakdowns by type of private legal employer are well established, with small firms paying the lowest (except for high-end boutiques) and large firms paying the most.[1] Once law school career services personnel find out the law firm's identity or size, they can make a reliable guess of the graduate's salary. A law school's posted salary numbers would be higher (and the response rate lower) if the school did not make follow-up salary inquiries to graduates in small firms or working on their own as solo practitioners.

Lower-ranked schools tend to have lower response rates because the numbers are poor (hence the reluctance of graduates to provide it) and obtaining the information would harm the school's salary profile (hence the reluctance of schools to get it). That explains the downward slope.

Evidence for allocating a portion of the blame for low response rates on law schools comes from the outliers. A number of lower-ranked schools have relatively high response rates: Texas Southern (97 percent); Charlotte (86 percent); and La Verne (85 percent). The performance of these schools shows that even relatively low salaries will be reported in large numbers if an effort is made. There is another way to see this. Compare the disparate performance among several schools ranked eighty-fourth (in a tie) by *US News*: Louisiana State (99 percent) and Arkansas (94 percent) have high response rates, while Seattle (25 percent), Hofstra (34 percent), and Santa Clara (50 percent) have low response rates. The only explanation—aside from incompetence by the latter law schools—for such a great disparity is a less than diligent effort on the part of the school to obtain the salary numbers of all graduates.

This matters, again, because it produces a distorted picture for prospective students who are trying to get a sense, before they make a huge investment of time and money, of what they are likely to earn on the back end. Santa Clara lists stunningly high earnings for its graduates in full-time private jobs: $110,000 (twenty-fifth percentile); $160,000 (median); $160,000 (seventy-fifth percentile). These numbers are high not because the class did so well but because the response rate was so low. Indeed it appears that the 2009 class at Santa Clara did poorly when one also considers that (notwithstanding the listed 85 percent employment rate) only 42 percent of the graduates got jobs as lawyers, and 45 percent of *these* jobs were part time. An educated guess is that the above numbers reflect the salaries of at most fifty graduates out of a class of 259.

The problem is not just that prospective students are unlikely to grasp all of this but that the actual employment results and earnings for the entire class cannot be reconstructed from the information provided. Law schools with low response rates are hiding the ball under the guise of providing a lot of detailed information. A bunch of law schools are doing this. Seattle and Hofstra have alluringly high salary numbers based on low response rates. Loyola Chicago looks really good at $108,376 (twenty-fifth percentile), $112 ,000 (fiftieth percentile), $152,981 (seventy-fifth percentile), although only 29 percent of the graduates in private full-time jobs provided salary information. Numbers like these are bait for the unwary.

New York Law School is a useful example because its dean disclosed in an interview the real numbers behind the veil, allowing us see the size of the disparity. They post dazzling employment numbers in their *US News* profile: $60,000 (twenty-fifth percentile), $160,000 (median), $160,000 (seventy-fifth percentile). Those unbelievably good salaries for graduates from a low-ranked school are explained by the low 28 percent response rate. When asked about these numbers, Dean Richard Matasar defended them as accurate but he admitted that they are incomplete. More detailed data are provided on the law school website. "In these materials and in our conversations with students and applicants," Matasar asserted, "we explicitly tell them that most graduates find work in small to medium firms at salaries between $35,000 and $75,000."[2] These painfully low salary numbers that Matasar says "most" graduates earn are drastically different from the giddily high numbers advertised.

Although Matasar grants that three or four years ago students might have been deceived by the $160,000 figure (a significant admission in itself), that is no longer the case, he insists. "Students are not stupid and they're not naïve."[3]

He is right that most prospective students today, after the drumbeat of bad news about law schools, are probably aware that they cannot trust the advertised salary numbers—a sad statement about the diminished credibility of law schools—but that is not an answer to the crucial problem. A person thinking about attending NYLS might realize that the numbers are inflated without realizing by how much and without knowing what the true figures are. The information provided on the NYLS employment statistics page on its website nowhere clearly states the range identified by Matasar. Nor does NYLS directly inform its students that only 62 percent of the class of 2009 (nine months after graduation) had obtained jobs as lawyers, and 27 percent of these lawyer jobs were part time. Despite the dismal job situation for its graduates, NYLS reaped a big increase in enrollment in the 2009 entering class, jumping up to 736 entering students from 565 the year before. How many of these people would have paid nearly $150,000 in tuition for three years (plus another $50,000 living expenses) if they were explicitly provided with full and accurate job data? It is too late, of course, to communicate this information to the incoming crop of students *after* they arrive.

While the focus here is mostly on lower-ranked law schools, problems exist at higher-ranked law schools as well, and students going to these schools must make the same hard decision about return on investment. The absolute best salary numbers a school can report are $160,000 at all three earning quartiles of the graduating class (twenty-fifth percentile; median; seventy-fifth percentile). That is especially enticing because it represents that students throughout the class (at least to the twenty-fifth percentile point) are landing top-paying jobs, which lessens the urgency of scoring top grades.

There are thirteen members of the exclusive Triple $160,000 Club. But not all are equal members. Harvard, NYU, and Chicago have 100 percent response rates. Pennsylvania (99 percent) and Columbia (98 percent) are also impressively high. The response rates hold up for Berkeley (95 percent) and Stanford (94 percent), tailing off a bit with Yale (92 percent) and Northwestern (91 percent), and then stretching downward for Virginia (86 percent) and Cornell (86 percent).

Two schools have response rates much lower than others in the group: George Washington (75 percent) and Georgetown (69 percent). If we assume that many of the nonresponding graduates of these latter two schools did not earn $160,000, which is likely, then both fall out of the coveted group, and they would look more like a bunch of schools with a lower 25 percentile salary but higher response rates (Duke, Michigan, Texas, UCLA, Fordham). For that matter, Cornell and Virginia, and even Northwestern and Yale, could fall out as well if a significant number of the nonresponsive graduates earned below $160,000, and if the schools barely hit that number for the twenty-fifth percentile with the responses that it had. Prospective students have no way of knowing how much to discount the advertised numbers of any of these schools.

Finally, we cannot disregard the possibility that all of these numbers all across the board, which are based on self-reporting by the law schools, are puff. In March 2011, Forbes asked Payscale—which has a large body of information from people who want to compare earnings with others similarly situated—to examine its database for the median salaries of recent law graduates from ninety-eight law schools.[4] It had salary information on 8,500 law graduates in the private sector within five years of graduation, 90 percent of whom were working as lawyers. No law school had graduates in private jobs earning a median salary of $160,000. Columbia graduates topped the list with a median salary of $157,000, and Virginia was second at $137,000. Median salaries quickly fell away—Yale was twelfth at $105,000; George Washington was twenty-second at $83,000. Graduates showed median salaries that were $30,000, $50,000, $70,000, and more, below the medians advertised by their law schools. Sixteen law schools—including many with median salaries listed between $130,000 and $160,000—had graduates whose earnings came in around half of what the school claimed. The biggest gap was for Seton Hall, with an advertised median of $145,000 but a Payscale median of $64,500.

Strictly speaking, these medians are not directly comparable because the advertised medians are from 2009, whereas the Payscale data search looked at employed law graduates from 2006 to early 2011 (both cover full-time jobs in private employment). That said, law schools have tended to list the same numbers consistently across this five-year period.

What could explain such a huge disparity for so many schools? One possible contributing factor is that the lawyer layoffs in the past few years swept away a number of high-earning graduates who were previously counted as employed by law schools. Another factor is that many graduates voluntarily leave corporate law firms within six years, moving to lower paying (less hours-driven) positions. These two explanations, though likely a part of it, would not appear to be sufficient to explain such an earnings chasm across so many schools. Another possible explanation is that the Payscale database has a downward bias that massively under-represents true medians. What would produce this is unclear, but that might be some of what's at work here. People who register on Payscale are seeking comparable employment information and as group might be more displeased about compensation than people who do not use the site.

The most obvious possible explanation is that law schools—including top schools—have been inflating the salaries of their graduates. Thirteen law schools had Payscale medians that were close to their advertised medians—a few thousand dollars below or above. If the database was systematically underreporting medians, for some reason these schools were not affected. They are from all over: University of San Francisco, DePaul, Northeastern, Utah, Penn State, New Mexico, Kansas, Oklahoma, Marquette, Oregon, Louisville, LSU, and Buffalo. The one characteristic this group has in common (aside from a heavy representation of public schools) is that their advertised medians were not extravagant, between $50,000 and $75,000.

Looking at schools with the largest disparities, two patterns emerge. The top fifteen schools all report a $160,000 median, and further-down schools in large legal markets report $160,000 medians as well (Santa Clara, Hastings, Brooklyn, Fordham, New York Law School, Boston University, Boston College, George Washington, and Catholic). These patterns suggest that reported medians are determined, in the first instance, less by the actual salaries of the midpoint of the graduating class in private firm jobs than by what immediate competitors claim. If a school's peers are claiming a $160,000 median, then that school finds a way to report the same. Outright fabrication might not be necessary to achieve this—aggressive massaging will do.

Law schools stand behind their employment numbers but they have given skeptics ample reason to scoff. A popular law blog, *Above the Law*, ridiculed UCLA law school for job data on its website, "claiming that 97.9% of its class of 2010 was employed within 9 months of graduation, at a median starting salary of $145K. . . . we've gotten so used to *educators* misleading us that the concept of one of them telling truth seems like we're asking too much."[5] George Mason claims on its website that 99 percent of the class of 2010 was employed nine months after graduation with a median starting salary in private practice of $130,000.[6] This is not credible in light of the horrendous job market. George Mason supplies no information on how many graduates are employed in lawyer jobs and how many are full-time jobs. A footnote at the bottom of the page says that "52% of employed graduates provided reportable salary information." Without information on what percentage of people in private practice reported their salaries there is no way to gauge the reported median, but it undoubtedly represents a small proportion of the class. Many law schools continue to report incomplete and misleading numbers at this writing

(December 2011)—an act of defiance in the face of the sharp public criticism of these practices.[7]

This is all the more disturbing because law students are lectured by their professors about professional ethics while law schools fail to live up to the spirit of the same standards. Rule 7.1 of the ABA *Model Rules of Professional Conduct* specifies that "a lawyer shall not make a false or misleading communication about the lawyer or the lawyer's services."[8] Law schools insist that they are telling the truth, but that is not enough. "Truthful statements that are misleading are also prohibited by this Rule. A truthful statement is misleading if it omits a fact necessary to make the lawyer's communication considered as a whole not materially misleading."[9] The information put out by many law schools fails this standard. The final defense left to law schools is that these rules do not apply to the "services" supplied by legal educators. That argument, while likely to prevail in disciplinary proceedings against us, amounts to a surrender of our professional standing.

DEBT AND JOB PROSPECTS OF LAW SCHOOLS

The most problematic combination is a law school with high average indebtedness among graduates, a low percentage of lawyer jobs, and a low salary on graduation. Since advertised salary numbers are unreliable and not comparable owing to low and varying reporting rates, I will focus on law schools that combine the highest average debt among graduates with the lowest percentage of graduates landing lawyer jobs. A low rate of lawyer jobs is a sign of the market weakness of the degree, and graduates who do not land lawyer jobs generally get lower pay than those who do.

I have matched three lists from the graduating class of 2009: the seventy law schools with highest average indebtedness among graduates (ranging from $100,000 to $132,000); the seventy law schools with the lowest percentage of the class landing "JD required" jobs (ranging from 26 percent to 62 percent); and the seventy law schools with the lowest percentage levels of reporting private full-time salaries (ranging from 5 percent to 50 percent). This is an arbitrary cutoff, which considers about one-third of law schools in each category. (The data are from the class of 2009 because numbers in all categories are still unavailable for 2010.) Although there is some consistency in these groupings over time, different years and different cutoffs would produce different lists and a different order—there are a few schools not on the list that are hardly distinguishable from those that made the cut.

These are the schools that landed in the first two categories (twenty-seven in all), set forth in order of the highest average debt, with an asterisk next to law schools that were also in the third category (fifteen of the twenty-seven) to flag especially unrepresentative advertised salary numbers: Thomas Jefferson,* New York Law School,* American University, John Marshall (Chicago),* Vermont,* Roger Williams,* Golden Gate,* Stetson,* New Hampshire, Charleston School of Law,* Atlanta's John Marshall,* Catholic, San Francisco,* Nova Southeastern, Florida Coastal,* Regent, Suffolk, Chapman,* Pennsylvania State, Valparaiso,* Barry, New England, DePaul, Denver, Santa Clara,* Oklahoma City, Widener.*

What places a school on the list is a combination, for the class of 2009, of high debt and difficult job prospects. Notice that this is not limited to low-ranked schools, as several on the list are in the top one hundred (American is usually around fifty). People who attend these schools are not fated to suffer poor results; from every one of these schools, graduates will emerge who go on to successful careers. Rather, the message here is that students who attend these law schools, at their current pricing levels, face tough odds of landing a legal job that pays a salary adequate to manage the average debt incurred at that law school.

A CALCULATION THAT PROSPECTIVE STUDENTS SHOULD MAKE

The best way for a prospective student to work this through in connection with a particular school is to make a few basic assumptions. To illustrate, I will provide a comparison of a 2010 graduate from New York University Law School (elite) and from New York Law School (nonelite), again both named Sarah. The income of NYU Sarah is $160,000, taken from the school's advertised median, which is reliable given its high reporting rate. The income of NYLS Sarah is $75,000, taken from Dean Matasar's statement that most graduates at firms earn starting salaries between $35,000 and $75,000 (its advertised numbers are too unrepresentative to rely on).

The average debt of graduates from both law schools was around $120,000, so that will be the debt of our Sarahs.

An online paycheck calculator provides net pay numbers by subtracting city, state, and federal taxes and social security and Medicare.[10] Using this, NYU Sarah's take-home income will be $102,300, while NYLS Sara's after-tax income will be $52,100. Their monthly loan payments under the standard ten-year repayment plan will be $1,400, totaling $16,800 in loan payments per year. Subtracting loan payments from take-home pay leaves NYU Sarah with $85,500 and NYLS Sarah with $35,300.

Rent is the next largest expense. New York City is famously pricey, with the average monthly rent for a studio in Manhattan at $2,400.[11] But let's say they each wanted to live more frugally, so instead they rented comfortable one-bedroom apartments in Brooklyn or Queens for $2,000 (a one-bedroom would be $3,000 in Manhattan), with a yearly rent of $24,000.[12] Subtracting rent leaves NYU Sarah with discretionary income of $61,500 and NYLS Sarah with $11,300.

Dividing these numbers by twelve gives a monthly discretionary income for NYU Sarah of $5,100—she will be doing fine financially. Her NYU law degree should pay off nicely for Sarah, assuming she stays in her corporate law job long enough to pay down her debt to a more manageable size.

NYLS Sarah's monthly discretionary income is $950. That might sound like a sufficient sum for "discretionary" spending, but one must factor in basic expenses: food, transportation, clothing, dry cleaning, utilities, telephone bill, cable bill, and so forth. After paying that out, NYLS Sarah will have little left over and no margin for unexpected expenses or setbacks.

She won't complain too much, however, because she knows many of her classmates did not get legal jobs, and many that did had lower salaries. An NYLS graduate who earns a salary of $50,000 would have $36,500 after taxes. The standard loan payment (on the average debt) and monthly rent come to $40,800, exceeding that graduate's income. If he were to find an apartment for $1,500 in a low-rent neighborhood (safety concerns aside), after rent and loan payments he would have $142 per month left over to spend on everything else. He would have no choice but to enter IBR.

To make a calculation like this, a prospective student needs a loan payment calculator, a net income calculator, and average rent information for whatever city one plans to reside in. These tools and information are available online. They must also have a solid estimate of the debt they will carry on graduation. With all that in hand, anyone who attempts to make this calculation, however, will still be stymied by schools that provide sketchy or misleading employment information—as many now do.

It is possible to determine a salary figure if one focuses on the firm size graduates land in. At lower-ranked schools, a significant proportion of graduates who obtain jobs as lawyers work in firms of two to ten lawyers. In New York, the median salary of a firm this size is $50,000; the median for firms with up to fifty lawyers is $62,000.[13] Setting aside the 35 percent chance of not landing a lawyer job at all, these would be realistic anticipated salary numbers for a prospective student thinking about a school like New York Law School. We know from the above calculation that this would not work for someone with $120,000 in debt, but a person with $40,000 debt will be okay.

WHAT PROSPECTIVE STUDENTS SHOULD CONSIDER

Law school is not a secure path to financial security—that much is obvious. Yet we need lawyers and a legal career can be rewarding financially and satisfying personally. Taking the leap into law school can pay off, keeping a few key issues in mind.

It is especially risky to attend a law school at which a significant percentage of graduates do not land full-time jobs as lawyers. This is the "JD Required" category. If only one out of two (or fewer) graduates get jobs as lawyers from a given school, that is a warning to stay away from that school. If 30 percent of the class does not obtain lawyer positions, graduates from there will struggle to find work. A low placement rate in full-time lawyer jobs suggests not just that jobs are hard to come by out of that school but also that starting salary, if one does land a lawyer job, will likely fall in the $40,000–$65,000 range at best.

Holding the level of debt down is crucial. A debt of $50,000 is fairly manageable regardless what happens coming out of law school. Debt at this level, while formidable, will neither dictate career choices nor substantially affect other aspects of life. A debt of $100,000, in contrast, imposes severe financial pressure to land a corporate law job. Outside the top-ten law schools, the odds of achieving this are less than even, and they quickly diminish the further one goes down the hierarchy. Outside the top one hundred or so law schools the chance of landing a corporate law job is virtually nil. Short of a corporate law job, a person with this level of debt must obtain a salary above the national average, which most law graduates fail to achieve. A $150,000 debt is unwise for anyone not at a top-five school. Many law graduates whose debt exceeds these benchmarks will nonetheless be okay financially (especially if they have a spouse who works), but many more will struggle—and there is no way beforehand to tell which group a person will fall into.

Attending a flagship state school that is priced below $20,000 is a sound choice if one wants to practice in that state. These schools usually have placement strength in the local legal market, and the relatively cheaper price will help keep debt down.

Another way to keep debt down is through scholarships. Law schools compete for students through discounting, which will increase as the number of applicants declines. Students can get a sense of their discount price (based on their LSAT/GPA profile) at a given school on the Law School Numbers website.[14] Schools that are having difficulty filling a class may offer scholarships to everyone who asks—and it might make sense for prospective students to not commit too early because schools struggling to meet their enrollment or LSAT/GPA targets may be more willing to increase their scholarship offers later in the season. Close attention should be paid to the requirements for retaining the scholarship. If a significant number of students annually forfeit their scholarships at the end of the first year for failing to meet the specified GPA, prospective students are on notice that there is a real risk of losing the discount, pushing up cost (and debt).

Law school ranking has significance if a prospective student is aiming for a corporate law job in one of the major legal markets. If that is the objective, then attending a top-ranked school is essential. Outside of top schools and corporate law jobs, the ranking has diminishing significance. One should not automatically assume that it is worth paying a great deal more to attend, for example, a school ranked fiftieth over a school ranked eightieth; the ranking difference does not necessarily translate into significantly better employment prospects. What matters most are where a prospective student hopes to work and whether a given law school places well in that locale.

For some students, it may be prudent to leave after the first year—or perhaps even after the first semester. Dropping out carries the stigma of failure; it is hard to walk away after expending thousands of dollars and putting in eight months of hard work. However, the dual prospect of high debt and diminished job possibilities means such an option should not be ruled out. Any student who enters law school banking on landing a corporate law job will know by the end of the first year whether that is possible. If a student forfeits a substantial scholarship by failing to meet the qualifying GPA at the completion of the first year, he or she is looking at a major increase in the cost of completing the law degree. Students around the bottom of the class after the first year at a bottom-ranked law school will know that their chance of landing a job as a lawyer after graduation, unless they have connections, is not good. Students in any of these positions should reevaluate. Walking away with $40,000 debt and no law degree beats leaving after two more years of lost earnings with $120,000 debt and a job that does not pay the bills.

To write such discouraging words, words that will dash the dreams of some people who always wanted to be a lawyer, is disheartening. Still, there are people who feel compelled to attend law school no matter how daunting the odds might be. To them I say, Godspeed.

THIRTEEN

Alarms for Law Schools

The word is getting out. There are several strong indications that prospective students are increasingly turning away from law school. The number of applicants to law school is in a multiyear decline that began in 2005, before the crash in the legal market, long before 2011, our *annus horribilis* of unflattering public exposure. Sustained declines in applicants to law school have occurred in each of the past three decades.[1] In the eighties and nineties the number of applicants rebounded nicely after about a half-dozen down years. But the combination of high tuition and a tight job market for lawyers points toward a prolonged reduction this time.[2]

When the "Great Recession" hit in 2008, law schools should have reaped a major boost in applicants. Traditionally, law school has served as a refuge to which recent college graduates and the newly unemployed flock in poor economic times. That appeared to be playing out again when the number of LSAT tests taken in 2008–9 jumped by nine thousand over the previous year and, then, by a whopping twenty thousand more in 2009–10.[3] In successive years, these were the highest number of LSATs ever taken. Law schools, it appeared, would once again enjoy fat times during an economic recession.

It was not to be. Demand for law school remained weak throughout. The spectacular rise in the number of LSATs administered produced an anemic increase in the actual number of applicants. There were 3,200 additional applicants to law school in the first year and only 1,300 additional applicants in the second.

This is contrary to recent historical patterns. Figure 13.1 shows that over the past twenty years law school enrollment has risen in sync every time the general rate of unemployment has gone up—until this time. When

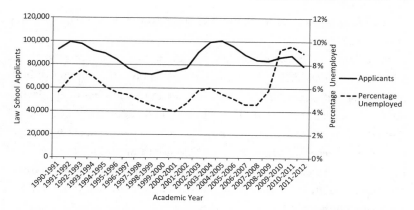

Fig. 13.1. Law school applicants and unemployment. Sources: Law School Admission Council and American Bar Association, *Official Guide to ABA-Approved Law Schools* ([Newtown, PA]: ABA-LSAC, 2011); Bureau of Labor Statistics, "Labor Force Statistics from the Current Population Survey," http://www.bls.gov/cps/prev_yrs.htm.

general unemployment shot up in 2008–9, law schools saw relatively few additional applicants, unlike previous bouts of joblessness.

After a slight upturn in the number of applicants during the worst part of the recession, it quickly turned down again despite a continuation of high unemployment. Two decades of synchronization between rising unemployment and rising law school applicants for some reason uncoupled. While separating on the upside, however, the synchronization reasserted itself on the downside—when unemployment declined so did the number of applicants to law school. This suggests that when the economy improves the number of applicants to law school will decline further.

Another striking sign that the recession-induced bump in applicants was just a blip in a longer decline shows up in the Google trend line. Google trend lines register the number of times people search for a term or phrase or subject. Many people interested in attending law school will search "LSAT." The Google trend line for LSAT searches over the past eight years slopes steadily downward. The last peak in the number of law school applicants was 100,600 in 2004. Thereafter, the number of applicants declined each year until 2009 and 2010. The Google trend line shows that the general decline in applicants coincided with a steady drop in "LSAT" searches over this period. The recent two-year bump in applicants hardly registers on the LSAT search chart. And the slope is still trending downward.

What ultimately matters to law schools is not how many times the LSAT is administered but how many people apply—the number of bodies seeking seats. In 2004, the previous peak in the number of applicants, the test was taken 147,600 times, netting 100,600 applicants. In 2009–10, the test was taken 171,500 times, but only 87,900 people actually applied. Comparing these two years, 2004 saw twenty thousand fewer LSATs administered, yet nearly thirteen thousand more applicants to law school. The 2009–10 data show that there has been a dramatic fall in the ratio of applicants to the number of tests taken.

One explanation is that nowadays more people take the LSAT multiple times. A rule change in 2007 allowed law schools to count only the highest LSAT score a student achieves; previously the student's reported score would be an average of the results. By eliminating the risk that they might reduce their score with a lower result the second time around, this rule change encouraged people to take another shot at the test. (On its end, LSAC would obtain more revenue if more people repeated the test.) Prior to the rule change, about 20 percent of test takers in a given year would repeat the test; in recent years about 30 percent repeat the test.[4]

To get an accurate sense of demand, therefore, we must focus on the number of people who take the test and go on to apply to law school. Therein lay another ominous sign for law schools. From 1994–95 through 2004–5, between 75 percent and 80 percent of the people who took the LSAT went on to apply to law school.[5] A high proportion of applicants makes sense because a significant investment of time and money goes into preparing for and taking the test. After 2003–4, when 78 percent of the people who took the test went on to apply, the yield of applicants to test takers has declined *every single year*. In the two most recent years, 2009–10 and 2010–11, only about 63 percent of the test takers applied to law school.[6] That is the lowest percentage for as far back as available records extend, substantially below the 80 percent yield a decade ago.

Worse still for law schools, this trend began before the recession in the legal market and before the recent spate of bad publicity about law schools. It is not possible to know for certain why people who made the effort to take the LSAT have been turning away from law school in greater numbers—and they began to do so even when law schools were advertising employment rates in the 90 percent range with six-figure salaries. The most plausible explanation is that rising tuition—which by the mid-2000s had reached an average of $30,000 at private law schools—has been pushing down demand for at least a half-dozen years. Unaware of or unconcerned about slackening demand, law schools continued to hike prices.[7]

This sustained decline in yield suggests that applicants, by relying heavily on what score they achieve to determine whether to apply, are rationally responding to the extraordinary emphasis law schools place on LSAT scores. LSAT score determines the law school rank-range a potential candidate will have a shot at. Because merit-based scholarship offers are a function of LSAT score (along with GPA), furthermore, the expected cost of law school is contingent on test results. The lower yield of applicants to test takers in recent years implies that a significant proportion of people are deciding that the range of law schools they would be eligible to attend and the expected tuition reduction that attaches to their score are not worth it.

There is no reason to think that the decline in yield of applicants to test takers will halt. A 2011 poll of people considering law school found that the top issue for 73 percent of respondents was finding a job that would allow them to pay off their student loans.[8]

The bad news for law schools does not end there. More people are apparently deciding to forgo the LSAT entirely. Since October 2010, the number of LSATs administered has declined substantially from the previous year for seven consecutive tests (the LSAT is administered four times a year).[9] The June 2011 and October 2011 tests showed the highest percentage yearly declines on record (−18.7 percent and −16.9 percent). Consistent with these indicators, the number of applicants to law school dropped by 11 percent in 2011, and early signs point toward a further double-digit decline in 2012.

A renewed downturn in the number of applicants will have immediate ramifications because a significant number of schools were already accepting a high percentage of applicants in 2010. That year, twenty law schools accepted between 45 percent and 49 percent of the students who applied; twenty-two schools accepted between 50 percent and 59 percent of applicants; and seven schools had an acceptance rate of 60 percent or higher (Cooley was the highest at 83.3 percent).[10] Added together, nearly a quarter of law schools in the country accepted close to half or more of their applicants. This was *before* the latest decline in the number of applicants.

To see how rapidly the situation can deteriorate, consider a scenario modeled on a lower-ranked law school in the Midwest. In 2010, it accepted roughly a thousand of the fifteen hundred people who applied, with two hundred students enrolling—an acceptance rate of two-thirds and a yield of one-fifth. Let's assume, reasonably, that the school requires around two hundred students (at scholarship discounted rates) to produce sufficient revenue to pay its bills and that its yield will remain constant. Assuming also that the school suffered a 10 percent decline in applicants in 2011 along with many law schools, to enroll the same number of students it must accept three out of four applicants. In the next couple of years, if the number of applicants to the school falls by one-third from its 2010 level, to make its target enrollment of two hundred, it *must accept every student who applies.* No responsible law school can do that. As the ratio of acceptances to applicants rises, student qualifications in the entering class fall. The only way to stave off a decline in student quality is to shrink class size. That reduces revenue which, in turn, requires a reduction in expenditures.

Several portents of this squeeze have begun to appear, although the full data are not yet in. A poll taken by the Law School Admission Council found that "45 percent of the 143 law schools that responded said they had fallen short of their enrollment targets" for the 2011 entering class.[11] A number of law schools announced that they were downsizing, whether voluntarily or because they could not fill their class.[12]

The fate of Illinois law school (which occurred before its falsification came to light) is perhaps a leading indicator of challenges ahead. Every student in the Illinois 2011 entering class, including every student admitted off the waitlist, received a scholarship.[13] When everyone gets a scholarship, that constitutes a de facto tuition reduction. In addition, the incoming class was 20 percent smaller than the previous year. Despite this, the median LSAT of the entering class fell four points (167 to 163)—a breathtaking collapse. Years of effort by Illinois to raise its median LSAT score were wiped out in a single stroke. If Illinois, a top-twenty-five law school, is having trouble making its desired enrollment and student profile targets, other law schools are likely struggling as well.

Law schools are caught in the grip of two reinforcing declines: fewer people are taking the LSAT test and fewer people who take the test go on to apply to law school. If this continues, law schools, especially those at the lower end of the rankings, will not be able to fill their classes with qualified candidates. They may be forced to cut the price—if not explicitly, then by offering scholarships throughout the entire incoming class.

Not only will law schools work harder to fill their first-year classes with desirable students, but they also face a formidable challenge at the end of the first year in hanging on to the students they initially brought in. The transfer phenomenon detailed in chapter 8 is stripping away revenue and a significant percentage of the best performers. Lower-ranked schools cannot easily make up these losses because they are not desirable transfer destinations themselves. Law schools that suffer a net transfer loss of 10 percent of the class will be downsized against their wishes. This occurred with the Midwest law school used as the example above. Its 2010 entering class of two hundred students was reduced to a class of 180 after the first year. Each departure represents a two-year loss of revenue, even for those students who paid discounted rates.

Another loss law schools will witness going forward is the departure of students who drop out after receiving poor grades in the first semester or first year. The economic risk of law school is substantial enough that for some the stigma attached to leaving will be outweighed by the dual prospect of heavy debt and poor likelihood of gainful employment. If this bears out, attrition rates will rise.

Law schools have pumped up tuition in the past two decades on the assumption that demand for a legal education is highly price inelastic. That faith was handsomely rewarded. The factors outlined above, however, suggest that about five or six years ago we crossed an invisible threshold to softening demand.

Veteran legal educators remain unperturbed. "Every 10 years we hit a trough in which doomsayers predicted that enrollments would decline and that law schools would go out of business," said Rudy Hasl, the dean of Thomas Jefferson law school.[14] "We always bounce back." Recent history supports his equanimity—a law school going out of business is rare, although it has happened. No matter how bad the news, it appears that enough people with a fervent desire to attend law school come along each year to keep schools afloat.

The quality and operation of law schools *are* at stake, however. When the number of applicants falls, with all else equal, three standard approaches exist. (1) Increasing scholarships to maintain quality (losing revenue), while keeping enrollment constant. (2) Shrinking enrollment to maintain quality, losing revenue. (3) Keeping enrollment and scholarship levels constant, consequently taking in a weaker class, but maintaining revenue. These alternatives assume a trade-off exists between revenue and quality: the first two give up revenue to maintain quality, the third sacrifices quality to maintain revenue. A school with declining applications that is determined to maintain quality may combine the first two, cutting price and shrinking enrollment, multiplying the revenue hit.

When an applicant-decline crunch slams a law school, the expected trade-off does not deliver—revenue *and* quality both go down. That is what walloped Illinois in 2011. The school gave scholarships to everyone in the entering class, overspending its scholarship budget by $200,000; its enrollment dropped from 228 to 184; and *still* its median LSAT fell four points.[15] As a result, it lost considerable revenue and student quality fell.

If this devastating combination were to happen to a law school several years running, it would soon be hobbled. The student body would be markedly less capable than before and resources would be tight. To survive, schools at the bottom of the law school hierarchy that suffer this fate will enroll students who should not be in law school. That is how law schools will keep their doors open, if they can. Signs of this are already appearing. Only 33.3 percent of the 2011 graduates of Thomas Jefferson passed the California bar exam (down from 76.2 percent in 2008)—a shockingly low success rate.[16]

FOURTEEN

Going Forward

n 2009 and 2010, an estimated 9,500 lawyers were let go from the 250 largest firms.[1] "This is the biggest two-year decline in the 33-year history of the survey," found the *National Law Journal*.[2] Many of the laid-off lawyers were young associates. Law firms deferred the hiring dates of new lawyers and slashed the number new positions at many firms by half or more.[3] The sharp contraction at large law firms reverberated throughout the job market. Graduates who might have obtained high-end corporate law jobs in previous years sought legal employment of any kind, pursuing positions in regional law firms, government legal jobs, or anything they could find. Unprecedentedly high numbers of recent graduates took temporary and part-time legal positions.[4] More than a third of law graduates didn't get lawyer jobs at all (within nine months after graduation). Three years on, there is no sign of improvement. A survey by *American Lawyer* of the two hundred leading firms found, "87 percent of respondents said that 2011's incoming class will be the same size or smaller than their (usually already reduced) 2010 class."[5]

Law schools responded to this abysmal job environment by *increasing* the number of students they enrolled in 2009, and yet again in 2010— thereby promising to throw out even more law graduates onto the saturated employment pool three years hence.

Law school defenders characterize the withering criticism of the past two years as the lashing out of unhappy graduates who fail to understand that law schools are not to blame for their travails. Things were fine before and will be fine once again when the economy recovers, their thinking goes. When that happens—soon, they hope—the current bitterness will subside and law schools can continue on as before. As further evidence of this, they point out that the number of lawyers per capita has actually fallen in recent years as law school enrollment, although increasing, has not kept pace with the growth of the population.[6] Law schools can ride out the storm. No radical changes are necessary.

A STRUCTURAL CHANGE IN THE LEGAL MARKET?

Scholars of the legal profession are debating whether the current situation involves long-term structural changes in the market for legal services or whether it is merely a cyclical event, after which things will go back to the way they were. If the latter, some argue, law schools should not overreact. Debates like this, which point to patterns, incipient developments, and forward indicators, cannot be conclusively resolved. Only a generation hence can we tell which side has the better argument.

Professor William Henderson (with coauthor Rachel Zahorsky), a leading scholar in the field who sees this as a structural shift, found that law firm employment had reached a plateau in 2004. "Between March 2004 and March 2008, several months before the Wall Street meltdown that initiated an unprecedented wave of law firm layoffs, the nation's law firm sector had already shed nearly 20,000 jobs."[7] When measured in terms of growth rate as a percentage of gross domestic product, the legal sector has been in decline since the mid-2000s.[8] That this happened during supposedly boom times signals an internal restructuring within the corporate legal sector. Larry Ribstein, another proponent of the structural change thesis, argues in his article "The Death of Big Law" that the large law firm business model is unraveling under demands from knowledgeable clients and greater competition.[9] More sweepingly, Richard Susskind has cataloged manifold technological and other changes that are taking away swaths of legal work and shifting the balance of power to clients, pondering the possible demise of the profession in his book *The End of Lawyers?*[10] In *The Vanishing Lawyer*, Thomas Morgan chronicles the economic pressure on lawyers created by the shifting legal market and how it is contributing to the decline of the legal profession.[11]

While there is much to what these scholars are saying, for immediate purposes it is more pertinent to pay attention to specific indications of what the job market for lawyers will look like in the next five to ten years.

Surveys of hiring partners in major firms find that several recent changes are likely to remain after legal business rebounds.[12] A significant proportion of clients refuse to pay high billing rates for new associates and are unlikely to relent.[13] Law firms, consequently, are hiring fewer new associates and relying more heavily on paralegals and contract attorneys to do basic work. Contract attorneys work on a per job basis—directly for the law firm or through a temp agency—and are paid $25–$30 an hour to handle document review tasks, often in Spartan (low overhead) basement or warehouse conditions. Contract attorney work is billed to clients at $60–$70, substantially below the $200–$300 per hour billing rates of new associates.[14] Graduates from well-regarded as well as lower-down schools take contract jobs these days—the employment market is *that* bad—earning as much as $50,000 annually when consistently employed. About half of the law firms polled admit to using contract attorneys and expect that it will remain a permanent part of their staffing.[15] Clients are happier with the lower billing rates for this work and law firm partners like its flexibility and cheaper cost to the firm. In another move to reduce costs, a few large firms have created in-house versions of outsourcing, setting up satellite offices in cheaper locales staffed by "career associates" who do the same work as traditional associates but at half the pay.[16] Contract attorneys and career associates will remain after the legal market improves because they are cost efficient for law firms and the savings wrung in these ways will enhance partner shares while keeping clients satisfied. Additional cost savings that reduce the need for new associates are likely to occur with the continued development of electronic document-processing technology and with more sophisticated offshore providers of legal services.[17]

The global managing partner of a major law firm confirmed the durability of these changes: " As the recession starts to reverse itself, there will be some movement away from the super-heightened awareness of cost, but this recession gave buyers of legal services enough time to appreciate that they could get the same quality of service for less than before the recession. The better, faster, cheaper concept is very much here to stay."[18] The hiring partner of another top corporate law firm said the same: "the efficiency of law practice has just changed dramatically in the past five years. We don't have to have these armies of young associates. It's good for the clients, it's good for everybody."[19] When business comes back to the corporate sector, "law firms will not return to the recruiting and hiring patterns that preceded the recession," concluded two law professors in an article elaborating on the "new normal" in the corporate legal market.[20]

The hiring market for corporate lawyers picked up a bit toward the end of 2011 but only for experienced associates, not rookies. A poll found that law firms were seeking lateral hires who are "professionals with a solid portfolio of clients and business development skills."[21] The poll also revealed "high demand" for experienced paralegals "with litigation and e-discovery backgrounds."[22] This is another indication that work formerly done by starting associates is devolving away. Meanwhile, "the job market for newly minted lawyers has yet to catch up with supply. Firms still are not recruiting entry-level associates in significant numbers, and many summer associate programs have been reduced or put on hold."[23]

Changes in the delivery of legal services are also squeezing the low end of the legal market. LegalZoom provides forms and guidance online that allow people to prepare their own divorce, write a will, incorporate a business, file for a patent or trademark, and much more—at a cost significantly below what lawyers would charge. In low-income communities, one can find "immigration assistance" or "divorce assistance" services that help people fill out and file the necessary documents at low rates. The organized bar's monopoly over legal services, which it polices through the vigorous enforcement against the "unauthorized practice of law," is fraying at the edges.

Law professors who fixate on the declining rate of lawyers per capita to argue that we do not have a glut of lawyers fail to appreciate that there can be an oversupply of lawyers if the previous per capita amount was already too high, or if the number of available lawyer jobs is declining because nonlawyers or computers are taking away work formerly handled by lawyers.[24]

Perversely, the United States has an oversupply of law graduates at the same time that a significant proportion of the populace—the poor and lower middle class—go without legal assistance. This is reaching crisis proportions. A recent study by the Legal Services Corporation—a government-funded program to provide legal assistance for low-income people—found that nearly a million cases (one out of every two seeking assistance) were rejected by legal-aid programs owing to insufficient resources.[25] Less than one in five low-income people with legal problems are served by an attorney.[26] These unmet legal needs involve divorces, child custody, eviction from rental property or foreclosure, workplace problems, disputes over insurance claims, and more. State courts across the country have reported alarming numbers of people who go without lawyers in civil cases: in New Hampshire 85 percent of all civil cases in district court and 48 percent of cases in superior court are self-represented, and 97 percent of domestic violence cases involve one party without a lawyer; in Utah 81 percent of respondents in family law cases are unrepresented; in California 90 percent of defendants in eviction cases are unrepresented; in Massachusetts at least 100,000 litigants in civil matters represented themselves; in DC 98 percent of respondents in paternity suits and 97 percent of respondents in housing cases do not have lawyers.[27] Significant unmet legal needs coexists with significant numbers of lawyers who cannot find jobs because American society lacks the public infrastructure to deliver affordable legal services on a mass scale, and recent law graduates cannot earn enough income on this kind of work to sustain a private practice.

THE FUNDAMENTAL PROBLEM

Whether the current situation involves a structural or cyclical shift in the delivery of legal services, there will be a substantial oversupply of lawyers either way. Law schools have created a systemic mismatch between the number of graduates and available jobs that predates the crash. During the glory hiring days of the mid-2000s many graduates were still not getting lawyer jobs. Unless legal business experiences an unprecedented boom—which no one is predicting—the excess of grads over jobs will remain. As long as this oversupply continues, earnings at the lower end of the legal market will continue to stagnate.

Skeptics ask, If a large oversupply predated the crash, why was so little said about it before? There are two answers. Before the crash that hit the corporate law market, graduates who failed to land lawyer jobs almost entirely came from mid- and lower-ranked schools, destined for the lower hemisphere of law jobs. In an elite-focused legal academy and legal profession, to put it frankly, no one cares about these people or those types of jobs. They faded away after leaving school, legal educators oblivious to their fate. Only when the problem touched elite graduates and the corporate legal market did we pay attention to the phenomenon.

The second answer is that, although debt was building a decade ago, many graduates who did not land lawyer jobs could survive financially. That is no longer true. And with debt now topping $100,000 for many, the failures today are not just graduates who never make it into the profession but also many of those who do. A law school graduate with the average amount of debt cannot get by on the average pay. This is why we are hearing more about it. The economics of it are broken in a way that was not true a decade ago.

Law schools are producing streams of economic casualties.

What if anything can be done?

A DIFFERENTIATED LEGAL EDUCATION SYSTEM

The wisdom of the members of the bar who a century ago argued on behalf of a differentiated system of legal education—wanting to allow research-oriented law schools to coexist alongside law schools that focus on training good lawyers at a reasonable cost—has been confirmed by subsequent events. Unfortunately, they lost the battle to elite legal educators who imposed their standard on all. The research brand of law schools became the model imposed and enforced through AALS and ABA standards. Accredited law schools today have a three-year curriculum taught by law professors who are scholars more than lawyers, while the bar incessantly complains that graduates are inadequately prepared for the practice of law.

The proposition that students could be trained for practice solely in law school was wrongheaded from the outset. The best way to learn how to practice law is to actually do it. Lawyers learn by being given tasks, struggling to do them, watching others around them, and learning from mistakes. No amount of classroom learning, skills training, and simulations can substitute for the real thing, though an excellent education helps graduates become proficient more quickly. After trial by fire, a capable law graduate gets up to speed in relatively short order. A great deal of legal work is routine; new tasks are learned as they come.

The century-long condemnation of law schools by the bar for doing a poor job of training lawyers misses the larger truth of their own objection. Law schools are doomed to fall short because a student ultimately can learn to practice only *in* practice. A large array of practice settings and specialized knowledge exists. Each must be learned by engaging in that practice, although certain basic skills are transferrable.

The rise of in-house clinical programs in law schools is an implicit admission of the original error. It cannot, however, be more than a patch. Law schools, at great expense, create artificial practice settings within an academic institution although actual settings exist in the world of legal practice. The economic inefficiency of this arrangement places an upper limit on the expansion of clinics that will keep law schools inadequate to the task.

The bar's position a century ago made consummate sense: two years of book learning followed by a one-year apprenticeship, then admission to the bar. The Carrington Report of four decades ago, which proposed three years of an undergraduate education followed by two years of law school, was also sensible. A law degree is an undergraduate degree in most countries.

The essential change could be achieved in a stroke. The current ABA-imposed minimum of 1,120 classroom hours can be reduced by a third, instead mandating 747 hours of instruction.[28] Law schools are already allowed the flexibility to admit students without a bachelor's degree, as long as the student has completed three years of college, and even this requirement can be waived "if the applicant's experience, ability, and other characteristics clearly show an aptitude for the study of law."[29]

A few additional changes will open the way to differentiation. The standards and official interpretations written in for the benefit of faculty must be deleted: those that mandate law schools to rely heavily on tenure-track full-time faculty, those that require support for faculty research, and those that provide job security for professors.[30] The entire set of rules relating to the law library must be deleted. These rules require law schools to maintain unnecessarily expensive library collections and a large support staff; the book-on-the-shelf library is virtually obsolete in the electronic information age.

With this handful of targeted changes, law schools would be free to construct a curriculum that focuses on training students to become lawyers. They will design programs to suit their particular mission and niche in the legal education market. Many law schools will continue to offer tenure, job security, and research support—others will not. Some degree programs will be two years, others will remain at three, with clinical components; some will be heavily doctrinal, others will be skills oriented. One-year degrees (the current LLM) will be widely available for an additional year of specialization in a chosen subject. Schools will offer two-year and three-year program options for students, incentivizing schools to create a third year that adds significant value.

Differentiation across the market for legal education—currently suppressed by ABA standards—would arise. The law school parallel—in program and pricing—of vocational colleges and community colleges will come into existence, many of two-year duration. Research-oriented law schools will remain as they are. Practice-oriented schools will be staffed by experienced lawyers teaching full time or as adjuncts; research institutions will be staffed by scholars mainly engaged in research; other schools will be staffed by both types.

Prospective students will be able to pick the legal education program they want at a price they can afford. A law graduate who wishes to engage in a local practice need not acquire, or pay for, the same education as a graduate aiming for corporate legal practice. This is not the race to the bottom prophesied by AALS. It simply recognizes that every law school need not be a Ritz-Carlton. A Holiday Inn–type law school would provide a fine education for many, adequate for the type of legal practice they will undertake. Differentiation will create affordable avenues to becoming a lawyer. Standards will still exist to insure a quality legal education, and anyone who wishes to become a lawyer will have to pass the bar exam.

This is not to say that this plan is without any dangers. Reducing the mandatory curriculum from three to two years raises the specter of increasing the flow of lawyers onto an already oversupplied market. A shorter and cheaper training period invites that result. Ideally this would make more lawyers available to fill unmet legal needs at a more affordable price, but there is no assurance that it would work out that way.

The one year reduction is severable from the other proposals. Law school differentiation will come about if the other proposed deletions of the standards go through.

If none of these changes are made to the rules, schools that avowedly embrace the mission of training capable lawyers at an affordable price can still accomplish this by transforming the third year into a genuine year of practice experience.[31] Law schools can place students on a wholesale basis in already-existing practice settings (law firms, government legal offices, courthouses, etc.), as many law schools already do through "externship" programs. This is more cost efficient than in-house clinics. Law school personnel responsible for these programs will not be scholars but experienced staff lawyers-supervisors who monitor outplaced students.

A more ambitious program would involve the participation by law schools, in partnership with government-funded agencies, with the delivery of legal services to the middle class and poor at low cost. Under currently existing "hybrid" programs, a clinical professor has an office at the practice setting and works with the students on location. If understaffed legal services offices were offered the full-time assistance of the third-year class of local law schools, that would help fill unmet legal needs while the students get useful training. Privately financed, privately run versions of low-cost legal services are also possible, in conjunction with law schools, in areas like immigration services, tax services, employment problems, and a variety of other common tasks on which third year students can hone their practice skills.[32]

Whichever the external setting, students would work as lawyers at an office earning basic wages (which would require a rule change in order to implement)—reviving a form of apprenticeship. Think of the lawyer equivalent of residency programs for graduates out of medical school. Law school staff and attorneys in the office would maintain oversight and provide advice, but students would handle much of the work themselves. Many third-year students already work part-time in law offices—this would amount to an institutionalized version of that. The responsibility of the law school would be to secure placement opportunities in practice settings while running a supplemental educational component on the side. Tuition for the third year can be reduced to a level commensurate with the extent of the outplacement and supervision services provided by the school.

These reforms will not pass easily. Path dependence, inertia, and entrenched economic interests, especially on the part of law professors and law schools, will conspire against them. The proposals will seem radical and outrageous to the legal educators who people the ABA Section on Legal Education and the Association of American Law Schools.

ANOTHER ROUTE TO OPENING UP CHANGE THAT BYPASSES THE ABA

There is a way to prompt a wave of changes that bypasses the ABA: eliminate the requirement that only graduates from ABA accredited law schools may sit for the state bar exam. State supreme courts imposed this requirement in the good faith belief that accreditation would be utilized to insure quality standards. As earlier chapters show, accreditation efforts, while meeting this charge, have also been used to serve the interests and commitments of law professors and law schools. "Quality" was defined less in terms of an affordable legal education and more in terms of an academic-oriented law school.

This is not lost on state supreme court justices. The Montana Supreme Court in 2002 denied the request of a graduate of an unaccredited law school in California for a waiver to sit for the Montana bar. Two dissenting justices lashed out at law schools and the ABA: "No empirical data has been offered to suggest that the ABA standards correlate in any way to a quality legal education. What is evident is that the monopoly given to this private trade association to set standards for law schools increases the cost of legal education, burdens new members of the profession with debt that limits their options for professional and public service, hampers innovations in the area of legal education, discriminates against 'working faculty' with practical professional experiences to share with their students, and discriminates against non-conventional students and minorities who do not meet the arbitrary admissions standards imposed."[33] After recent disclosures about law schools, perhaps more state court justices will find these observations persuasive.

A handful of states, which have their own accreditation procedures, do not require graduation from an ABA accredited law school for admission to their bar. If the majority of states were to eliminate this requirement—a rule change by the highest court of each state—or at a minimum if the states with the largest legal markets were to do so, tuition at the lower-ranked law schools would fall. The "ABA accreditation" stamp allows a graduate to sit for the bar anywhere. This gives it the economic value that enables law schools to set tuition $20,000 or more above schools that lack the stamp. "There is no ABA-accredited law school in California with tuition under $30,000 per year," while tuition for eighteen California-accredited schools is around $10,000.[34] (This substantial pricing difference is not due entirely to the increased costs imposed by accreditation.) Without the ABA accreditation entry barrier, accredited law schools would forfeit their premium pricing power. ABA accreditation, which certifies a minimum quality level, could continue to exist, but in the nature of a seal of approval, like the current status of AALS accreditation.

The main impact of this change would be felt at the lowest-ranked schools. Instead of paying $30,000–$40,000 annual tuition for the privilege to take the bar everywhere it would be $15,000–$20,000. This reduction would readjust the debt to expected income mismatch that creates long odds against students who attend these schools. Low-ranked accredited law schools would slash their tuition or go under.

FEDERAL LOAN ELIGIBILITY REQUIREMENTS

Another route to change would entail modifications by Congress and the Department of Education of the rules for federal loan eligibility. If rules similar to those the Department of Education applies to for-profit vocational colleges to qualify for federal loans were applied to law schools, a number of schools would be in the danger zone. Under these regulations, "a program would be considered to lead to gainful employment if it meets at least one of the following three metrics: at least 35 percent of former students are repaying their loans (defined as reducing the loan balance by at least $1); the estimated annual loan payment of a typical graduate does not exceed 30 percent of his or her discretionary income; or the estimated annual loan payment of a typical graduate does not exceed 12 percent of his or her total earnings."[35] It appears likely that a sizable number of law schools fail the second and third metrics—which says something about the economics of legal education. The key metric is the first—a low bar that is hard for a school to fail. Assuming it applies to IBR, law graduates whose income-based payment rates do not cover the monthly interest, while technically not in default, will not be reducing the loan balance at all.

Losing federal loan eligibility would be the death penalty. To stay alive, law schools in the danger zone would reduce their tuition, increase their financial aid, or bolster their loan-forgiveness programs. The key to IBR is student debt level, which law schools would have to carefully monitor out of self-preservation. If need be, law schools would provide graduates with direct assistance in repaying their federal loans. The fate of law schools would then be aligned with the fate of their graduates.

CAPPING FEDERAL LOAN TOTALS BY SCHOOL

To affect the overall dynamic of rising tuition and debt requires a more fundamental change. Previously, the federal government guaranteed student loans made by private lenders, but now it loans money directly to students. When lending the money, the government makes no evaluation of whether the borrower is likely to repay the loan. A student who borrows to attend Thomas Jefferson or Cooley gets the same treatment as a student who borrows to attend Harvard Law School, notwithstanding the fact that a far greater proportion of the former will not repay the loan. A private lender would soon go out of business if it operated this way, but in the student loan context this policy is justified as "providing access."

While well intentioned, it is not necessarily beneficial to the people it purports to help, since many of them end up burdened with massive debt and no legal job or a salary inadequate to make the loan payments. The federal loan program is justified in terms of access for students but it is more aptly perceived as a funding program for law schools, with students serving as conduits. Law schools compete for federal dollars that they obtain through student intermediaries. The law school processes and approves the loan request—in effect granting itself money—which it forwards to the government to receive payment. The money goes directly from the government to the law school. All of the risk in this arrangement is borne by the students in the first instance and by the taxpayers thereafter. Law schools extract their financial payoff up front.

Legal educators will find this an offensive way to characterize the law school operation, ignoring the educational service law schools provide. But it captures the economic relationship between law schools, students, and federal loan money. Cooley law school graduates from 2008 to 2011 had a combined debt of over $300 million, nearly all of it directly from the federal government or backed by federal guarantees. To increase its take, Cooley opens additional branches, increasing the number of students it enrolls. The total debt for Georgetown law graduates in this same period was over $270 million. New York Law School, American, and Harvard law graduates had upward of $200 million in debt. George Washington and New York University law graduates had nearly $200 million. Suffolk, Fordham, Loyola Marymount, and Columbia law graduates had combined debt of $160 million–$180 million. These figures cover only four years. The total debt of 2010 law graduates alone exceeded $3.6 billion.

Enormous sums of money thus flow from the federal treasury to law school bank accounts. Law schools have the ability to increase this flow unilaterally—to disgorge more money from the federal government—by raising tuition and enrolling more students, as many law schools have been doing without restraint. Florida Coastal, a for-profit law school intelligently responding to the economic incentives, extracts an ever-larger sum of federal dollars, going from $28 million in 2008, to $33 million in 2009, to $45 million in 2010, by increasing its enrollment every year. Four hundred students graduated from Florida Coastal in May 2010. A few months later the school enrolled a double-sized new entering class of eight hundred students, each bringing federal dollars in tow. After attrition, the debt for the class of 2013 will likely exceed $60 million.

Providing access to legal careers *is* essential. The legal system will suffer if only the wealthy can attend law school. But the price to the students and to the government will continue to rise unless something is done to crimp the ability of law students to pay whatever asking price is set by law schools.

One commonly suggested way to deal with the situation is to set a cap on how much an individual student can borrow from the federal government tied to the rate of inflation. That would slow tuition increases. But to obtain additional revenue law schools can take in more students—as they have been doing—which would exacerbate the difficulty graduates have finding jobs and would increase the total sum of money supplied by the government.

A better solution is to set an across-the-board per-school cap for federal loans: say $60 million per class for each law school. That is a generous amount of public money. It could be set lower or higher. A cap imposes the greatest immediate restraint on large law schools. Schools above or near the limit will be forced to control enrollment as well as tuition. In theory the smaller schools will be free to increase their tuition and enrollment, but in practice they will be restrained as well. Any school that increases its enrollment risks a decline in student quality, which harms a school's standing. The cap will also indirectly control tuition increases. With schools like Harvard and Columbia already at the cap unable to increase their tuition (and enrollment), law schools below them in the hierarchy also cannot charge higher tuition because students would balk. Once the top is restrained, the prestige-market pricing system will dampen tuition increases all through the chain. Yale's tuition can go up because its enrollment is relatively low, but with Harvard and Columbia topped out, other schools beneath them cannot rise.

Along with the cap, there must be no federal guarantee of private loans to attend law school, and any such private loans must be eligible for discharge in bankruptcy. This would put the risk on lenders, which would not loan money to students who are unlikely to repay (at least not without charging prohibitive interest rates).

The remaining option for schools squeezed by the cap that wish to increase their revenue stream is to loan money directly to the students themselves. This is another way of aligning their interests with the fate of their students. Low-ranked law schools are unlikely to extend such credit because they are well aware of the high likelihood of nonpayment.

The main downside of the cap is that schools will place a premium on letting in rich folks who don't need to borrow. That is problematic, to be sure, but there is no clean solution to the high tuition–high enrollment problem. Schools that have a genuine commitment to providing access can help reduce the debt problem by allocating a greater proportion of financial aid to need-based scholarships. All things considered, a hard cap would seem to be the most viable way to control tuition and enrollment, while still providing access.

CHANGE BROUGHT BY MARKET FORCES

Change will come even if none of the above reforms are enacted. The economic model of law schools is unsustainable. At the current rate of tuition increase, in 2020 annual tuition at top law schools will be $70,000 and average tuition at mid- and lower-ranked private schools will be $50,000. The former is conceivable—the latter is not. Economic rationality eventually has its way even when multiple sources of market distortion collude to prop up a system beyond its expiration date.

The most powerful mechanism for reform will be a fall in applicants. In 2004, there were fifty-two thousand more applications than the number of people who enrolled. In 2011, the margin of applicants over enrollment had fallen to around thirty thousand. If the number of applicants declines by the same percentage in 2012, unless law schools slash enrollment, the margin will be about twenty thousand. As the margin of applicants over seats gets smaller, a greater number of schools will be forced to accept a higher proportion of the people who apply. The qualifications of incoming classes will deteriorate. Schools will be downsized whether they want to or not.

Law schools all throughout the hierarchy will feel the squeeze. The competition for students—for federal dollars—will intensify. Most law schools heretofore have extended merit scholarship offers mainly to applicants with LSAT scores above the median for *US News*–ranking purposes. When law schools have difficulty filling their classes, however, bottom-half students become desirable in straight-up revenue terms. A student paying half price is better than an empty seat bringing in no federal dollars. If discounting extends throughout the class, a tuition reduction will be in place, even if unannounced. Schools will turn to alternative sources of revenue if they can—endowments, transfers, and LLM students (especially international students).

All law schools, if the fall in applicants persists, will be forced to trim costs. The faculty portion of the budget is the largest expense item. The growth of law faculties will slow, and may even reverse, with a greater proportion of courses taught by cheaper adjuncts and professors on contract. Full-time professors will be asked to teach more courses—this is already happening at the college level—and undertake a greater share of other responsibilities.[36] Less money will go into research. The age of indulgence for law schools will make way for a time of pain.

HOPE FOR THE FUTURE

Unless they combine forces in an economic storm that sweeps away the current model, none of the changes advocated or predicted above will rectify the warped economic arrangement that law schools have created. Law school will remain expensive, and many graduates will find it hard to find work that allows them to service their debt.

There is little reason for optimism that law schools will change on their own. Consider the path of the newly created UC Irvine Law School. California did not need another law school. With great fanfare, Irvine was rolled out and justified as a unique institution—one that will train skilled, ethical attorneys and imbue students with the spirit of public service.[37] Out of the gate, the school had a $20 million gift from a local businessman. A prominent liberal constitutional law scholar from Duke University School of Law, Erwin Chemerinsky, was hired to lead the school. He recruited a lineup of professors from top-twenty-five law schools. With the help of major donors, the inaugural class was offered three years of tuition-free law school, producing a class with impressive LSAT/GPA medians. To keep up the quality, the second class got 50 percent tuition reductions, and the third class got 33 percent reductions. The explicit goal was to create an immediate top-twenty law school, an unprecedented feat. "We have the chance to build something very special: the ideal law school for the 21st century," said Chemerinsky.[38] "We have a wonderful opportunity in that we have a blank slate."[39]

A wonderful opportunity it was. But what they ended up doing was chase a prestige ranking, spending their seed money to recruit top scholars and students with high LSAT scores, following the standard template for all top law schools: a research institution with a heavy dose of clinics.

Any doubt about this was dispelled when Irvine announced its tuition going forward: $44,347 for residents and $54,192 for nonresidents.[40]

Adding expenses, law students who pay full price to attend Irvine will put out $200,000 for their law degree. To insure that its LSAT/GPA scores remain high, the law school will implement the standard reverse–Robin Hood scholarship arrangement to have the bottom half of the class subsidize the top half. After the initial scholarship classes pass through, Irvine law graduates will duly take their place among graduates with $100,000 or more in average debt. They will struggle like all the other graduates to obtain positions offering salaries commensurate with this debt. They will feel powerful economic pressure to secure high-paying corporate law jobs, regardless of a desire to engage in public service. The ten-year loan-forgiveness period for public-service jobs is an attractive escape from the debt, but students cannot count on getting these highly competitive jobs. Corporate law jobs are obtained during the fall of the second year while public-service jobs typically are handed out in the second semester of the third year or after graduation. A student in substantial debt would take a huge risk to pass up a corporate law job in the hope of later landing a public-service job.

In economic terms Irvine law school is nothing new. Avowedly progressive law professors with ample resources and a clean slate, setting out to build a school focused on public service, reproduced an institution that loads students with debt and channels them to the corporate law sector. This squandered opportunity demonstrates how difficult it is to break away from the distorted economic model that so dominates the thinking of legal academics.

Where they went wrong was in setting out to create an *elite* law school. This goal condemned the project. Affordability and elite status are mutually exclusive under current circumstances. Competition over *US News* rankings has warped law school economics, and Irvine jumped into it with gusto, doing its utmost to land high in the ranking sweepstakes. Had their goal instead been to create an excellent law school that trains top-quality lawyers at an *affordable price*—which California lacks—a different design would have resulted.

What might that have looked like? For starters, Chermerinsky would have had to sell the vision of affordable excellence, recruiting top faculty who were willing to accept less pay (more in line with professors in other departments) to make that vision a reality; professors would have had practice experience as well as have been excellent scholars; they would teach two classes a semester, leaving ample time to write; the entering class would be capped at two hundred students; the third year would entail externships in excellent public-service work settings; tuition would be set below $20,000; there would be no merit scholarships; the $20 million seed money would create an endowment for need-based scholarships, supplemented by fund raising. With the "UC" name, a reasonable price, outstanding professors, and a public-service mission, quality students would have enrolled. And graduates would leave law school with manageable debt levels that would enable them to eschew the corporate law route if they so desired. This would have been the ideal school for the twenty-first century. The only problematic element in an otherwise realistic plan would have been recruiting enough top professors who would teach four courses and accept lower pay—we constantly advocate public service but doing it ourselves is another matter.

The remaining hope lies in public law schools that continue to embrace the mission of providing a quality education at lower cost. A host of top public law schools, foremost Berkeley, Michigan, Virginia and UCLA, have abdicated their public mission in order to pursue rankings, following the expensive private research-university model. Irvine did that right off. Other top public schools, like Texas, Illinois, and Minnesota, are moving rapidly in this direction. As the recent fiascos at Texas and Illinois illustrate, getting in the prestige race, trying to compete on even terms with top private schools that have greater resources and a higher pay scale, can twist a school apart. Schools in the prestige race are all running faster while they remain in the same relative place. The students are forced to borrow more money to pay for all this without any improvement in their job opportunities at the end. It is the professors who benefit the most as their salaries rise thanks to recruitment wars and the benefits spread for internal equity reasons to the rest of the faculty.

There are many excellent state law schools that continue to charge tuition well below $20,000. North Carolina, Alabama, Georgia and Georgia State, Wisconsin, Utah, Florida and Florida State, Tennessee, Temple,

University of Kentucky, Oklahoma, Kansas, New Mexico, Louisiana State, Buffalo, Nebraska, Hawai'i, West Virginia, Louisville, Missouri, and a few more, fall in this category. These schools have resisted the distorting pull of *US News* competition, secure in their position as flagship state schools with a strong presence in the local legal market. They regularly lose their top scholars to lateral recruitment from better-paying higher-ranked schools, but that does not diminish their operation or standing.

Attending these law schools at resident rates can still make economic sense. If private law school tuition continues to rise, reasonably priced public schools will win away a greater share of excellent students in head-to-head competition, getting stronger while the private schools they compete with weaken. Graduates of affordable public law schools, less burdened by onerous debt, will have more freedom and flexibility throughout the course of their careers, giving them a better chance to do great things with their degrees. Public school graduates who do not obtain lawyer jobs will have a better chance to build a successful career outside of law than private law school graduates in the same predicament, who will suffer under their double-sized debt.

Affordable public schools are the final sensible corner of legal academia. The biggest threat to their existence is a withdrawal of public subsidies, whether out of budget-cutting imperatives or as a backlash at law schools for their misdeeds.

A Few Last Words

This has been a difficult book to write. I have many friends and colleagues in legal academia. At almost every turn I wrote things I thought might offend or irritate people I admire. Early on I resolved that this book could be written only if I protected no one, including myself. I hope it is clear from what I have written that I am as responsible as everyone else for the situation in which we find ourselves in legal academia. I, too, benefit, with a generous salary that my students pay for with debt. When I name names in the text, identifying schools (including my own) and individuals, I'm not calling out people for wrongdoing, but telling a story in which we are all involved.

What compelled me to write this book is the conviction that the current economic barrier to a legal career is one of the most important social justice issues of our age. It is increasingly more difficult for people from all spectra of society to become lawyers—and especially hard for people from modest economic backgrounds to get in to and afford an elite law school. Raised by school-teacher parents who taught me to live within my means, I doubt that I would have gone to law school today. The size of the prospective debt would have been too much. When I went to law school thirty years ago, with tuition at $5,000, I gave nary a thought to my cumulative $15,000 debt ($35,000 in inflation adjusted dollars). I was able to decline a corporate law job and instead work, first, as a public defender and, later, as a lawyer in a developing country—immensely rewarding experiences—with no financial reservations because my monthly loan payments were easily manageable despite relatively low pay. Not so for today's graduates.

A generational aspect to the situation must be highlighted. Law professors who attended law school up to and including the eighties enjoy the best of both worlds. We paid in when the price of law school was relatively low, and we entered our prime earning years when law professor pay leapt to a higher level (with the exception of public law schools that have re-strained tuition). Compare that with our younger colleagues on faculties who graduated from law school in the 2000s when tuition at elite schools crossed the $40,000 mark. They get the benefit of the higher professor pay scale but their buy-in price was so steep and their resultant debt levels so high—a degree of magnitude more than their senior colleagues (who also earn much more)—that they are in a financial squeeze. We will soon see law professors who enter income-based loan repayment programs (those at nonprofit schools qualify for the public-service version).

This bears mention because, if the escalation in the price of a legal education is to be contained, law professors must take less and do more. Faculties must shrink. Raises must be tempered, though in an uneven way: the senior generation of professors—twenty-plus years out of law school—must accept less to allow our younger colleagues to have more. For many accomplished and hard-working full professors, this will be hard to swallow. But those of us in this position cannot say we are un-derpaid for what we do. Over the years I have heard many law professors utter "This is the best job in the world." So it is.

There will be legal educators who remain unconvinced that the eco-nomics of legal education are as badly askew as I argue in this book. Enough uncertainty and information gaps are present in the case I pre-sent to allow a skeptic to demur. As a final argument, I ask every reader who is a legal educator to take this simple "Law School Value Test." Let's say your best friend since high school calls you one day for advice. Her youngest daughter, Sarah, wants to be a lawyer. Your school is the best one Sarah got into. Your friend and her husband (a teacher and a nurse) used up their savings and borrowed as much as they could to help Sarah get through college debt free. If Sarah attends your law school, she will leave with $100,000 debt ($70,000 debt if you are at a public school). Your friend asks, "Please tell me—should Sarah go to your law school?"

Many law professors at many law schools across the country are selling a degree to their students that they would not recommend to people close to them.

APPENDIX A

List of Abbreviations

AALS	Association of American Law Schools
ABA	American Bar Association
ALDA	American Law Deans Association
BLS	Bureau of Labor Statistics
CLEA	Clinical Legal Education Association
DCL	Doctor of Civil Law
DOJ	Department of Justice
GPA	Grade Point Average
IBR	Income Based Repayment
JD	Juris Doctor/Juris Doctorate
LLB	Bachelor of Laws
LLM	Master of Laws
LSAC	Law School Admission Council
LSAT	Law School Admission Test
ML	Master's Degree in Law
NALP	National Association for Law Placement
SALT	Society of American Law Teachers
US NEWS	*U.S. News and World Report*

APPENDIX B

List of Law Schools Referenced

IN-TEXT REFERENCE	OFFICIAL NAME
Alabama	University of Alabama School of Law
Albany	Albany Law School
American	American University Washington College of Law
Appalachian	Appalachian School of Law
Arizona State	Arizona State University College of Law
Arkansas	University of Arkansas at Little Rock William H. Bowen School of Law
Atlanta's John Marshall	Atlanta's John Marshall Law School
Ave Maria	Ave Maria School of Law
Baltimore	University of Baltimore School of Law
Barry	Barry University—Dwayne O. Andreas School of Law
Berkeley	University of California Berkeley School of Law
Boston College	Boston College Law School
Boston	Boston University School of Law
Brooklyn	Brooklyn Law School
Buffalo	SUNY Buffalo Law School
California Western	California Western School of Law
Capital	Capital University Law School
Cardozo	Benjamin N. Cardozo School of Law
Catholic (DC)	Catholic University of America's Columbus School of Law
Chapman	Chapman University School of Law
Charleston	Charleston School of Law
Charlotte	Charlotte School of Law
Chicago	University of Chicago Law School
Cleveland-Marshall	Cleveland-Marshall College of Law
Columbia	Columbia Law School
Cooley	Thomas M. Cooley Law School
Cornell	Cornell Law School
Creighton	Creighton University School of Law
CUNY	City University of New York School of Law

Dayton . . . . University of Dayton School of Law

Denver . . . . University of Denver College of Law

DePaul . . . . DePaul University College of Law

Detroit Mercy . . . . University of Detroit Mercy School of Law

Drake . . . . Drake University Law School

Drexel. . . . . Drexel University Earle Mack School of Law

Duke. . . . . Duke University School of Law

Emory. . . . . Emory University School of Law

Florida . . . . University of Florida Fredric G. Levin College of Law

Florida A&M. . . . . Florida A&M University College of Law

Florida Coastal . . . . Florida Coastal School of Law

Florida International . . . . Florida International University College of Law

Florida State. . . . . Florida State University College of Law

Fordham. Fordham University School of Law

Georgia. . . . . University of Georgia School of Law

Georgia State . . . . Georgia State University College of Law

George Mason . . . . George Mason University School of Law

Georgetown . . . . Georgetown University Law Center

George Washington (GW). . . . . . George Washington University Law School

Golden Gate. . . . . Golden Gate University School of Law

Gonzaga . . . . Gonzaga University School of Law

Hamline . . . . Hamline University School of Law

Harvard . . . . Harvard Law School

Hastings . . . . University of California Hastings College of Law

Hawaii . . . . University of Hawai'i at Mānoa
William S. Richardson School of Law

Hofstra . . . . Maurice A. Deane School of Law at Hofstra University

Illinois . . . . University of Illinois College of Law

Iowa . . . . University of Iowa College of Law

Irvine . . . . University of California Irvine School of Law

John Marshall . . . . John Marshall Law School [Chicago]

Kansas . . . . University of Kansas School of Law

La Verne. University of La Verne College of Law

Liberty . . . . Liberty University School of Law

Louisiana State . . . . Louisiana State University Law Center

Louisville . . . . Louis D. Brandeis School of Law at University of Louisville

Loyola Chicago . . . . Loyola University Chicago School of Law

Loyola Marymount. . . . . Loyola Law School Los Angeles

Maine . . . . University of Maine School of Law

Marquette. . . . . Marquette University School of Law

Massachusetts School of Law . . . Massachusetts School of Law at Andover

Miami. . . . . University of Miami School of Law

Michigan . . . . University of Michigan Law School

Michigan State. . . . . Michigan State University College of Law

Minnesota . . . . University of Minnesota Law School

Mississippi College . . . . Mississippi College School of Law

Missouri. . . . . University of Missouri School of Law

NC Central . . . . North Carolina Central University School of Law

Nebraska . . . . University of Nebraska College of Law

New England. . . . . New England Law Boston

New Hampshire . . . . University of New Hampshire School of Law

New Mexico. . . . . University of New Mexico School of Law

North Carolina . . . . University of North Carolina School of Law

Northeastern . . . . Northeastern University School of Law

Northern Illinois. . . . . Northern Illinois University College of Law

Northwestern . . . . Northwestern University Law School

Notre Dame. . . . . Notre Dame Law School

Nova Southeastern . . . . Nova Southeastern University Law Center

NYLS . . . . New York Law School

NYU (or New York University). . New York University School of Law

Ohio Northern . . . . Ohio Northern University Pettit College of Law

Ohio State . . . . Ohio State University Michael E. Moritz College of Law

Oklahoma . . . . University of Oklahoma College of Law

Oklahoma City . . . . Oklahoma City University School of Law

Oregon . . . . University of Oregon School of Law

Pace. . . . . Pace Law School

Pacific (McGeorge). . . . . University of the Pacific McGeorge School of Law

Penn . . . . University of Pennsylvania Law School

Penn State . . . . Pennsylvania State University Dickinson School of Law

Pepperdine. . . . . Pepperdine University School of Law

Phoenix . . . . Phoenix School of Law

Quinnipiac. . . . . Quinnipiac University School of Law

Regent . . . . Regent University School of Law

Roger Williams . . . . Roger Williams University School of Law

Rutgers—Camden . . . . Rutgers School of Law—Camden

Rutgers—Newark . . . . Rutgers School of Law—Newark

St. John's. . . . . St. John's University School of Law

St. Mary's . . . . St. Mary's University School of Law

St. Thomas (Minnesota). . . . . University of St. Thomas School of Law

San Francisco . . . . University of San Francisco School of Law

Santa Clara. . . . . Santa Clara University School of Law

Seattle. . . . . Seattle University School of Law

Seton Hall . . . . Seton Hall University School of Law

Southern Illinois. . . . . Southern Illinois University School of Law

South Texas . . . . South Texas College of Law

Southwestern. . . . . Southwestern Law School

Stanford . . . . Stanford Law School
Stetson . . . . Stetson University College of Law
Suffolk . . . . Suffolk University Law School
Syracuse . . . . Syracuse University College of Law
Temple . . . . Temple University James E. Beasley School of Law
Tennessee . . . . University of Tennessee College of Law
Texas Southern . . . . Texas Southern University Thurgood Marshall
                                               School of Law
Texas Wesleyan . . . . Texas Wesleyan School of Law
Texas . . . . University of Texas School of Law
Thomas Jefferson . . . . Thomas Jefferson School of Law
Toledo . . . . University of Toledo College of Law
Touro . . . . Touro College Jacob D. Fuchsberg Law Center
Tulane . . . . Tulane University Law School
Tulsa . . . . University of Tulsa College of Law
UCLA . . . . University of California Los Angeles School of Law
University of DC . . . . University of the District of Columbia
                                               David A. Clarke School of Law
University of Kentucky . . . . University of Kentucky College of Law
USC . . . . University of Southern California Gould School of Law
Utah . . . . University of Utah S. J. Quinney College of Law
Valparaiso . . . . Valparaiso University Law School
Vanderbilt . . . . Vanderbilt University Law School
Vermont . . . . Vermont Law School
Villanova . . . . Villanova University School of Law
Virginia . . . . University of Virginia School of Law
Washington and Lee . . . . Washington and Lee University School of Law
Washington University . . . . Washington University School of Law
Western New England . . . . Western New England University School of Law
Western State . . . . Western State University College of Law
West Virginia . . . . West Virginia University College of Law
Whittier . . . . Whittier Law School
Widener . . . . Widener Law (Wilmington)
Wisconsin . . . . University of Wisconsin Law School
Yale . . . . Yale Law School

NOTES

PROLOGUE

1. William L. Prosser, "Lighthouse No Good," *Journal of Legal Education* 1 (1948): 257, quote at 259.

2. See Jeffrey L. Harrison, "Post-Tenure Scholarship and Its Implications," *University of Florida Journal of Law and Public Policy* 17 (2006): 139; Michael I. Swygert and Nathaniel E. Gozansky, "Senior Law Faculty Publication Study: Comparisons of Law School Productivity," *Journal of Legal Education* 35 (1985): 373.

3. See Robert J. Tepper and Craig G. White, "Academic Early Retirement: Do Tenure Buyout Payments Warrant Unique Employment Tax Treatment?" *Oklahoma City University Law Review* 35 (2010): 169.

4. A survey of deans was conducted asking what they would do to professors who were underperforming in various different scenarios. The most common response was to withhold extra benefits rather than to impose any sanctions; revocation of tenure was a rare response. William G. Hollingsworth, "Controlling Post-Tenure Scholarship: A Brave New World Beckons?" *Journal of Legal Education* 41 (1991): 141.

5. American Bar Association, Section of Legal Education and Admissions to the Bar, *ABA Standards for Approval of Law Schools and Interpretations* (Chicago: ABA, 1996), interpretation 205-1.

CHAPTER ONE

1. United States v. American Bar Association, Civil Action No. 95-1211 (US Dist. Ct., June 27, 1995).

2. See John S. Elson, "The Governmental Maintenance of the Privileges of Legal Academia: A Case Study in Classic Rent-Seeking and a Challenge to our Democratic Ideology," *St. John's Journal of Legal Commentary* 15 (2001): 269, quote at 271.

3. American Bar Association, Section of Legal Education and Admissions to the Bar, *Standards for Approval of Law Schools and Interpretations* (Chicago: ABA, 1996), standard 404.

4. Ibid., standard 405(b).

5. United States v. American Bar Association, Competitive Impact Statement.

6. Ibid., 2.

7. "Adequate" facilities were regulated by standard 701; student-faculty ratios were governed by standard 201 (*Standards for Approval.*).

8. In 1953, the chairman of the Section on Legal Education, Homer Crotty, openly advocated this use of the accreditation process, recounting, "As one dean who appeared before us said, 'The advisor to the Section is in a far better position to speak to the president of my university than I am. He can say things to the president that I cannot, and still remain dean'" (Homer D. Crotty, "Law School Salaries—a Threat to Legal Education," *Journal of Legal Education* 6 [1953]: 166, quote at 172).

9. Steven A. Holmes, "Justice Department Forces Chances in Law School Accreditation," *New York Times*, June 28, 1995.

10. "Law Professor Salaries Outpace Inflation," *National Jurist* (February 1999), 10.

11. "A Short History of the American Law Deans Association," http://www.americanlaw deans.org/images/A_Short_History_of_the_America.pdf.

12. United States v. American Bar Association, Competitive Impact Statement.

13. Debbie Goldberg, "ABA Settles Antitrust Case over Certifying Law Schools, *Washington Post*, June 28, 1995, A02.

14. Bushnell's confidence was vindicated when the Federal Court of Appeals ruled against Massachusetts School of Law's lawsuit against the ABA for violating antitrust laws. See Massachusetts School of Law v. American Bar Association, 107 F.3d 1026 (1997). However, the court did not rule that the ABA had not engaged in anticompetitive practices; it ruled that the harmful consequences of a denial of accreditation were caused by states that decided to adopt ABA accreditation, and states are not covered by antitrust law. For a detailed argument that these practices do violate antitrust laws, see George B. Shepherd and William G. Shephard, "Scholarly Restraints? ABA Accreditation and Legal Education," *Cardozo Law Review* 19 (1998): 2019.

15. Written comments of Millard Ruud, Exhibit 12 of "United States' Response to Public Comments," in United States of America v. American Bar Association (http://www.justice.gov/atr/cases/f1000/1035.htm).

16. *Standards for Approval*, standard 405(a), interpretation 1. The germ of this provision was first set forth in a 1953 article by Homer Crotty, the Chairman of the Section on Legal Education, lamenting low salaries for law professors. Crotty recommended that "no school shall be added to the approved list hereafter unless its salary level is equal to or exceeds the national median of law school salaries" (Crotty, "Law School Salaries," 171).

17. *Standards for Approval*, standard 405(a), interpretation 2.

18. Ken Myers, "Law Profs: Poor No More, Pay is Up," *National Law Journal*, October 18, 1993, 15.

19. ABA, "Law School Tuition, 1985–2009," http://www.americanbar.org/content/dam/aba/migrated/legaled/statistics/charts/stats_5.authcheckdam.pdf.

20. Ibid.

21. The following quotations are taken from United States v. American Bar Association, Civil Action No. 85-1211, 60 FR 63766-01 (1995), "Notices."

22. Elson repeats these charges in John S. Elson, "The Governmental Maintenance of the Privileges of Legal Academia: A Case Study in Classic Rent-Seeking and a Challenge to Our Democratic Ideology," *St. John's Journal of Legal Commentary* 15 (2001): 269.

23. See United States v. American Bar Association, 2006-1 Trade Cases P 75295.

24. On the high costs that follow from this unified model, see Marina Lao, "Discrediting Accreditation? Antitrust and Legal Education," *Washington University Law Quarterly* 79 (2001): 1035.

25. Roger C. Cramton, "Demystifying Legal Scholarship," *Georgetown Law Journal* 75 (1986): 1, quote at 13n45.

26. Tom Stabile, "Are Your Professors Cheating You?" *National Jurist* (October 1999), 26.

27. A number of unaccredited schools graduate lawyers at a much lower cost. See Daniel Morrissey, "Saving Legal Education," *Journal of Legal Education* 56 (2006): 254, esp. 271–74. These schools have lower bar pass rates (though not much lower than the worst accredited schools), but this is likely a function of the caliber of students who now attend these schools, rather than of the schools themselves.

CHAPTER TWO

1. Big Think Editors, "Stanford Law's Larry Kramer on the Law School Revolution," August 2, 2010, http://bigthink.com/ideas/21630.

2. The Carrington Report, reprinted as app. A in Herbert L. Packer and Thomas Ehrlich, *New Directions in Legal Education* (New York: McGraw Hill, 1972), 139.

3. Ibid., 136–42.

4. Jerold Auerbach, "Enmity and Amity: Law Teachers and Practitioners, 1900–1922," in *Law in American History*, vol. 5 of Perspectives in American History, ed. Donald Fleming and B. Bailyn (Cambridge, NY: Cambridge University Press, published for the Charles Warren Center for Studies in American History, Harvard University, 1971), 573.

5. Harry S. Richards, "Progress in Legal Education," in *Handbook of the Association of American Law Schools and Proceedings of the . . . Annual Meeting*, vol. 15 (1915) 60, quote at 63.

6. See Alfred Z. Reed, *The Study of Legal Education* (New York: Carnegie Foundation, 1921), chap. 16. This account of events relies heavily on Reed's book, which is the definitive work on the development of legal academia.

7. See Russell N. Sullivan, "The Professional Associations and Legal Education," *Journal of Legal Education* 4 (1952): 401.

8. J. Newton Fiero, "Minutes of Section on Legal Education," *Report of the Annual Meeting of the American Bar Association* 23 (1900): 421, esp. 449–50.

9. Christopher C. Langdell, quoted in G. Edward White, "The Impact of Legal Science on Tort Law, 1880–1910," *Columbia Law Review* 78 (1978): 213, quote at 220.

10. William A. Keener, "Methods of Legal Education," *Yale Law Journal* 1 (1892): 143, quote at 144.

11. Alfred Z. Reed, *Training for the Public Profession of the Law* (New York, 1921), 290.

12. Ibid., 291.

13. Reed, *Study of Legal Education*, 11.

14. On the negative reaction to Reed's report, see Auerbach, "Enmity and Amity," 588–92.

15. "Report of the Special Committee to the Section of Legal Education and Admissions to the Bar of the American Bar Association," *Annual Report of the ABA* 44 (1921): 679, at 687–88.

16. See, regarding the overlap of members between AALS and the ABA's Section on Legal Education, Edward T. Lee, "Proceedings of the Section of Legal Education and Admissions to the Bar," *Annual Report of the ABA* 44 (1921): 656, at 667.

17. Ibid., 666.

18. Ibid., 668.

19. Charles F. Carusi, quoted in ibid. 662–65.

20. "Report of the Special Committee to the Section of Legal Education," 684.

21. Laura I. Appleman and Dan Solove, "Debate Club: Abolish the Third Year of Law School?" *Legal Affairs*, September 19, 2005, at http://www.legalaffairs.org/webexclusive/debate club_2yr0905.msp.

22. Daniel J. Morrissey, "Saving Legal Education," *Journal of Legal Education* 56 (2006): 254, quote at 269. Morrissey quotes a report showing that Latino and Black law graduates have the highest levels of debt (Ronit Dinovitzer and Bryant G. Garth, *After the JD: First Results of a National Study of Legal Careers* [Overland Park, KS: NALP Foundation of Law Career Research and Education; Chicago: American Bar Foundation, 2004], 72).

CHAPTER THREE

1. "Faculty Resolutions Opposing the Elimination of Tenure and Security of Position," SALT, at http://www.saltlaw.org/contents/view/3-2011_ABA.

2. The many resolutions and letters are posted at American Bar Association, "Standards Review," under the heading "Comments on the Comprehensive Review," http://www.americanbar .org/groups/legal_education/committees/standards_review.html.

3. American Bar Association Section of Legal Education and Admissions to the Bar Standards Review Committee, "Security of Position, Academic Freedom and Attract and Retain Faculty," interpretation 405-1 (emphasis added).

4. See William Deresiewicz, "Faulty Towers: The Crisis in Higher Education," *Nation*, May 4, 2011.

5. Letter of Michael A. Olivas, AALS President to Hewlett H. Askew, Consultant on Legal Education, March 28, 2011, http://www.aals.org/advocacy/Olivas.pdf; emphasis added.

6. Ibid., 4.

7. Ibid., 9.

8. ABA, "Security of Position, Academic Freedom and Attract and Retain Faculty," standard 405 (c); emphasis added.

9. Ibid., interpretation 405-6.

10. For background, see Peter A. Joy and Robert R. Kuehn, "The Evolution of ABA Standards for Clinical Faculty," *Tennessee Law Review* 75 (2008): 183.

11. Robert Kuehn, CLEA Letter to Dean Polden, October 25, 2010, 2, http://www.american bar.org/content/dam/aba/migrated/2011_build/legal_education/committees/standards_ review_documents/comment_security_of_position_clea_october_2010.authcheckdam.pdf.

12. Ibid., 7.

13. Karen Sloan, "ABA Panel Considering Boosting Job Protections for Nontraditional Faculty," *National Law Journal*, July 11, 2011, http://www.law.com/jsp/nlj/PubArticleNLJ.jsp? id=1202500221368&ABA_panel_considering_boosting_job_protections_for_nontraditional_ faculty&slreturn=1&hbxlogin=1.

14. See Robert R. Kuehn and Peter A. Joy, "Lawyering in the Academy: The Intersection of Academic Freedom and Professional Responsibility," *Journal of Legal Education* 59 (2009): 97.

15. Michael A. Olivas, "2012 AALS Annual Meeting Theme: Academic Freedom and Academic Duty," https://memberaccess.aals.org/eweb//DynamicPage.aspx?webcode=2012Aa mwhy&Reg_evt_key=d4a06b1f-994e-4ffe-b5ea-548f57898594&RegPath=EventRegFees.

16. Karen Sloan, "Membership Changes May Take Law School Accreditation Panel in New Direction," *National Law Journal*, October 19, 2011, http://www.law.com/jsp/nlj/PubArticleNLJ .jsp?id=1202519462357.

17. H. Resse Hansen, "Presidents' Messages: Letter to ABA Standards Review," June 1, 2010, http://www.aals.org/services_newsletter_presAug10.php.

CHAPTER FOUR

1. Association of American Law Schools, *Proceedings of the Annual Meeting* (Washington, DC: AALS, 1910), 6 (statement made by Frank Irvine); see also John C. Townes, "Organization and Operation of a Law School," *Proceedings of the Annual Meeting* (Washington, DC: AALS, 1910), 53–76, esp. 61.

2. Henry M. Bates et al., "Report of the Committee on the Status of the Law Teacher," *Handbook of the Association of American Law School and Proceedings* (Washington, DC: AALS, 1920), 166–77, esp. 173–75.

3. Herman Oliphant and the AALS Executive Committee, "Symposium on Legal Research in Law Schools, *Handbook of the Association of American Law School and Proceedings* (Washington, DC: AALS, 1923), 99–117, esp. 99, 117.

4. Paul W. Brosman et al., "Special Committee on Faculty and Students," *Handbook of the Association of American Law School and Proceedings* (Washington, DC: AALS, 1937), 347–50, esp. 347.

5. Herman Oliphant and Percy B. Bordwell, "Legal Research in Law Schools," *American Law School Review* 5 (1923): 293, 298.

6. John Kirkland Clark, "A Contrast: The Full-Time Approved Law School Compared with the Unapproved Evening School," *American Bar Association Journal* 20 (1934): 505, esp. 505 (150 out of 200-plus schools responded).

7. Benjamin Franklin Boyer, "The Smaller Law Schools: Factors Affecting Their Methods and Objectives," *Oregon Law Review* 20 (1941): 281 (99 out of 108 schools responded).

8. AALS, Special Committee on Law School Administration and University Relations, *Anatomy of Modern Legal Education* (St. Paul, MN: West, 1961), 310 (91 percent response rate).

9. Ibid.

10. Ibid., 302n3.

11. See Boyer, "The Smaller Law Schools," 289.

12. See Ralph W. Aigler, "AALS Presidential Address: Legal Education and the Association of American Law Schools," *Texas Law Review* 5 (1927): 111, esp. 114.

13. AALS, *Anatomy of Modern Legal Education*, 303.

14. Ibid., 357–60.

15. Ibid., 352.

16. American Bar Association, Section of Legal Education and Admissions to the Bar, *Standards for Approval of Law Schools and Interpretations* (Chicago: ABA, 1996), standards 404, 405.

17. Ibid., standard 405, interpretation (5).

18. Elliot E. Cheatham, "The Law Schools of Tennessee, 1949," *Tennessee Law Review* 21 (1949): 283, quote at 290.

19. Mary Kay Kane, "Some Thoughts on Scholarship for Beginning Teachers," *Journal Legal Education* 37 (1987): 14, quote at 16; emphasis added.

20. See, e.g. Roscoe Pound, "Some Comments on Law Teachers and Law Teaching," *Journal of Legal Education* 3 (1951): 519.

21. Deborah Jones Merritt, "Research and Teaching on Law Faculties: An Empirical Exploration," *Chicago-Kent Law Review* (1998): 765, 803–4. Surveys were sent to all 832 professors hired during this period; there were 477 responses.

22. Ibid., 803–7.

23. Ibid., 807.

24. Gordon Smith, "Law Professor Teaching Loads," *The Conglomerate* (blog), April 12, 2005, http://www.theconglomerate.org/2005/04/law_professor_t.html.

25. Theodore P. Seto, "Understanding the *U.S. News* Law School Rankings," *Southern Methodist University Law Review* 60 (2007): 493, quote at 546.

26. See Bridget Crawford, "Optional Reduced Teaching Load for Increased Faculty Productivity: One School's Experiment," *The Faculty Lounge* (blog), January 20, 2011, http://www.thefacultylounge.org/2011/01/opting-in-to-a-reduced-teaching-load-for-increased-faculty-productivity.html (describing the program at Pace Law school; a commenter indicated that the same option exists at Wisconsin).

27. Seto, "Understanding the *U.S. News* Law School Rankings," 186.

28. Edward Rubin, "Should Law Schools Support Faculty Research?" *Journal of Contemporary Legal Issues* 17 (2008): 139, esp. 142.

29. William F. Massy and Robert Zemsky, "Faculty Discretionary Time: Departments and the 'Academic Ratchet,'" *Journal of Higher Education* 65 (1994): 1.

30. See Gordon C. Winston, "The Decline in Undergraduate Teaching," *Change* 26 (1994): 8; Mary Frank Fox, "Research, Teaching, and Publication Productivity: Mutuality versus Competition in Academia," *Sociology of Education* 65 (1992): 293.

31. Winston, "The Decline in Undergraduate Teaching."

32. Derek Bok, "Reclaiming the Public Trust," *Change* 24 (1992): 12.

33. See Massy and Zemsky, "Faculty Discretionary Time"; Winston, "The Decline in Undergraduate Teaching"

34. Chris Klein, "Feeding Frenzy for Prof Stars," *National Law Journal*, September 8, 1997, A1. New York University Law School dean John Sexton is widely seen as a major impetus in this competition. For an article describing Sexton's aggressive recruiting and its impact on other institutions, see Joshua L. Kwan, "Faculty Tempted by Perks at Other Schools," *Harvard Crimson*, June 4, 1998.

35. See Benjamin Franklin Boyer, "The Smaller Law Schools: Factors Affecting Their Methods and Objectives," *Oregon Law Review* 20 (1941): 281; Homer D. Crotty, "Law School Salaries—a Threat to Legal Education," *Journal of Legal Education* 6 (1953): 166, esp. 170.

36. See Clayton P. Gillette, "Law Faculty as Free Agents," *Journal of Contemporary Legal Issues* 17 (2008): 213.

37. One striking statistical indication of this is that full professors of law comprise a much higher percentage of the faculty on average than any other university department. Full law professors are 56.5 percent of the law faculty; the next highest percentages are 43.8 percent in engineering and 43.3 percent in agriculture; among the low categories are 20.4 percent in communications technology and 19.3 percent in health sciences. See College and University Professional Association for Human Resources, *National Faculty Salary Survey by Discipline and Rank in Four-Year Colleges and Universities* (Washington, DC: College and University Professional Association for Human Resources, 2008), 16.

38. See Merritt, "Research and Teaching on Law Faculties," 812–15.

39. Ibid., 809.

40. Ibid.

41. I know one law professor who publishes poetry and almost no legal scholarship, and about ten others who are active, and in several instances prolific, novelists.

42. College and University Professional Association for Human Resources, *Community College Faculty Salary Survey* (College and University Professional Association for Human Resources, 2008), 12. The survey indicates that this load has remained constant for years.

43. Even in 1920 law professors earned more than other professors. See Bates et al., "Report of the Committee on the Status of the Law Teacher," 174.

44. Crotty, "Law School Salaries," 166.

45. Ibid., 167.

46. AALS, *Anatomy of Modern Legal Education*, 256 (twenty-five schools did not answer this inquiry).

47. Ibid., 257.

48. Ibid., 308.

49. *Annual Report of the Consultant on Legal Education to the American Bar Association, 1990–1991*, 11.

50. See Bates et al., "Report of the Committee on the Status of the Law Teacher," 175.

51. Crotty, "Law School Salaries," 168.

52. See William D. Ferguson, "Economics of Law Teaching," *Journal of Legal Education* 19 (1967): 439.

53. "It's Not over Yet: The Annual Report on the Economic Status of the Profession, AAUP," *Academe*, 96, no. 2 (March–April 2011): 14, at http://www.aaup.org/AAUP/pubsres/academe/2011/MA/zreport/zreport.htm.

54. See *National Faculty Salary Survey*, 14–15.

55. For charts comparing professor pay to judges and lawyers, see Alvin L. Goldman, "More on the Economics of Law Teaching," *Journal of Legal Education* 19 (1966): 451.

56. See Richard Redding, "Where Did You Go to Law School? Gatekeeping for the Professoriate and Its Implications for Legal Education," *Journal of Legal Education* 53 (2003): 594. A substantial majority of law professors attended elite institutions and were successful students.

57. See Gillette, "Law School Faculty as Free Agents," 217 (noting that salary increases for law professors picked up in the early to mid-1980s).

58. Ken Myers, "Law Profs Poor No More, Pay Is Up," *National Law Journal*, October 18, 1993, 15.

59. See Jack Crittenden, "Why Is Tuition Up? Look at All the Profs," *National Jurist*, March 2010, 40.

60. US Supreme Court, *2008 Year-End Report on the Federal Judiciary* (Washington, DC: Supreme Court, 2009).

61. Form 990, New York Law School, Guidestar Nonprofit Reports, http://www2.guidestar .org/.

62. "Public Employees in the Twin Cities and Minnesota: Law School," (for salary year 2007), StarTribune.com, http://ww3.startribune.com/dynamic/salaries/employees.php?dpt_code=Law&ent_code=UMTC.

63. See Larry Sager's resignation letter to law faculty, December 8, 2011, posted at Miriam Rozen, "Sager Out Earlier Than Expected as UT Law Dean," *Texas Lawyer*, December 8, 2011, http://www.law.com/jsp/tx/PubArticleTX.jsp?id=1202534984121&slreturn=1.

64. See open records request for information relating to Larry Sagers, reprinted at Reeve Hamilton and Morgan Smith, "UT President Asks Law School Dean to Resign Immediately,"

Texas Tribune, December 8, 2011, http://www.texastribune.org/texas-education/university-of-texas-system/dean-ut-law-signs-letter-resignation/.

65. See Ralph K. M. Haurwitz, "Chancellor Orders Review of UT Law School Foundation Funds," *American Statesman*, December 9, 2011, http://www.statesman.com/news/local/chancellor-orders-review-of-ut-law-school-foundation-2023572.html.

66. See Hamilton and Smith, "UT President Asks Law School Dean to Resign Immediately"; and Rozen, "Sager Out Earlier Than Expected as UT Law Dean."

67. See "Survey Information," *Salt Equalizer*, June 2010, http://www.saltlaw.org/userfiles/SALT%20salary%20survey%202010%20--%20final.pdf. The numbers provided understate actual compensation because law professors supplement their nine months salaries with summer research grants.

68. This figure is taken from Crittenden, "Why Is Tuition Up?"

69. The list, which was released in Massachusetts School of Law's suit against the ABA, was posted online by *National Jurist* ("Professor Salaries"; article on file with author). The top forty paying schools in 1994–95 that supplied salaries for the 2008 survey were Pace, Rutgers—Newark, Rutgers—Camden, Michigan, Harvard, Minnesota, and Touro. As these numbers suggest, in addition to elite law schools, schools located around New York City also tend to pay more. The top ten schools by average professor salaries in 1994–95 in order were: Fordham, Harvard, NYU, Columbia, and Hofstra.

70. See Josh Barbanel, "Recruiting with Real Estate," *New York Times*, January 20, 2008.

71. See open records request for information relating to Sagers (reprinted in Hamilton and Smith).

72. Pace Law School, 2010 Summer Research Grant Policy, at http://www.pace.edu/school-of-law/summer-research-stipend-and-assistant-policy.

73. See open records request for information relating to Sagers (reprinted in Hamilton and Smith).

74. Bureau of Labor Statistics, US Department of Labor, Occupational Outlook Handbook, 2010-11 Edition, Lawyers, http://www.bls.gov/oco/ocos053.htm.

75. "In Pictures: The Best Law Schools for Getting Rich," *Forbes*, http://www.forbes.com/2011/03/07/rich-law-school-grads-salaries-leadership-careers-education_slide.html.

76. The Southeastern Association of Law Schools (SEALS) is known to select attractive family venues for its annual gathering, holding conferences in 2010 at Breakers, Palm Beach, Florida, in 2011 at Hilton Head Marriott, South Carolina, in 2012 at the Ritz Carlton-Amelia Island, Florida, in 2013 at Breakers, Palm Beach, Florida. The annual AALS meeting regularly rotates through San Francisco, New Orleans, and Washington, DC. The 2012 meeting of the Law and Society Association is in Hawai'i.

77. Theodore Seto, "The Law School Pricing Problem," *TaxProf* (blog, ed. Paul Caron), July 5, 2011, http://taxprof.typepad.com/taxprof_blog/2011/07/seto-the.html#more.

78. See Gillette, "Law School Faculty as Free Agents," supra 220.

79. While the standards did not actually specify limits on the percentage of nontenured faculty, in practice in the inspection process they have been interpreted to not allow a significant proportion of the faculty to be in non-tenure-track positions.

80. See Letter of Michael A. Olivas, AALS President to Hewlett H. Askew, Consultant on Legal Education, March 28, 2011, http://www.aals.org/advocacy/Olivas.pdf.

81. Rubin, "Should Law Schools Support Faculty Research?" 141

82. Ibid., 141–45.

83. See Nancy B. Rapoport, "Eating Our Cake and Having it, Too: Why Real Change Is So Difficult in Law School," *Indiana Law Journal* 81 (2006): 359.

CHAPTER FIVE

1. Herman Oliphant, "Legal Research in Law Schools," *American Law School Review* 5 (1923): 293, quote at 298.

2. Comments of Albert J. Harno, in "Meeting of the Association of American Law Schools—1937," *American Law School Review* 8 (1937): 1106, quote at 1110.

3. Thomas F. Bergin, "The Law Teacher: A Man Divided Against Himself," *Virginia Law Review* 54 (2008): 637, esp. 638–39.

4. Owen M. Fiss, "Correspondence on the Critical Legal Studies Movement" (Owen M. Fiss to Paul Carrington), *Journal of Legal Education* 35 (1985): 24, quote at 24.

5. H. Reese Hansen, "Presidents' Messages: Letter to ABA Standards Review," http://www .aals.org/services_newsletter_presAug10.php/.

6. Alfred Z. Reed, *Training for the Public Profession of the Law* (New York, 1921); William M. Sullivan et al., *Educating Lawyers: Preparation for the Profession of Law* (New York: Wiley & Sons, 2007).

7. Reed, *Training for the Public Profession of the Law*, 257.

8. Robert MacCrate, ed., *Legal Education and Professional Development: An Educational Continuum* (Chicago: American Bar Association, Section of Legal Education and Admissions to the Bar, 1992), 4.

9. Adam Liptak, "Keep the Briefs Brief, Literary Justices Advise," *New York Times*, May 21, 2011.

10. Another in the series of derisive observations by judges is Adam Liptak, "When Rending Decisions, Judges Are Finding Law Reviews Irrelevant," *New York Times*, March 19, 2007. Harry T. Edwards, "The Growing Disjunction between Legal Education and the Legal Profession," *Michigan Law Review* 91 (1992): 34.

11. MacCrate, ed., *Legal Education and Professional Development*, 4.

12. Tom Smith, "A Voice, Crying in the Wilderness, and Then Just Crying," *The Right Coast* (blog), July 13, 2005, http://therightcoast.blogspot.com/2005/07/voice-crying-in-wilderness-and-then.html.

13. See David Hricik and Victoria Salzmann, "Why There Should be Fewer Articles Like This One: Law Professors Should Write More for Legal Decision-Makers and Less for Themselves," *Suffolk University Law Review* 38 (2004): 761.

14. Pierre Schlag, "Spam Jurisprudence, Air Law, and the Rank Anxiety of Nothing Happening (A Report on the State of the Art)," *Georgetown Law Journal* 97 (2009): 803, quote at 804.

15. See Karen Sloan, "Legal Scholarship Carries a High Price Tag," *National Law Journal*, April 20, 2011, at http://www.law.com/jsp/nlj/PubArticleNLJ.jsp?id=1202490888822 &slreturn=1&hbxlogin=1.

16. Judge Richard Posner's response to Schlag takes a more measured view, agreeing that a good deal of legal scholarship has limited instrumental value, but also contending that some areas are producing useful and insightful information. Richard A. Posner, "The State of Legal Scholarship Today: A Comment on Schlag," *Georgetown Law Journal* 97 (2009): 845.

17. On the exaggerated lack of interest of judges in law reviews, see Erwin Chermerinsky,

"Why Write?" *Michigan Law Review* 107 (2009): 881, quote at 884. Regarding court citations of law review articles, see David L. Schwartz and Lee Petherbridge, "The Use of Legal Scholarship by the Federal Courts of Appeals: An Empirical Study," *Cornell Law Review* 96 (2011): 101. Two limitations of the study should be kept in mind. They did not distinguish what percentage of articles were student pieces, and they did not consider the total pool of cases, leaving out unreported cases, which are a substantial bulk of the cases today (and proportionally less so in previous decades).

18. See Chemerinsky, "Why Write?" 886–87.

19. For a positive assessment of the value of this work, see Edward Rubin, "Should Law Schools Support Faculty Research?" *Journal of Contemporary Legal Issues* 17 (2008): 139, esp. 150–53.

20. See Mark Bauerlein, "The Research Bust," *Chronicle of Higher Education*, December 4, 2011, http://chronicle.com/article/The-Research-Bust/129930/.

21. Roughly one-third of the professors hired in the past decade at top ten schools hold PhDs. See Brent E. Newton, "Preaching What They Don't Practice: Why Law Faculties' Preoccupation with Impractical Scholarship and Devaluation of Practical Competencies Obstruct Reform in the Legal Academy," *South Carolina Law Review* 62 (2010): 105, esp. 131.

22. Joni Hersch and W. Kip Viscusi, "Law and Economics as a Pillar of Legal Education," Vanderbilt Law and Economics Research Paper No. 11-35, http://papers.ssrn.com/so13/papers.cfm?abstract_id=1907760.

23. See Paul L. Caron, ed., "Fellowships for Aspiring Law Professors (2011 Edition)," *Tax Prof* (blog), February 16, 2011, http://taxprof.typepad.com/taxprof_blog/2011/02/fellowships-for-aspiring-law-professors-2010–11-edition.html.

24. Newton, "Preaching What They Don't Practice," 129–30.

25. Richard E. Redding, "'Where Did You Go to Law School?' Gatekeeping for the Professoriate and Its Implications for Legal Education," *Journal of Legal Education* 53 (2003): 594, quote at 612.

26. See Robert J. Borthwick and Jordan R. Schau, "Gatekeepers of the Profession: An Empirical Profile of the Nation's Law Professors," *University of Michigan Journal of Law Reform* 25 (1991): 191.

27. John G. Hervey, "There's Still Room for Improvement," *Journal of Legal Education* 9 (1956): 149, quotes at 152, 151.

28. See Robert R. Kuehn and Peter A. Joy, "Lawyering in the Academy: The Intersection of Academic Freedom and Professional Responsibility," *Journal of Legal Education* 59 (2009): 97, esp. 98.

29. A harsh critique is Newton, "Preaching What They Don't Practice."

30. Roy Stuckey, *Best Practices for Legal Education* (New York: Clinical Legal Education Association, 2007), 16.

31. Ibid., 26.

32. Erwin Chemerinsky, "Why Not Clinical Education?" *Clinical Law Review* 16 (2009): 35.

33. See Susan P. Liemer, "The Quest for Scholarship: The Legal Writing Professor's Paradox," *Oregon Law Review* 80 (2001): 1007; Melissa H. Weresh, "Form and Substance: Standards for Promotion and Retention of Legal Writing Faculty on Clinical Tenure Track," *Golden Gate University Law Review* 37 (2007): 281.

34. See James Lindgren, "Fifty Ways to Promote Scholarship," *Journal of Legal Education* 49 (1999): 126.

35. Ibid., 134.

36. See Richard Buckingham, Diane D'Angelo, and Susan Vaughn, "Law School Rankings, Faculty Scholarship, and Associate Deans for Faculty Research," Suffolk University Law School Research Paper No. 07-23, http://ssrn.com/abstract=965032.

CHAPTER SIX

1. Paras D. Bhayani, "Kagan Stresses Growth," *Harvard Crimson*, September 21, 2006, http://www.thecrimson.com/article/2006/9/21/kagan-stresses-growth-harvard-law-school/. Isaac Arnsdorf, "At Harvard Law, New Competition for Yale," *Yale Daily News*, September 30, 2008, http://www.yaledailynews.com/news/2008/sep/30/at-harvard-law-new-competition-for-Yale.

2. Dean Heidi Hurd, "Appendix 36: 2006 Strategic Plan, University of Illinois College of Law," in Jones Day and Duff & Phelps, "Investigative Report, University of Illinois College of Law Class Profile Reporting," app.1, available at http://www.uillinois.edu/our/news/2011/Law/App.1–75.pdf, 8–10.

3. Brian Karlovitz, "Cornell Law School Announces Major Expansion in Permanent Faculty," *Cornell Daily Sun*, September 5, 2008, http://cornellsun.com/node/31300.

4. Cornell University, "Law School Restructuring and Planning Final Report Submitted to Provost Kent Fuchs By the Law School Planning Task Force: Executive Summary," November 3, 2009, http://www.cornell.edu/reimagining/docs/law-summary-1109.pdf.

5. Michael Froomkin, "Yes, We're Hiring," *Discourse.net*, January 30, 2010, http://www.discourse.net/2009/01/yes_were_hiring.html.

6. Elie Mystal, "Tuition Is Going up at Notre Dame Law (but Not as High as Some Other Places," *Above the Law*, November 9, 2010, http://abovethelaw.com/2010/11/tuition-is-going-up-at-notre-dame.

7. Association of American Law Schools, "2008–2009 AALS Statistical Report on Law Faculty," http://www.aals.org/statistics/2009dlt/gender.html.

8. American Bar Association, "Student Faculty Ratio: Semester System Schools, 1978–2009," http://www.americanbar.org/content/dam/aba/migrated/legaled/statistics/charts/stats_3.authcheckdam.pdf.

9. Cornell University," Law School Restructuring," 2.

10. These numbers are taken from "Law Schools Report," *National Law Journal*, February 28, 2011, http://www.law.com/jsp/nlj/PubArticleNLJ.jsp?id=1202483173162&slreturn=1&hbxlogin=1.

11. See Law School Admission Council and American Bar Association, *Official Guide to ABA-Approved Law Schools* ([Newtown, PA]: ABA-LSAC, 2012), 58, 59.

12. It may seem odd that a masters degree in law follows a juris doctor degree, but the explanation is historical. The basic law degree was initially an LLB, bachelor of law, but this was changed in the course of the twentieth century as an undergraduate degree became a prerequisite for entry to law school. The LLM degree, which followed LLB, retained the same name after the LLB was replaced by the JD.

13. These numbers are provided in the National Association of Law Placement, *NALP Directory of Law Schools* (Washington, DC: NALP, 2011).

14. Karen Sloan, "'Cash Cow' or Valuable Credential," *National Law Journal*, September 20, 2010.

15. The same thing also occurred during a fall in applications in the early 1980s, but I have limited the focus to the last twenty years for convenience. See David H. Vernon and Bruce I.

Zimmer, "The Demand for Legal Education: 1984 and the Future," *Journal of Legal Education* 35 (1985): 261.

16. The data on applicants and enrollment are from American Bar Association and Law School Admission Council, *Official Guide to ABA Approved Law Schools* ([Newtown, PA]: ABA-LSAC, 2011), app. A, 870.

17. See David Segal, "Law School Economics: Ka Ching!" *New York Times*, July 16, 2011, http://www.nytimes.com/2011/07/17/business/law-school-economics-job-market-weakens-tuition-rises.html?pagewanted=all.

18. These numbers are provided in the 1998 Edition, *Official Guide to ABA Approved Law Schools* ([Newtown, PA]: ABA-LSAC, 1997), 450; and 2012 Edition, *Official Guide to ABA Approved Law Schools* ([Newtown, PA]: ABA-LSAC, 2011), 866. To be consistent with information used earlier in the text, I rely upon the AALS numbers for full-time professors, which is higher than the ABA numbers for reasons that are unclear.

19. See Richard Schmalbeck, "The Durability of Law School Reputation," *Journal of Legal Education* 48 (1998): 568.

20. 2002 Edition, *Official Guide to ABA Approved Law Schools* ([Newtown, PA]: ABA-LSAC, 2001); 302; 2012 Edition, *Official Guide to ABA Approved Law Schools*, 344.

CHAPTER SEVEN

1. David Segal, "Is Law School a Losing Game?" *New York Times*, January 8, 2011.

2. See U.S. News and World Report, *America's Best Graduate Schools* (Washington, DC: U.S. News and World Report, 2011), 28–29. Owing to a lag in the data, these figures were for nine months after graduation of the 2008 class.

3. For the 2012 ranking, *US News* altered both of the rules to limit gaming. Now the employment rate is based solely on graduates who have jobs, divided by the total number in that class. Robert Morse and Sam Flanigan, "Law School Rankings Methodology," *US News and World Report*, March 14, 2011, http://www.usnews.com/education/best-graduate-schools/articles/2011/03/14/law-school-rankings-methodology-2012.

4. "Law School Rankings," *US News and World Report*, March 10, 1997. The pre-1997 rankings consistently show this distribution pattern; in the early years it was common to have twenty or more schools report placement rates below 70.

5. See "Law School Rankings," *US News and World Report*, April 11, 2005. Only seven of the top 136 schools reported employment rates below 90 percent.

6. For a summary of conditions in the legal market at the time, see Center For Career Strategy, Northwestern Law, "Market Trends," http://www.law.northwestern.edu/career/markettrends/.

7. See NALP, *Jobs and JDs: Employment and Salaries of New Law Graduates, Class of 2009* (Washington, DC: NALP, 2011); "Class of 2010 Graduates Saddled with Falling Average Starting Salaries as Private Practice Jobs Erode," NALP press release, July 7, 2011, http://www.nalp.org/classof2010_salpressrel. For the 2007 percentage, see NALP, *Jobs and JDs: Employment and Salaries of New Law Graduates, Class of 2007* (Washington, DC: NALP, 2008). The actual percentage of graduates who landed jobs is lower than these figures because they exclude people whose employment status is unknown.

8. NALP, *Jobs and JDs: Employment and Salaries of New Law Graduates, Class of 2007* (Washington, DC: NALP, 2009), 26.

9. "Class of 2010 Graduates Saddled."

10. NALP, *Jobs and JDs . . . Class of 2009*, 13.

11. "Class of 2010 Graduates Saddled."

12. Job openings are a combination of new legal positions generated by growth in the legal market and replacement positions created by departures (retirement, death, leaving the practice). The Bureau of Labor Statistics uses a 2 percent rate of departure for law. Between 2008 and 2010, when lawyers were laid off, there was, rather than growth, a contraction of 18,886 jobs, so the openings in those years came from replacement. Joshua Wright, "Data Spotlight: New Lawyers Glutting the Market," Economic Modeling Specialists, Inc., http://www.economicmodeling.com/2011/06/22/new-lawyers-glutting-the-market-in-all-but-3-states/. Ongoing lawyer oversupply, using EMS statistical analysis, was highlighted in Catherine Rampell, "The Lawyer Surplus, State by State," New York Times, June 27, 2011. http://economix.blogs.nytimes.com/2011/06/27/the-lawyer-surplus-state-by-state/. Detailed data on lawyer overproduction are maintained by Matt Leichter, "Law Graduate Overproduction," Law School Tuition Bubble, http://lawschooltuitionbubble.wordpress.com/original-research-updated/law-graduate-overproduction/.

13. Defending the practice, Northwestern law dean David Van Zandt remarked, "I don't think it's unethical if you're giving value to your students" (Alex Wellen, "The $8.87 Million Maneuver," New York Times, July 31, 2005). What this response fails to address is the ethics of misinforming prospective students about genuine job placement results.

14. See letter of Dean John Gotanda, to Villanova Law School Alumni, reprinted at Elie Mystal, "Villanova Law 'Knowingly Reported' Inaccurate Information to the ABA," http://abovethelaw.com/2011/02/villanova-law-school-knowingly-reported-inaccurate-information-to-the-aba/. Regarding the discrepancy in LSAT scores, see Karen Sloan, "Law Schools' Credibility at Issue," National Law Journal, September 19, 2011, http://www.law.com/jsp/nlj/PubArticleNLJ.jsp?id=1202514708103&slreturn=1.

15. Letter of Senator Barbara Boxer to Stephen Zack, reprinted at "Boxer Calls on American Bar Association to Ensure Accurate and Transparent Data Reporting by Law Schools," press release, March 31, 2011, http://boxer.senate.gov/en/press/releases/033111b.cfm.

16. David Segal, "Law Students Lose the Grant Game as Schools Win," New York Times, April 30, 2011.

17. For simplicity, this illustration ignores the fact that a number of nonscholarship students will land above the cutoff GPA as well. When this is factored in, a greater number of scholarship students will fail to make the necessary grade. An excellent explanation of the allocation of scholarships can be found in Jerome Organ, "How Scholarship Programs Impact Students and the Culture of Law School," Journal of Legal Education 61 (2011): 173.

18. Among the 137 schools Organ (ibid.) found policies on, 107 imposed competitive qualifying cutoffs and twenty-seven did not. The majority of top-fifty schools did not. He was unable to find information on every school, but their practices are likely similar.

19. Sarah Randag, "Grads Sue New York Law School and Cooley Law, Saying They Inflated Job and Salary Stats," ABA Journal, August 10, 2011, http://www.abajournal.com/news/article/grads_sue_new_york_law_school_and_cooley_law_saying_they_inflated_job_and_s/.

20. See Joe Palazzalo, "A Dozen Law Schools Hit with Lawsuits over Job Data," Wall Street Journal, February 2, 2012, http://blogs.wsj.com/law/2012/02/01/a-dozen-law-schools-hit-with-lawsuits-over-jobs-data/.

21. Letter from Senator Charles E. Grassley to Stephen N. Zack, July 11, 2011, http://grassley.senate.gov/about/upload/2011-07-11-Grassley-to-ABA.pdf.

22. Karen Sloan, "University of Illinois Investigating Whether College of Law Fudged Figures," National Law Journal, September 12, 2011, http://www.law.com/jsp/nlj/PubArticleNLJ

.jsp?id=1202514109913&University_of_Illinois_investigating_whether_College_of_Law_fudged_figures&slreturn=1&hbxlogin=1.

23. "College of Law Profile Data Inquiry Identifies Discrepancies in Three Additional Years," University of Illinois, press release, September 28, 2011, http://www.uillinois.edu/our/news/2011/Sept28.Law.cfm.

24. Wellen, "The $8.78 Million Maneuver."

25. Sloan, "Law Schools' Credibility at Issue."

26. Ibid.

27. For details on this arrangement, see Brian Tamanaha, "Why Law Schools Need External Scrutiny," *Balknization* (blog), October 7, 2011, http://balkin.blogspot.com/2011/10/why-law-schools-need-external-scrutiny.html.

28. See "Coburn, Boxer Call for Department of Education to Examine Questions of Law School Transparency," US Senator Barbara Boxer, press release, October 14, 2011, http://boxer.senate.gov/en/press/releases/101411.cfm.

29. Karen Sloan, "ABA Gives Ground on Law Schools Graduate Jobs Reporting Data," *National Law Journal*, December 5, 2011, http://www.law.com/jsp/nlj/PubArticleNLJ.jsp?id=1202534457162&ABA_gives_ground_on_law_schools_graduate_jobs_data_reporting&slreturn=1.

30. The problem of misleading employment numbers by law schools was well known long before the *Times* series began, but the ABA did nothing. See Brian Z. Tamanaha, "Wake Up, Fellow Law Professors, to the Casualties of Our Enterprise," *Balkinization* (blog), June 13, 2010, http://balkin.blogspot.com/2010/06/wake-up-fellow-law-professors-to.html.

31. John F. O'Brien, "With Much to Celebrate, Room to Improve in Legal Education," *National Law Journal*, November 1, 2011, http://legaltimes.typepad.com/lawschoolreview/2011/11/with-much-to-celebrate-room-to-improve-in-legal-education.html#comments. O'Brien made these comments in his capacity as the chair of the ABA Section on Legal Education and Admissions to the Bar.

32. Karen Sloan, "Unruly 'Scam Bloggers' Are Changing Legal Education, A Researcher Says," *National Law Journal*, June 29, 2011, http://www.law.com/jsp/nlj/PubArticleNLJ.jsp?id=1202498922216&Unruly_scam_bloggers_are_changing_legal_education_researcher_argues&slreturn=1&hbxlogin=1.

33. Fernando Rodriguez, *Third Tier Reality* (blog), http://thirdtierreality.blogspot.com/.

34. Paul Campos, *Inside the Law School Scam* (blog), http://insidethelawschoolscam.blogspot.com/.

35. Segal, "Is Law School a Losing Game?" 6–7.

36. A superb study of the impact of *US News*, based on over two hundred interviews of law faculty and students, is Michael Sauder and Wendy Espeland, *Fear of Falling: The Effects of U.S. News and World Report Rankings on U.S. Law Schools*, LSAC Research Report Series, 2007 (Newtown, PA: Law School Admission Council, 2009) (available at http://www.lsac.org/LsacResources/Research/GR/GR-07-02.pdf).

37. US Government Accountability Office, *Higher Education: Issues Related to Law School Cost and Access* (Washington, DC: GAO, 2010).

38. Michael Sauder and Ryon Lancaster, "Do Rankings Matter? The Effects of *US News and World Report* Rankings on the Admissions Process of Law Schools," *Law and Society Review* 40 (2006): 105.

39. The placement success of lower-ranked schools in large legal markets, like New York and Washington, DC, exceeds their relative rank because of their proximity to employers.

See William D. Henderson and Andrew P. Morriss, "Student Quality as Measured by LSAT Scores: Migration Patterns in the *U.S. News* Rankings Era," *Indiana Law Journal* 81 (2006): 163, esp. 188–90.

40. See "Law Schools Report: Our Annual Survey of the Law Schools That *NLJ* 250 Law Firms Relied on the Most to Fill Their First-Year Associate Classes," *National Law Journal*, February 28, 2011, http://www.law.com/jsp/nlj/PubArticleNLJ.jsp?id=1202483173162.

41. See Brian Leiter, "Top Producers of New Law Teachers, 2003–2007," and "Where Current Faculty Went to Law School," both in *Brian Leiter's Law School Rankings* (blog), http://www.leiterrankings.com/jobs/2008job_teaching.shtml and http://www.leiterrankings.com/jobs/2009job_teaching.shtml, respectively.

42. Sauder and Lancaster, "Do Rankings Matter?" 127–28.

43. Ibid., 129.

44. For an excellent breakdown of the ranking, see Brian Leiter, "The *US News* Law School Rankings: A Guide for the Perplexed," *Brian Leiter's Law School Rankings* (blog), May 2003, http://www.leiterrankings.com/usnews/guide.shtml.

45. Gary J. Greener, "Law School Ranking: A Look Behind the Numbers," *NALP Bulletin*, July 2005. The response rate for the 2012 ranking was only 14 percent. See Robert Morse and Sam Flanigan, "Law School Rankings Methodology," *US News and World Report*, March 14, 2011, http://www.usnews.com/education/best-graduate-schools/articles/2011/03/14/law-school-rankings-methodology-2012.

46. The drop might not even be related to Emory, but to shifts at other schools that had repercussions for Emory. *US News* assigns every school a relative place on a scale from 0 to 100, so shifts in one position, even some distance away, shuffles others. This effect is explained in Theodore P. Seto, "Understanding the U.S. New Law School Rankings," *Southern Methodist University Law Review* 60 (2007): 493, esp. 508–21.

47. This is roughly the difference between schools ranked in the upper twenties and lower twenties.

48. One study found that LSAT score explains 90 percent of the overall difference in ranks. See Stephen P. Klein and Laura Hamilton, "The Validity of the *U.S. News and World Report* Ranking of ABA Law Schools," February 18, 1998, http://www.aals.org/reports/validity.html.

49. See Sauder and Lancaster, "Do Rankings Matter?" 116.

50. Brian Leiter, "More on the *US News* Rankings Echo Chamber," *Leiter Reports: A Philosophy Blog*, April 1, 2005, http://leiterreports.typepad.com/blog/2005/04/more_on_the_us_.html.

51. "LSAT Scores: Disturbing Discrepancies," *U.S. News & World Report*, March 20, 1995, 82.

52. Dale Whitman, "Doing the Right Thing," *AALS Newsletter*, April 2002.

53. Wellen, "The $8.78 Million Maneuver." Although Lexis-Nexis and Westlaw charge law schools sharply reduced rates for access to online legal research, Illinois reported an "expenditure" of $8.78 million for these services, an estimate of its fair market value rather than the $75,000–$100,000 that Illinois actually paid.

54. Robert Morse and Sam Flanigan "What Happened with Brooklyn Law School?" Morse Code—Inside the College Rankings, May 18, 2009, http://www.usnews.com/education/best-graduate-schools/articles/2011/03/14/law-school-rankings-methodology-2012.

55. See Bob Morse and Sam Flanigan, "Law School Rankings Methodology," US News, http://www.usnews.com/education/best-graduate-schools/articles/2011/03/14/law-school-rankings-methodology-2012. I have broken the factors down using the categories provided by Sauder and Espeland, *Fear of Falling*, 5.

56. Dean Heidi Hurd, "Appendix 36: 2006 Strategic Plan, University of Illinois College of Law," in Jones Day and Duff & Phelps, "Investigative Report, University of Illinois College of Law Class Profile Reporting," app. 1, available at http://www.uillinois.edu/our/news/2011/Law/App.1–75.pdf.

57. "Strategic Plan," 8–10.

58. Ibid., 12.

59. Ibid.

60. Ibid.

61. See Jones Day and Duff & Phelps, "Investigative Report," 36.

62. On estimating of raw scores, see ibid., 34–39, and esp. App. 22; for strategies to surpass nearby competitors, ibid., 34–39.

63. Ibid., 38.

64. Ibid., 39.

65. Segal, "Is Law School a Losing Game?"

CHAPTER EIGHT

1. See William D. Henderson and Andrew P. Morriss, "Student Quality as Measured by LSAT Scores: Migration Patterns in the *U.S. News* Rankings Era," *Indiana Law Journal* 81 (2006).

2. See Paul F. Kirgis, "Race, Rankings, and the Part-Time Free Pass," *Journal of Legal Education* 54 (2004): 395.

3. Amir Efrati, "Law School Rankings Reviewed to Deter 'Gaming,'" *Wall Street Journal*, August 26, 2008, http://online.wsj.com/article/SB121971712700771731.html?mod=googlenews_wsj.

4. See Bill Henderson and Jeff Lipshaw, "The Empirics and Ethics of USNWR Gaming," *Legal Profession Blog*, August 26, 2008, http://lawprofessors.typepad.com/legal_profession/2008/08/posted-by-jeff.html.

5. See American Bar Association and Law School Admission Council, *Official Guide to ABA-Approved Law Schools* ([Newtown, PA]: ABA-LSAC, 2008),. Brooklyn's statistics are on 138–39; GW's are on 306–7. The current statistics are taken from the 2012 ed. of the same publication. Both schools now grant fewer admits to part-time students and their yield is much lower than previously (which suggests less generous scholarship offers).

6. Blacks score about ten points lower on the LSAT on average than whites do. See "News and Views: The Widening Racial Scoring Gap on Standardized Tests for Admission to Law School," *Journal of Blacks in Higher Education* (2006), http://www.jbhe.com/news_views/51_graduate_admissions_test.html. See also Michael Sauder and Wendy Espeland, "Rankings and Diversity," *Southern California Review of Law and Social Justice* 18 (2009): 587; Lenard M. Baynes, "The LSAT, *US News and World Report*, and Minority Admissions," symposium issue, *St. John's Law Review* 80 (2006): 1; John Nussbaumer, "Misuse of the Law School Admissions Test, Racial Discrimination, and the De Facto Quota System for Restricting African American Access to the Legal System," *St. John's Law Review* 80 (2006): 167.

7. Law school administrators confirm that this homogenization in admissions around LSAT/GPA profiles has occurred. Michael Sauder and Wendy Espeland, *Fear of Falling: The Effects of U.S. News and World Report Rankings on U.S. Law Schools*, LSAC Research Report Series, 2007 (Newtown, PA: Law School Admission Council, 2009) (available at http://www.lsac.org/LsacResources/Research/GR/GR-07-02.pdf).

8. See Jeffrey L. Rensberger, "Tragedy of the Student Commons: Law Student Transfers and Legal Education," *Journal of Legal Education* 60 (2011): 616, esp. 618.

9. See Leslie A. Gordon, "Transfers Bolster Elite Schools," *ABA Journal*, December 1, 2008, http://www.abajournal.com/magazine/article/transfers_bolster_elite_schools/.

10. Rensberger, "Tragedy of the Student Commons," 625.

11. Ibid., at 634.

12. The latest figures were provided in Memorandum to Senator Charles Grassley, Section of Legal Education and Admissions to the Bar, attachment 4, July 20, 2011, http://online.wsj .com/public/resources/documents/ABAmemo.pdf. See also "Internal Grants and Scholarships: Total Dollar Amount Awarded. 1991–2008," Section of Legal Education and Admissions to the Bar, http://www.americanbar.org/content/dam/aba/migrated/legaled/statistics/charts/stats_4 .authcheckdam.pdf.

13. See David Segal, "Law Students Lose the Grant Game as Law Schools Win," *New York Times*, April 30, 2011.

14. ABA-LSAC, *Official Guide to ABA-Approved Law Schools* ([Newtown, PA]: ABA-LSAC, 2011), 133, 277.

15. Founded in 2003, Law School Numbers is a "publicly accessible database of user-supplied law school applicant information with the intent of helping other applicants judge their chances in the upcoming law school admissions cycle" (http://www.lawschoolnumbers .com/).

16. Memorandum to Senator Charles Grassley, attachment 4.

17. *Annual Report of the Consultant on Legal Education to the American Bar Association, 2000–2001*, 18.

18. These numbers are from the ABA. See Memorandum to Senator Charles Grassley, attachment 4.

19. See Martha Daughtrey et al., *Report of the Special Committee on the U.S. News and World Report Rankings, Section on Legal Education and Admissions to the Bar* (Chicago: ABA, 2010), http://ms-jd.org/files/f.usnewsfinal-report.pdf.

20. Sauder and Espeland, *Fear of Falling*, 11–12.

21. A study of tuition discounting in universities found that, as tuition rose, a greater portion of tuition discounts went to the wealthy—who performed better on merit measures like SAT—so needy students were actually doing worse in financial terms even with increases in aid. Jerry Sheehan Davis, *Unintended Consequences of Tuition Discounting*, New Agenda Series, vol. 5, no. 1 (Indianapolis: Lumina Foundation for Education, 2003).

22. Sauder and Espeland, *Fear of Falling*, 12.

23. Linda F. Wightman, "Beyond FYA: Analysis of the Utility of SAT Scores and UPGA for Predicting Academic Success in Law School," Law School Admission Council Report 99-05 (2000), http://www.lsac.org/LSACResources/Research/RR/RR-99–05.asp.

24. These LSAT numbers are taken from the law school rankings in US News and World Reports, *Best Graduate Schools*, 2012 ed. (Washington, DC: US News and World Reports, 2011).

25. For explanations, see Financial Aid Staff, *Stanford Law School Financial Aid Handbook, 2011–12* (Stanford, CA: Stanford Law School, 2011), http://www.law.stanford.edu/program/ tuition/jd/doc/2011/Handbook2011–12.pdf; *Yale Law School Financial Aid Policies, Programs, and Procedures, 2011–2012* (New Haven, CT: Yale Law School, 2011), http://www.law.yale.edu/ documents/pdf/Financial_Aid/FinAidHandbook.pdf.

26. I have rounded off the figures to the nearest thousand. For the average indebtedness of the class of 2010, see "Whose Graduates Have the Most Debt?" *US News*, http://grad-schools .usnews.rankingsandreviews.com/best-graduate-schools/top-law-schools/grad-debt-rankings.

27. "List of Law Schools Attended by Supreme Court Justices," Wikipedia, http:// en.wikipedia.org/wiki/List_of_law_schools_attended_by_United_States_Supreme_Court_ Justices#Harvard_Law_School.

28. See "Where Current Law Faculty Went to Law School," *Brian Leiter's Law School Rankings*, http://www.leiterrankings.com/jobs/2009job_teaching.shtml. According to Leiter, as of 2008, Harvard had 993 and Yale had 712 of their graduates in law professor positions, with Columbia the next closest school in number at 308.

29. Richard H. Sander, "Class in American Legal Education," *Denver University Law Review* 88 (2011): 631, esp. 637.

30. Ibid., 639.

31. See "Whose Graduates Have the Most Debt?"

32. David Leonhardt, "How Elite Colleges Still Aren't Diverse," *New York Times*, March 29, 2011, http://economix.blogs.nytimes.com/2011/03/29/how-elite-colleges-still-arent-diverse/.

33. See Don Peck, "Can the Middle Class Be Saved?" *Atlantic Magazine*, September 2011, http://www.theatlantic.com/magazine/archive/2011/09/can-the-middle-class-be-saved/8600/.

CHAPTER NINE

1. John B. Kramer, "Will Legal Education Remain Affordable, by Whom, and How?" *Duke Law Journal* 1987 (1987): 240, esp. 240.

2. *Annual Report of the Consultant on Legal Education to the American Bar Association, 1988–1989*, 4.

3. Kramer, "Will Legal Education Remain Affordable?" 240.

4. Ibid., 241.

5. See Matt Leichter, "The Law School Debt Bubble," *Law School Tuition Bubble* (blog), October 17, 2011, http://lawschooltuitionbubble.wordpress.com/2011/10/17/the-law-school-debt-bubble-53-billion-in-new-law-school-debt-by-2020/.

6. See, e.g., Daniel J. Morrissey, "Saving Legal Education," *Journal Legal Education* 56 (2006): 254, esp. 262n34.

7. Ann Davis, "Graduate Debt Burden Grows of All Professionals, Law Grads Have Complied the Worst Loan Default Record," *National Law Journal*, May 22, 1995.

8. *National Jurist* Editors, "Lawopoly: Pass Go, Borrow Money, Pay Tuition," *National Jurist*, February 1999, 14.

9. Unless otherwise indicated, tuition numbers are taken from the American Bar Association, "Law School Tuition, 1985–2009," http://www.americanbar.org/content/dam/aba/ migrated/legaled/statistics/charts/stats_5.authcheckdam.pdf.

10. The first two figures are from Yale University Office of Institutional Research, "University Tuition Rates, 1976–1999," November 15, 2000, table L-1, http://oir.yale.edu/node/ 214/attachment.

11. See Matt Leichter, "Private Law School Tuition Projections," *Law School Tuition Bubble* (blog), February 1, 2011, http://lawschooltuitionbubble.wordpress.com/original-research-updated/tuition-projections/.

12. Kramer, "Will Legal Education Remain Affordable?" 262.

13. According to the *National Jurist*, average debt of law students upon graduation 1999 was $55,000. *National Jurists* Editors, "Lawopoly," 14. It is not clear whether this amount included undergraduate debt.

14. American Bar Association, "Average Amount Borrowed for Law School, 2001–2009," http://www.americanbar.org/content/dam/aba/migrated/legaled/statistics/charts/stats_20.authcheckdam.pdf.

15. American Student Assistance, "Student Loan Debt Statistics," Graduate Students, http://www.asa.org/policy/resources/stats/default.aspx#GraduateStudents.

16. See William D. Henderson and Rachel M. Zahorsky, "The Law School Bubble: How Long Will it Last if Law Grads Can't Pay Bills?" ABA Journal, January 1, 2012, http://www.abajournal.com/magazine/article/the_law_school_bubble_how_long_will_it_last_if_law_grads_cant_pay_bills/ This figure is a weight-adjusted calculation based on the total debt numbers of each law school provided in "Whose Graduates Have the Most Debt?" US News Education: Grad Schools, http://grad-schools.usnews.rankingsandreviews.com/best-graduate-schools/top-law-schools/grad-debt-rankings.

17. See Project on Student Debt, "Average Student Debt for Class of 2010 Tops $25,000 in Tough Job Market," press release, http://projectonstudentdebt.org/files/pub/Student_Debt_and_the_Class_of_2010_NR.pdf. See also Peter Taylor et al., "Is College Worth It? College President, Public Assess Value, Quality and Mission of Higher Education," Pew Research Center: Social and Demographic Trends, May 16, 2011, 44, http://www.pewsocialtrends.org/2011/05/15/is-college-worth-it/.

18. See "Whose Graduates Have the Most Debt."

19. "The New JD: Just Debt, Job Disabled, Justifiably Depressed?" *Connecticut Law Tribune*, August 24, 2011, reprinted at http://www.law.com/jsp/tx/PubArticleTX.jsp?id=1202512320980; see *Law School Survey of Student Engagement: Law School Report, 2009* (Bloomington, IN: Indiana University, Bloomington, Center for Postsecondary Research; Association of American Law Schools; Carnegie Foundation for the Advancement of Teaching, 2009); 29 percent expect to graduate with debt above $120,000.

20. Cecelia Cappuzi Simon, "R.O.I.," *New York Times*, July 22, 2011, http://www.nytimes.com/2011/07/24/education/edlife/edl-24roi-t.html?pagewanted=1&_r=1&src=rechp.

21. Sandy Baum and Saul Schwartz, *How Much Debt Is Too Much? Defining Benchmarks for Manageable Student Debt*, (New York: The College Board, 2006), 12, http://professionals.collegeboard.com/profdownload/pdf/06-0869.DebtPpr060420.pdf (emphasis added).

22. See FinAid, http://www.finaid.org/.

23. NALP, "Class of 2010 Graduates Saddled with Falling Average Starting Salaries as Private Practice Jobs Erode," press release, July 7, 2011, http://www.nalp.org/classof2010_salpressrel.

24. The following numbers are from "Law Schools Report: The *National Law Journal's* Annual Survey of the Law Schools That NLJ 250 Law Firms Relied on the Most to Fill Their First-Year Associate Classes," *National Law Journal*, February 28, 2011, http://www.law.com/jsp/nlj/PubArticlePrinterFriendlyNLJ.jsp?id=1202483173162.

25. "The NALP Salary Curve Morphs with the Class of 2010," August 2011, http://www.nalp.org/salarycurve_classof2010.

26. This is an approximation that assumed that most people who get this salary report it. The 10 percent estimate is calculated based upon the numbers provided in the highest earning categories in the NALP data. See NALP, "Class of 2010 National Summary Report," http://www.nalp.org/uploads/NationalSummaryChartforSchools2010.pdf.

27. See Bill Henderson, "The End of an Era: The Bi-Modal Distribution for the Class of 2008," *Legal Profession Blog*, June 29, 2009, http://lawprofessors.typepad.com/legal_profession/2009/06/the-end-of-an-era-the-bi-modal-distribution-for-the-class-of-2008.html.

28. See Bernard A. Burk and David McGowan, "Big but Brittle: Economic Perspectives on the Future of the Law Firm in the New Economy," *Columbia Business Law Review* 1 (2011): 1, esp. 20–21.

29. "Lawyers," in *Occupational Outlook Handbook, 2010–2011* (Washington, DC: US Bureau of Labor Statistics, 2011), http://www.bls.gov/oco/ocos053.htm#earnings.

30. See NALP, "Class of 2010 National Summary Report," http://www.nalp.org/uploads/NationalSummaryChartforSchools2010.pdf.

31. See "Employment Market for Law School Graduates Wavers," *NALP Bulletin*, July 2010, http://www.nalp.org/july10trendsgradempl. The percentage employed as lawyers is obtained by multiplying the number of employed in jobs requiring a JD with the number of graduates employed. I thank Law School Transparency for the data.

32. This estimated departure rate covers 2008–18, which is different from the 2000–2010 period, but the method of calculation would produce similar numbers. See "Replacement Needs, 2008–2018," *Employment Projections* (Washington, DC: US Bureau of Labor Statistics, 2010), table 1.10, http://www.bls.gov/emp/ep_table_110.htm; "Estimating Occupational Replacement Needs," *Employment Projections* (Washington, DC: US Bureau of Labor Statistics, 2011), http://www.bls.gov/emp/ep_replacements.htm.

33. For a more detailed analysis making the same point, see Matt Leichter, "Dear Prospective Law Students, Do Not 'Reasonably Rely' On Cooley's 'Report One,'" *AmLaw Daily*, November 3, 2011, http://amlawdaily.typepad.com/amlawdaily/2011/11/dear-prospective-law-students-do-not-reasonably-rely-on-cooleys-report-one.html.

34. There are no comprehensive current data on how many graduates take the bar. An exhaustive national study that tracked the entering class of 1991 found that 93 percent of graduates from ABA-approved law schools took the bar. Linda F. Wightman, *National Longitudinal Bar Passage Study* (Newtown, PA: Law School Admission Council, 1998), 6, http://www.unc.edu/edp/pdf/NLBPS.pdf. My assertion assumes that this percentage has not fallen over time.

35. See Curtis M. Caton and Frank M. Coffin, *Lifting the Burden: Law Student Debt as a Barrier to Public Service* (Chicago: ABA, 2003), 38–39 (results of a survey shows reluctance of both students and advisers).

36. See Higher Education Act of 1965, 20 U.S.C. § 1098. For an informative article on federal loan legislation and loan forgiveness programs, see Philip G. Schrag and Charles W. Pruett, "Coordinating Loan Repayment Assistance Programs with New Federal Legislation," *Journal of Legal Education* 60 (2011): 583.

37. See Federal Student Aid, *Income Based Repayment Questions and Answers* (Washington, DC: US Department of Education, 2010), 3–4.

38. I am treating gross income as equivalent to adjusted gross income because for most earners they will be the same.

39. This is 15 percent of ($63,000—$27,465) spread over twelve months.

40. As before, I am assuming a consolidated loan rate of 7.25. This assumption is based on consolidating the rates of the two main types of federal loans, Stafford Loans (6.8 percent) and GradPlus Loans (7.9 percent). I am rounding numbers to the nearest hundred.

41. Two-thirds of law students surveyed in 2009 expected to graduate with debt $60,000 or higher (*Law School Survey of Student Engagement*).

42. This is an adjusted mean provided by NALP. Salaries at small firms are underreported compared to larger firms, so the average overstates the actual mean, which NALP corrects with an adjusted mean.

43. If Bob was single, he would still qualify. One-hundred-fifty percent of the poverty line for a single person is $16,335. The IBR payment would be $1,046.

44. See American Student Assistance, "Student Loan Debt Statistics," http://www.asa.org/policy/resources/stats/default.aspx (88.6 percent of students borrow to finance law school). Henderson and Zahorsky estimate that 85 percent of the class of 2010 graduated with debt, Henderson and Zahorsky, "The Law School Bubble," see alsoCaton and Coffin, *Lifting the Burden*, 17, showing the steady rise in the past two decades of the percentage of students in debt.

45. This estimate is calculated by adding together the graduates in the four highest earning categories of listed by NALP. See NALP, "Class of 2010 National Summary Report," http://www.nalp.org/uploads/NationalSummaryChartforSchools2010.pdf.

46. Philip G. Schrag, "Federal Student Loan Repayment Assistance for Public Interest Lawyers and Other Employees of Governments and Nonprofit Organizations," *Hofstra Law Review* 36 (2007): 27, 41.

47. See Philip G. Schrag, "The Federal Income-Contingent Repayment Option for Law Student Loans," *Hofstra Law Review* 29 (2001): 733, 830–31.

48. A perverse incentive is hidden within the details of IBR. Any student who anticipates going into and remaining in IBR has no economic incentive not to borrow (and spend) freely while in law school because the maximum monthly payment is tied to income, not level of debt, and the full balance will be discharged after twenty-five years. See Matt Leichter, "A Hypothetical Class of 2014 Law Student's Journey into Debt," *Law School Tuition Bubble* (blog), September 5, 2011, http://lawschooltuitionbubble.wordpress.com/2011/09/05/a-hypothetical-class-of-2014-law-student%E2%80%99s-journey-into-debt/.

49. See Heather Wells Jarvis, *Financing the Future: Responses to the Rising Debt of Law Students*, 2nd ed. (Washington, DC: Equal Justice Works 2006).

50. Higher Education Act of 1965, 20 U.S.C. §§1078-3, 1087, 1098. An excellent analysis of the act is Schrag, "Federal Student Loan Repayment Assistance."

51. NALP, "Thomas Jefferson School of Law: Class of 2010 Summary Report," June 2011, http://www.tjsl.edu/sites/default/files/files/NALP-Employment-Report-Salary-Survey-Class-2010%282%29.pdf.

52. See NALP, *Jobs and JDs . . . Class of 2009*, 81–84.

53. The ABA provided loan default rates on nineteen stand-alone law schools: all but one had a default rate below 2.2. The exception was Atlanta's John Marshall, with a 2008 rate of 7.1. See Memorandum to Senator Charles Grassley, from Section of Legal Education and Admissions to the Bar, American Bar Association, attachment 5, July 20, 2011, reprinted at http://online.wsj.com/public/resources/documents/ABAmemo.pdf.

54. For a detailed exploration of the economic implications of IBR for debtors and the government, see Matt Leichter, "A Hypothetical Class of 2014 Law Student's Journey into Debt," *Law School Tuition Bubble* (blog), September 5, 2011, http://lawschooltuitionbubble.wordpress.com/2011/09/05/a-hypothetical-class-of-2014-law-student%E2%80%99s-journey-into-debt/.

55. Matt Leichter, "2010 Law Grad Debt at $3.6 Billion," *Law School Tuition Bubble* (blog), October 11, 2011, http://lawschooltuitionbubble.wordpress.com/2011/10/11/2010-law-school-grad-debt-at-3-6-billion/#comment-1011. Leichter made this calculation by multiplying the

number of graduates from each law school by average debts levels and the percentage of the class in debt.

56. Aaron N. Taylor, "Why Law School Is Still Worth It," *National Jurist*, October 11, 2011, http://www.nationaljurist.com/content/why-law-school-still-worth-it. (Taylor is a professor at Saint Louis University Law School.)

CHAPTER TEN

1. For an excellent discussion of the implications of this jump, see Bill Henderson, "The End of an Era: The Bi-Modal Distribution for the Class of 2008," *Legal Profession Blog*, June 29, 2009, http://lawprofessors.typepad.com/legal_profession/2009/06/the-end-of-an-era-the-bi-modal-distribution-for-the-class-of-2008.html.

2. On salary increases, see Law School Admission Council and American Bar Association, *Official Guide to ABA-Approved Law Schools* ([Newtown, PA]: ABA-LSAC, 2012), 871.

3. The dean of Baltimore Law School, Philip Closius, resigned in mid-2011 on the grounds that the university was taking 45 percent of the law schools tuition. The university president disputed this account, saying that 42 percent was taken and all but 13 percent of this amount was to cover expenses incurred by the law school. Childs Walker, "University of Baltimore President Responds to Ousted Dean," *Baltimore Sun*, August 1, 2011, http://www.baltimoresun.com/news/maryland/bs-md-law-dean-response-20110801,0,1206152.story.

4. See *Annual Report of the Consultant on Legal Education to the American Bar Association, 1990–1991*, 11 (emphasis added).

5. Daniel Indiviglio, "Chart of the Day: Student Loans Have Grown by 511% since 1999," *Atlantic Monthly*, August 16, 2011, http://www.theatlantic.com/business/archive/2011/08/chart-of-the-day-student-loans-have-grown-511-since-1999/243821/. See also Andrew Hacker and Claudia Dreyfuss, "The Debt Crisis at American Colleges," *Atlantic Monthly*, August 17, 2011, http://www.theatlantic.com/business/archive/2011/08/the-debt-crisis-at-american-colleges/243777/.

6. The dean of George Washington Law School lists the same factors in his explanation for high tuition; see Paul Berman, "Thinking about Law School Tuition," *Conversations with the Dean of the George Washington University Law School* (blog), August 30, 2011, http://20thandh.org/2011/08/30/thinking-about-law-school-tuition/.

7. Henry E. Riggs, "The Price of Perception," April 13, 2011, http://www.nytimes.com/2011/04/17/education/edlife/edl-17notebook-t.html?_r=1&scp=1&sq=Henry%20riggs&st=cse.

8. See Riggs, "The Price of Perception."

9. Danny Jacobs, "Closius on Debt, the Future of Law Schools," *Daily Record*, November 21, 2010, http://thedailyrecord.com/ontherecord/category/maryland-lawyer/.

CHAPTER ELEVEN

1. A recent poll of students currently applying for law school or considering applying found that 37 percent had wanted to be a lawyer since childhood; 32 percent were in high school when they decided to apply. Executive summary of study done by Veritas Prep, "Inside the Mind of Law School Applicants," summarized at Karen Sloan, "The Bloom Is Coming off the Rose for Prospective Law Students," *National Law Journal*, October 26, 2011, http://www.law.com/jsp/nlj/PubArticleNLJ.jsp?id=1202520270239&The_bloom_is_coming_off_the_rose_for_prospective_law_students&slreturn=1.

2. Paul Berman, "Thinking about Law School Tuition," *Conversations with the Dean of the George Washington University Law School* (blog), August 30, 2011, http://20thandh .org/2011/08/30/thinking-about-law-school-tuition/.

3. Jennifer Cheeseman Day and Eric C. Newburger, *The Big Payoff: Educational Attainment and Synthetic Estimates of Work-Life Earnings*, Current Population Reports (Washington, DC: US Census Bureau, July 2002), http://www.census.gov/prod/2002pubs/p23–210.pdf .

4. Peter Taylor et al., "Is College Worth It? College President, Public Assess Value, Quality and Mission of Higher Education," Pew Research Center: Social and Demographic Trends, May 16, 2011, 91; available at http://www.pewsocialtrends.org/2011/05/15/is-college-worth-it/.

5. Ibid., 109.

6. Anthony P. Carnevale, Stephen J. Rose, and Ban Cheah, *The College Payoff: Education, Occupations, Lifetime Earnings* (Washington, DC: Georgetown University, Center on Education and the Workforce, 2010).

7. See ibid., 17, 19.

8. Taylor et al., "Is College Worth It?" 84.

9. Carnevale et al., *The College Payoff*, 22.

10. Ibid., 10.

11. Dean Berman is not alone among deans in using an unrealistically long projected career. Richard Matasar also cited a forty- to fifty-year career. Richard A. Matasar, "Law School Costs, Educational Outcomes, and a Reformer's Agenda," *New York Law School* (blog), http:// www.nyls.edu/news_and_events/matasars_response_to_nytimes.

12. Ronit Dinovitzer et al., *After the JD II: Second Results from a National Study of Legal Careers* (Chicago: American Bar Foundation; Dallas: NALP Foundation for Law Career Research and Education, 2009), 15.

13. On projected job openings, see "Employment by Occupation, 2008–2018," *Employment Projections* (Washington, DC: US Bureau of Labor Statistics, 2010), table 1.2, http://www.bls .gov/emp/ep_table_102.pdf .

14. Carnevale et al., *The College Payoff*, 6.

15. Taylor et al., "Is College Worth It?" 98.

16. See Herwig Schlunk, "Mamas Don't Let Your Babies Grow Up to Be . . . Lawyers," Vanderbilt Law and Economics Working Paper No. 09-29, October 30, 2009, 2, http://ssrn .com/abstract=1497044.

17. Taylor et al., "Is College Worth It?" 92, 94.

18. An excellent example of how this might be done in economic terms is Schlunk, "Mamas Don't Let your Babies Grow Up to Be . . . Lawyers." Another excellent example is Jim Chen, "A Degree of Practical Wisdom: the Ratio of Educational Debt to Income as a Basic Measure of Law School Graduates' Economic Viability," *William Mitchell Law Review* 38 (forthcoming 2012), http://papers.ssrn.com/sol3/papers.cfm?abstract_id=1967266.

19. On average earnings peaking after ten years, see Carnevale et al., *The College Payoff*, 5.

20. John P. Heinz, Robert L. Nelson, Rebecca L. Sandefur, and Edward O. Laumann, *Urban Lawyers: The New Social Structure of the Bar* (Chicago: Chicago University Press, 2005).

21. Ibid., 291, 315–20.

22 See Dinovitzer et al., *After the JD II*, 44.

23. Ibid., 42.

24. Ibid.

25. The income cutoff for IBR eligibility for a person with $100,000 debt is $110,000.

26. Dinovitzer et al., *After the JD II*, 54–60.

27. Ibid., 25.

28. See Tali Sharot, *The Optimism Bias: A Tour of the Irrationally Positive Brain* (New York: Random House, 2011).

CHAPTER TWELVE

1. See Ronit Dinovitzer et al., *After the JD II: Second Results from a National Study of Legal Careers* (Chicago: American Bar Foundation; Dallas: NALP Foundation for Law Career Research and Education, 2009), 43.

2. David Segal, "Law School Economics: Ka-Ching!" *New York Times*, July 16, 2011, http://www.nytimes.com/2011/07/17/business/law-school-economics-job-market-weakens-tuition-rises.html?_r=1&pagewanted=all.

3. Interview with Richard Matasar by Karen Sloan, "'Poster Child' Shares Frustration about Pace of Law School Reform," *National Law Journal*, July 26, 2011, http://www.law.com/jsp/nlj/PubArticleNLJ.jsp?id=1202508336129&slreturn=1.

4. Kurt Badenhausen, "Law School Graduates Do Not Make $160,000," *Forbes*, March 23, 2011, http://www.forbes.com/sites/kurtbadenhausen/2011/03/23/law-school-graduates-do-not-make-160000/.

5. Elie Mystal, "UCLA's Job Placement Numbers Strain Credulity, but Did You Read the Fine Print," *Above the Law* (blog), June 28, 2011, http://abovethelaw.com/2011/06/ucla-laws-job-placement-numbers-strain-credulity-but-did-you-read-the-fine-print/#more-79245 (emphasis in original).

6. "Class of 2010 Employment Statistics," George Mason University School of Law, March 2011, http://www.law.gmu.edu/assets/files/career/employment_stats_class_of_2010_updated_march_2011.pdf.

7. Law School Transparency, a nonprofit organization started by two law students, posts an index that rates each school on its job reporting data, showing that most schools continue to provide inadequate information to prospective students. Kyle McEntee and Patrick J. Lynch, "Winter 2012 Transparency Index Report," January 2012, http://www.lawschooltransparency.com/documents/Winter2012/Winter_2012_Index_Report.pdf.

8. ABA, House of Delegates, Committee on Drafting, *Amendments to Proposed Model Rules of Professional Conduct with Synopsis* ([Chicago]: ABA, 1983), rule 7.1: "Communication concerning a Lawyer's Services."

9. Ibid., comment 2.

10. To determine net pay numbers by subtracting city, state, and federal taxes and social security and Medicare, see the online calculator at the website Paycheck City, http://www.paycheckcity.com/covaliant/netpayHRatesCalculator.asp.

11. Joseph Alexiou, "Hey, College Kiddies! Welcome to the Island of the $2,417 Studio," *New York Observer*, http://www.observer.com/2010/real-estate/hey-college-kiddies-welcome-island-2417-studio.

12. See "Average Rental Prices in New York City," *nakedapartments blog*, http://www.nakedapartments.com/blog/average-rental-prices-in-nyc/.

13. NALP, *Jobs and JDs: Employment and Salaries of New Law Graduates, Class of 2009* (Washington, DC: NALP, 2010), 81, 83.

14. A sense of a student's discount price at a given school can be obtained using his or her LSAT/GPA profile at the website Law School Numbers, http://www.lawschoolnumbers.com/.

CHAPTER THIRTEEN

1. During the decline in the early eighties, like later declines, law schools reduced enrollment relatively little despite a significant drop in the number of applicants. Consequently, student qualifications fell. See David H. Vernon and Bruce I. Zimmer, "The Demand for Legal Education: 1984 and the Future," *Journal Legal Education* 35 (1985): 261.

2. The Google trend lines for "LSAT" and "LSAC," which counts the number of searches for these terms, presumably reflecting interest from prospective students, show a steady decline since 2004. See http://www.google.com/trends?q=lsat&ctab=0&geo=all&date=all& sort=0.

3. All of the numbers in the following discussion are derived from "LSAC Volume Summary" (2002–11), http://www.lsac.org/LSACResources/Data/lsac-volume-summary.asp; and "Legal Education Statistics from ABA-Approved Law Schools" (1984–2010), http://www .americanbar.org/groups/legal_education/resources/statistics.html. There are slight differences between these two sources because LSAC rounds numbers and the ABA does not. I have also rounded numbers.

4. See Laura A. Marcus, Andrea Thornton Sweeney, and Lynda M. Reese, *The Performance of Repeat Test Takers on the Law School Admissions Test: 2003–2004 through 2009–2010 Testing Years*, LSAT Technical Report 11-01 (Newton, PA: Law School Admission Council, 2011, http://www.lsac.org/lsacresources/Research/TR/TR-11-01.pdf).

5. Sources for figures on test takers and law school applicants are Law School Admission Council and American Bar Association, *Official Guide to ABA-Approved Law Schools* ([Newtown, PA]: ABA-LSAC, 2011); Law School Admission Council, LSAT Technical Report Series, 11-01 and 01-03, Jennifer R. Duffy, Susan P. Dalessandro, Lisa Anthony Stilwell, and Kimberly A. Swygert, "The Performance of Repeat Test Takers on the Law School Admission Test, 1994–95 through 2000–01 Testing Years," October 2001, http://www.lsac.org/lsacresources/ Research/TR/TR-01-03.pdf.

6. The percentage for 2010–11 is an estimate because the final numbers are not yet available.

7. Matt Leichter, "Private Law School Tuition Projections," *Law School Tuition Bubble* (blog), http://lawschooltuitionbubble.wordpress.com/original-research-updated/tuition-projections/.

8. Executive summary of study done by Veritas Prep, "Inside the Mind of Law School Applicants," summarized at Karen Sloan, "The Bloom Is Coming off the Rose for Prospective Law Students," *National Law Journal*, October 26, 2011, http://www.law.com/jsp/nlj/Pub ArticleNLJ.jsp?id=1202520270239&The_bloom_is_coming_off_the_rose_for_prospective_ law_students&slreturn=1.

9. See "LSATs Administered," LSAC Resources, http://www.lsac.org/lsacresources/Data/ lsats-administered.asp.

10. See U.S. News and World Report, *America's Best Graduate Schools* (Washington, DC: US News and World Report, 2011).

11. Katherine Mangan, "Law Schools on the Defensive over Job-Placement Data," *Chronicle of Higher Education*, October 21, 2011, A16, http://www.leclairryan.com/files/Uploads/ Documents/Law%20Schools%200n%20the%20Defensive%20over%20Job-Placement%20 Data%20-%20Chronicle%20of%20Higher%20Education%20-%20R.%20Smith%20 Quoted%20-%2010.16.11.pdf.

12. Three nonelite schools have announced reductions in class size, Albany and Touro by

ten students, and Creighton University School of Law by fifteen. See Joel Stashenko, "Two Deans Say They Will Trim Entering Classes, "*New York Law Journal*, March 4, 2011; Leslie Reed, "Too Many Lawyers. Too Few Jobs," *World Herald*, June 20, 2011.

13. The information about Illinois is taken from Jones Day, Duff & Phelps, "Investigative Report: University of Illinois College of Law Class Profile Reporting," November 7, 2011, 39, 4, http://www.uillinois.edu/our/news/2011/Law/Nov7.UofI.FinalReport.pdf.

14. Mangan, "Law Schools on the Defensive over Job-Placement Data."

15. Jones Day and Duff & Phelps, "Investigative Report," 77–80.

16. See Paul Caron, "July 2011 California Bar Exam Results," *Tax Prof Blog*, http://taxprof .typepad.com/taxprof_blog/2012/01/july-2011.html.

CHAPTER FOURTEEN

1. See "Law Firms: A Less Gilded Future," *Economist*, May 5, 2011, http://www.economist .com/node/18651114.

2. Leigh Jones, "Vanishing Act, Year II," *National Law Journal*, November 8, 2010, http:// www.law.com/jsp/nlj/PubArticleNLJ.jsp?id=1202474471365.

3. See "Entry-Level Recruiting Volumes Plunge, Some Start Dates Deferred," NALP press release, March 2, 2010, http://www.nalp.org/2009perspectivesonfallrecruiting. For an overview of the job reductions, see Bernard A. Burk and David McGowan, "Big but Brittle: Economic Perspectives on the Future of the Law Firm in the New Economy," *Columbia Business Law Review* 1 (2011): 1, esp. 27–36.

4. See NALP, "Class of 2010 Graduate Faced Worst Job Market since Mid-1990s: Longstanding Employment Patterns Interrupted," http://www.nalp.org/uploads/Classof2010 SelectedFindings.pdf.

5. See Claire Zillman, "Law Firm Leaders Survey 2010: The New Normal," *American Lawyer*, December 1, 2010, http://www.law.com/jsp/tal/PubArticleTAL.jsp?id=1202475032294& slreturn=1.

6. Theodore Seto, "Is the Sky Really Falling in Legal Education?" *TaxProf Blog*, July 1, 2011, http://taxprof.typepad.com/taxprof_blog/2011/07/seto-.html.

7. William D. Henderson and Rachel M. Zahorsky, "Law Job Stagnation May Have Started before the Recession—and It May Be a Sign of Lasting Change," *ABA Journal*, July 1, 2011, http://www.abajournal.com/magazine/article/paradigm_shift/. See Leigh Jones, "So Long, Farewell," *National Law Journal*, November 9, 2009. This suggests that the growth at the top was offset by an overall decline in the corporate law sector.

8. See Matt Leichter, "A Profession in Decline: BEA [Bureau of Economic Analysis] Legal Sector Data (1977–)," *Law School Tuition Bubble* (blog), http://lawschooltuitionbubble.word- press.com/original-research-updated/a-profession-in-decline/.

9. Larry Ribstein, "The Death of Big Law," *Wisconsin Law Review* 2010 (2010): 749.

10. Richard Susskind, *The End of Lawyers? Rethinking the Nature of Legal Services* (Oxford: Oxford University Press, 2009).

11. Thomas D. Morgan, *The Vanishing American Lawyer* (New York: Oxford University Press 2010). Morgan's book is a terrific study of the changes in the legal profession that covers some of the topics raised in this book, although my focus herein is specifically on the econom- ics of legal education, while Morgan ranges more broadly.

12. See Zillman, "Law Firm Leaders Survey 2010"; Thomas S. Clay and Eric A. Seeger, "Law Firms in Transition: An Altman Weil Flash Survey" (2010).

13. Ashby Jones and Joseph Palazzolo, "What's a First-Year Lawyer Worth? Not Much, Say a Growing Number of Corporate Clients Who Refuse to Pay," *Wall Street Journal*, October 17, 2011, B1.

14. Vanessa O'Connell, "Lawyers Settle for Temp Jobs: As Clients Seek to Cut Costs, the Field of 'Contract' Attorneys Expands," *Wall Street Journal*, June 15, 2011, B1.

15. Clay and Seeger, "Law Firms in Transition," 2.

16. Catherine Rampell, "At Well-Paying Law Firms, Some Legal Help Comes More Cheaply," *New York Times*, May 24, 2011.

17. These and other developments are elaborated in Henderson and Zahorksy, "Law Job Stagnation."

18. Statement of Gregory Jordan, Global Managing Partner of Reed Smith, quoted in Henderson and Zahorksy, "Law Job Stagnation."

19. Jennifer Smith, "Law Firms Keep Squeezing Associations," *Wall Street Journal*, January 30, 2012, (quoting Bill Dantzler, hiring partner at White & Case LLP), http://online.wsj.com/article/SB10001424052970203363504577186913589594038.html.

20. An excellent analysis of these changes, which explains why they are likely to remain, is Burk and McGowan, "Big but Brittle," quote from94.

21. *2010 Salary Guide: Your Resource for Compensation in the Legal Field* (Robert Half Legal, 2011), 4, http://www.roberthalflegal.com/salarycenters.

22. Ibid., 5.

23. Ibid., 4.

24. For a concise elaboration of the factors involved, see William Henderson, "Are We Asking the Wrong Questions about Lawyer Regulation," *Truth on the Market* (blog), September 19, 2011, http://truthonthemarket.com/2011/09/19/william-henderson-on-are-we-asking-the-wrong-questions-about-lawyer-regulation/.

25. *Documenting the Justice Gap in America: The Current Unmet Civil Legal Needs of Low-Income Americans* (Washington, DC: Legal Services Corporation, September 2009), 9.

26. Ibid., 18.

27. Ibid., 25–26.

28. The current minimum requirement for classroom hours can be found at American Bar Association, Section of Legal Education and Admissions to the Bar, *Standards for Approval of Law Schools and Interpretations* (Chicago: ABA, 1996), standard 304.

29. Ibid., standard 502 (a)(b).

30. Directives regarding the significant use of tenure-track full-time faculty by law schools can be found in ibid., standards 402, 403. Regulation of support for faculty research and job security for professors is found in ibid., standards 404, 404, 405.

31. The only additional change, on top of the ones proposed earlier, will be to pare the nine hundred hours of "in residence" classroom time mandated in ibid., standard 305(e), back to 750–800 hours.

32. A version of such private low-cost legal services based in law schools is proposed in Bradley Borden and Robert Rhee, "The Law School Firm," *South Carolina Law Review* 63 (2011): 1. Pace law school recently announced the creation of an "in-house law firm" where recent graduates (otherwise unemployed) will handle cases under the supervision of lawyers while getting training in the basics of starting up a practice. See Tierney Plumb, "Pace Law School Enters the In-House Law School Market, *National Jurist*, November 18, 201, http://www.nationaljurist.com/content/pace-law-school-enters-house-law-school-market. This model would also work for students in their third year.

33. First Professional Degree In re Culver, N.W.2ed (Mont. 2002), quoted in Fred P. Parker, "Litigation Update," *Bar Examiner*, May 2002.

34. "California's State Accredited and Unaccredited Law Schools and the Baby Bar," Top-Law-Schools.Com, http://www.top-law-schools.com/californias-law-school-baby-bar.html.

35. See U.S. Department of Education, "Obama Administration Announces New Steps to Protect Students from Ineffective Career College Programs," press release, June 2, 2011. http://www.ed.gov/news/press-releases/gainful-employment-regulations.

36. Robin Wilson, "Back in the Classroom: Colleges are Calling Off the Deals That Allowed Many Professors Time out from Teaching," *Chronicle of Higher Education*, October 21, 2011, 1.

37. See Erwin Chermerinsky, "Visions of Change," *Dean's Notes Archive* (blog) (University of California Irvine School of Law), http://www.law.uci.edu/visions_of_06.html.

38. Ibid.

39. Erwin Chemerinsky, "Keynote Speech: Reimagining Law Schools?" *Iowa Law Review* 96 (2011): 1461, quote at 1462.

40. University Registrar, University of California Irvine, "School of Law Fees 2011–12," http://reg.uci.edu/fees/2011–2012/law.html.

INDEX

Page numbers in italics indicate figures.